Edoardo Albert is a London-based writer of Italian and Sri Lankan extraction who specialises in history, religion and archaeology. His previous books include *Warrior: A Life of War in Anglo-Saxon Britain*, *The Perfect Sword: Forging the Dark Ages*, both of which he co-authored with Paul Gething, and *The Man Who Stopped the Sultan: Gabriele Tadino and the Defence of Europe*.

# BEDE

## The Man Who Invented England

EDOARDO ALBERT

BIRLINN

First published in 2026 by
Birlinn Limited
West Newington House
10 Newington Road
Edinburgh
EH9 1QS

*www.birlinn.co.uk*

ISBN 978 1 78027 839 1

British Library Cataloguing-in-Publication Data

A catalogue record of this book is available
on request from the British Library

Typeset by Initial Typesetting Services, Edinburgh

Papers used by Birlinn are from well-managed forests
and other responsible sources

Printed and bound by MBM Print SCS Ltd, Glasgow

# Contents

*For Robert Dudley,*
*who made it possible.*

*And Hugh Andrew,*
*who made it better.*

The main kingdoms of Britain in Bede's lifetime,
with important sites marked.

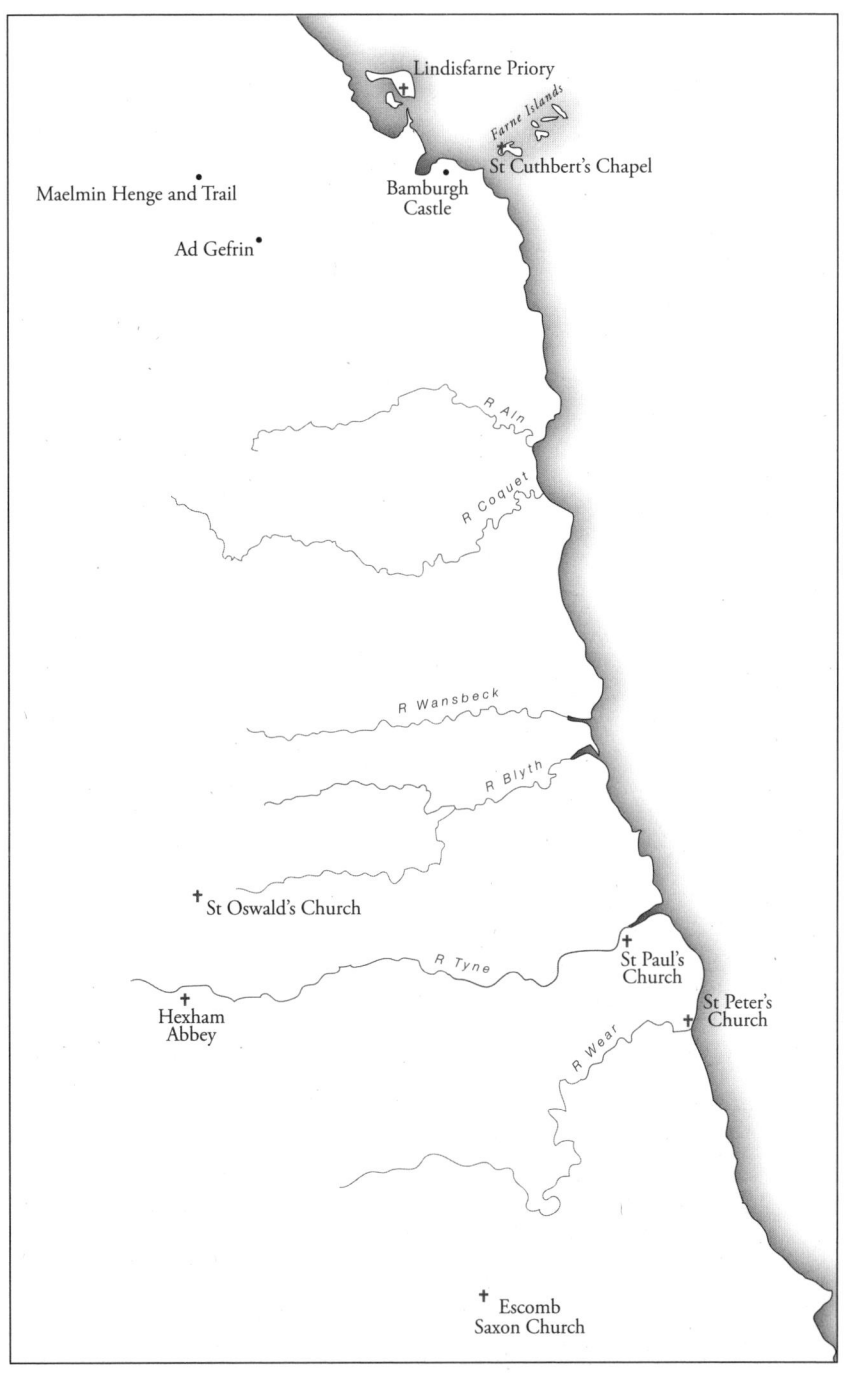

Bede's world: Bede, famously, didn't travel much, but he did regularly move between St Paul's and St Peter's, and visited Hexham and, probably, Lindisfarne.

# CHAPTER 1

# Plague

We alone remain.'

Although the boy heard the words, he could not drag his gaze up from the grave into which they had lain his friend.

'Bede.'

The name called the boy back to the present.

'So many of our brethren.'

Bede nodded. He could not speak. He looked up to the abbot.

Ceolfrith, standing on the far side of the grave, said nothing more. Bede watched as the wind, blowing in from the North Sea, tugged at the man's rough robe. It was cold, cold as his friend's body as they had carried him from the monastery to the cemetery, Abbot Ceolfrith holding him under the arms, Bede stumbling and trying not to drop his legs. They had walked alongside each other, the boy's body, wrapped in its grave cloth, slung between them.

Bede spoke. 'Sigetreow.'

'I know,' said Ceolfrith. He gazed around the little cemetery. 'I know the names of everyone here. They followed me here and I buried them here.'

'Sigetreow came from Wearmouth way. He was kind to me when my parents left me here.' Bede looked at the abbot. 'I cried when they went away.'

'That was six years ago. When you were seven.'

'I still remember. Sigetreow sat with me that night, when I cried and the other boys mocked me.'

'I was the same age when my parents gave me to the Church.' Ceolfrith looked at the boy standing on the other side of the grave. 'Will you promise not to tell anyone what I tell you now?'

Bede nodded, eyes wide at what secret the abbot might share with him.

'After my parents left me, I cried every night for a four week. I only stopped when the other oblates, fed up with my crying, dumped a bucket of water over me in the middle of the night.' Abbot Ceolfrith's face creased into a smile. 'So, you see, you are already braver than I.'

Not knowing what to say, Bede nodded.

'Good. I am glad you agree, because I have need of that bravery now.' Ceolfrith gestured Bede to his side, put a hand on his shoulder and gently turned him so that they were both facing the monastery.

The abbot looked again at the boy standing next to him. 'The plague has taken all our brethren. We alone remain. If this House of God is to survive, then we must continue its work. What is the work we do here, Bede?'

'We pray and we sing.'

'That is correct. We pray for the world, and we sing to the Lord, after the lesson of the psalmist who said, "Seven times a day do I praise thee." For our prayers and songs, one must ask, and others answer. Now, as we only remain, then I will ask, and you will answer.'

Bede stared incredulously at the abbot. 'B-but I do not know all the words, Master. I have only learnt some.'

'You will learn the rest. Of that I have no doubt. One day you shall speak the language of the Bible as fluently as our master, Benedict. But for the moment it will be sufficient to learn the responses.' The abbot smiled again. 'You will find that words sung are easier to remember than words spoken.'

'A-are you sure of this, Master?' The boy's face was solemn, eager and fearful at the same time.

'Yes, I am sure,' said Abbot Ceolfrith.

Bede nodded. 'Yes. Yes, I will.'

The man and the boy made their way back along the all-too-worn path from the cemetery to the church of St Paul.

Entering the stone building, the boy paused. The church was silent. Whenever he had come in here before, it had been a place of sound and smell: the voices of the monks, raised in chant, or the cantor singing alone; the scent of incense rising into the roof and, truth be told, making Bede cough and his eyes water.

Ceolfrith pointed to the bucket by the door. 'Wash your hands. Today, you will touch holy books: let there be no filth upon your fingers.'

Bede laved his hands. The abbot did the same, then led Bede along the nave to the choir area. There, benches lined each side of the church. Bede stopped to look at them.

Seeing him do so, Ceolfrith paused. 'I miss them, too. Now we must do the work of all, Bede. Are you ready?'

'Yes, Master, I am ready.'

'Very well. I will lead, you must make the response. Come, stand beside me. I will show the response in the breviary. You know your letters?'

'Yes, Master.'

'By the time we are finished here, you will know the meaning of the words as well as their sounds. But for now, I will help you. Listen, and I will prompt you when you are unsure.'

'Yes, Master.'

'*In nomine Patris, et Filii et Spiritus Sancti.*'

'Amen.'

The abbot's finger went to the page of the breviary, underscoring each word as he chanted it. Bede, concentrating furiously, sang the responses.

There were only two voices, but the deep bass of the abbot and the high tones of the boy wound through the church. It was not as full as the sound of the whole choir of monks singing together, but the two voices complemented each other.

At the end of the passage, the abbot lifted his finger from the page and looked down at Bede.

'Well done,' he said quietly.

Bede nodded.

'Ready to continue?'

Bede nodded again.

And the two voices were raised again, the sound of them threading through the deep shadows within the church and rippling in the light that shone through the windows.

*

It's still there. The church where a boy of thirteen stood beside his abbot, chanting the psalm against the rising dark 1,300 years ago, is still there. The church of St Paul, Jarrow, stands beside the River Don, looking out towards the North Sea. St Paul's sits at a bend in the river, where the Don's course turns from the east and runs north, to feed into the River Tyne some 500 yards away over a ridge that is now home to Jarrow Hall, a reconstructed Anglo-Saxon farm and village, as well as a museum to Bede.

Of course, the prospect from the church of St Paul has changed. The church itself has changed. It has been extended and enlarged over the centuries, with little of its original substance remaining. But it has survived. It survived the depredations of the Vikings in the tenth and eleventh centuries. It survived the despoliation of the sixteenth century. The church still stands, as enduring as the ideas of the boy who sang the Office beside his abbot, the sole survivors of a monastic expedition into the wasteland.

There have been many books about Bede in the centuries since his death but few deal much with his life, for the simple reason that there has been very little to tell. The monastic life is, by design, regular and calm. Not much happens and, in the sense of events of moment and significance, nothing much did happen during Bede's life: he prayed, he sang, he taught and he wrote. One of the very few 'events' to punctuate the apparent tranquillity of his life was the plague that struck the monastery at Jarrow in 686, killing all the monks present save for the abbot, Ceolfrith, and, according to the anonymous life of Ceolfrith, one small boy. Faced with the silence of the abbey, Ceolfrith trained the boy to sing the responses to the psalms, and the two of them continued the work of monks, praying through song, until reinforcements arrived from Wearmouth. Historians pretty well unanimously accept that the small boy was Bede, and that the period he spent together with Ceolfrith, holding the monastery in being, cemented a deep and enduring bond between the pair.

St Paul's, Jarrow, was one half of an unusual double monastery, with its other half at St Peter's in Wearmouth, and both houses were under the control of a single abbot.

During the rest of his life, Bede seldom stirred from the confines of these two houses. He must have walked the six miles between them many, many times. It's quite likely that he made the journey just as often by boat, sailing down the Don and into the Tyne, then turning south and hugging the coast to the mouth of the River Wear, where the church of St Peter also still stands, witness to the man who lived and taught and sang in both of them. It's important to remember that at this time, rivers and the sea were not barriers but highways, roads that were often quicker and easier to travel than their equivalents on land. The peoples to whom Bede traced his ancestry, the Angles, and their cousins the Saxons and the Jutes, had used the waterways of eastern England as channels to cut deep into the country they were coming to, rather as the Vikings would do in the century after Bede's death.

Because the epithet often applied to Bede is 'venerable' there is a tendency to imagine him living to a hoary old age, his hair white, hobbling to the library with the aid of a stick. But the 'venerable' of his title actually means 'worthy of veneration'. Bede lived a good life, certainly, but he was dead at 61 or 62, so he was by no means a particularly old man at his death, even by the standards of his time.

The veneration due to Bede resulted from his work. During the fifty-plus years he spent as a monk, Bede produced a huge body of written work, an output made all the more impressive when we remember how much more difficult it was for the monks of his community to commit words to the page than it had been in earlier times.

The derisory name of 'Dark Ages' applied to the period between the fall of the Western Roman Empire and the medieval period (in itself propaganda for apologists of the new fashions of the Renaissance) is almost wholly undeserved. The only way in which the appellation is merited is the lack of historical sources. But this was mainly due to the difficulty in finding a medium on which to actually write anything down. Papyrus, the mainstay of Roman writing, was cheap to produce, available in large quantities and easy to write upon – a bit like paper, really – but it was largely lost to Europe with the end of the Western Empire, and even more so when the armies of Islam conquered Egypt in 642.

For the regions of northern Europe, there was no equivalent to papyrus. Papyrus itself won't grow in the cold, wet climates of the region. Paper technology, imported from China, still lay in the future. The main mediums for writing were vellum and parchment. Both are made from animal skin. Parchment is made from the skin of calves, goats or sheep. Vellum, a finer writing medium, is made from calf skin. Being made from animal skins, the writing medium was expensive, although it was also more durable than papyrus or paper. In fact, because of this very durability, public Acts of Parliament were written on vellum to ensure their preservation right up until 2015. Since then, public Acts have been printed on archival paper.

Only having access to relatively expensive 'paper', writing was necessarily confined to fewer documents. Couple this with a loss of literacy outside the Church, and it's natural that this period is poorly documented. But beyond the pages of the few books, it was a time of rapid change, culturally and technologically. The slave-based economy of the Roman Empire gave way to the reciprocal obligations of lord and peasant. In Europe, Latin produced the polyglot Romance languages and their respective kingdoms, while in Britain, the Germanic language of the Anglo-Saxons slowly supplanted the Celtic languages of the Britons in the lowlands. And a group of unnamed smiths in Britain set about forging some of the most extra-ordinary swords ever made, while their brethren specialising in gold and jewels created the unparalleled examples of their craft found at Sutton Hoo and in the Staffordshire Hoard. Indeed, almost all the foundations for what would become England, Wales and Scotland were laid during these obscure centuries.

However, despite these achievements, the political chaos of these centuries resulted in a dearth of documents. For the whole of the period between the supposed departure of the Roman legions in 410 and the arrival of St Augustine in Kent in 597, we have basically three written works: Gildas' jeremiad against contemporary Britonnic kings and two letters by St Patrick. Gildas, a Briton, writing somewhere between 480 and 550, wrote in excellent, educated Latin, so it was still possible for the native Britons to receive education sufficient to write polished Latin. But even if there were other works produced, they did not survive the dislocations of the time.

Bede wrote the *Historia ecclesiastica gentis Anglorum* (*Ecclesiastical History of the English People*) in 731. In doing so, he brought Britain, and particularly the kingdoms that would later become England, out of the legends of his people and into history. To a writer, there's a certain bittersweet aspect of this re-emergence. While England re-entered history, the vast majority of the stories and myths of its people were lost to that history. The most eminent Anglo-Saxon scholar of the first half of the twentieth century, one John Ronald Reuel Tolkien, was intensely aware of this loss and set about writing his own version of these lost tales.[1]

In the Middle Ages, there developed a vast cycle of tales and poems, known as the Matter of Britain,[2] that purportedly told of the past of Britain, but these have their kernel in the stories of the Britons and their heirs, the Welsh, although by the time of the great Arthurian tales they had lost all connection to the historical roots.

The only surviving Anglo-Saxon epic, *Beowulf*, also tells of the Heroic Age, when men in boats might fetch up on a fresh shore and do great deeds and win for themselves a kingdom or an early grave.

People tell stories in different ways, and the ways of legend have truths of their own that have deep resonance within the human soul.

But the ways of history have their place, too. While their roots do not run as deep as those of myth – Herodotus wrote in the fifth century BC while the *Epic of Gilgamesh* probably first coalesced into a single story around 1800 BC – they now spread far and wide, underpinning much of the settlements upon which the modern world is based. While historians no longer exhibit the sort of hubris that once allowed us to claim to tell the absolute truth of what happened, we can still research the events, examine the motivations and interrogate our own perspective when writing of the past. While no single telling can reveal the whole truth, it might not be a vain hope to think that our many views of the past may come together to reveal something coherent of what went before.

With his *Ecclesiastical History*, Bede created the most enduring image of England's past. Historians and archaeologists have spent the last century refracting Bede's singular vista with their different lenses. Sometimes they have reversed the image, sometimes they have distorted it and sometimes they have refuted it. But Bede's is the framework upon which the whole endeavour rests, for without him, there is almost nothing.

So that is why I am writing this book. For Bede was the man who, wittingly or otherwise, invented England, and even today we rest upon the foundations he laid.

But the base that enabled Bede to become the towering intellectual figure of his era was laid by another man. His name was Benedict Biscop, and he is one of the most important but least known men in the history of England.

# CHAPTER 2

# The Making of a Monastery

I t had been a long journey. Taking ship from the old Roman port at Richborough in Kent, Biscop (c.628–690) – along with his companion in pilgrimage, Wilfrid, and the cohort of armed men necessary to deter brigands and thieves on the road – had arrived in Francia, en route to Rome. Given a letter of recommendation from Eorcenberht, king of Kent, they had sought out the king of the Franks, Clovis II.

Biscop[1] came from Northumbrian nobility; the Baducinga, according to Stephen of Ripon. As such, he had served as a gesith, a member of the warband that travelled with and supported King Oswiu. But in his 25th year, Biscop had decided to put aside the sword and leave the way of the warrior to embark on the pilgrim path to Rome. It would prove a longer road than he could have ever imagined, taking in a new name in religion and more miles than anyone of whom we have record before the Norse sailors of the tenth century.

The obvious place for Biscop to stop for advice on how to make his first journey was Canterbury. The archbishop there was Honorius, the last survivor of the original Augustinian mission to the Anglo-Saxons that had arrived in 597. Traditionally, Honorius succeeded to the archbishopric in 627 (although it's possible the date was later, around 634). By the time Biscop arrived in Canterbury, Honorius had ruled over the Church for 26 years. He most probably met the young Northumbrian in the spring or summer, for Honorius died on 30 September of that year. Alongside Honorius's own knowledge of the best routes for a pilgrim to Rome, there was continued contact between the two sees, allowing the clerics in Canterbury to advise Biscop as to his best course.

Biscop sought secular as well as religious advice, seeking out King Eorcenberht. The Kentish royal family had long-established links to the Merovingian kings in France, so gaining Eorcenberht's help for his pilgrimage would ensure Biscop a welcome when he crossed the Channel.

While at Eorcenberht's court, Biscop met another young man who was also set on going to Rome. Wilfrid[2] was a Northumbrian of equal social standing to Biscop but, it seems likely, considerably greater wealth. He would occupy a crucial position in the nexus between the religious and political worlds in Northumbria for the rest of his life, but here in Kent at the court of King Eorcenberht, Wilfrid was at the start of his tumultuous career. At twenty years old, he was five years younger than Biscop but was similarly set on making the long journey to Rome. As such, it was natural, and safer, for the two men to combine their travelling parties and make the trip together.

With letters of introduction safely tucked away in belt pouches, the two young men set off to one of the Kentish ports to find a ship to take them to France. We don't definitively know which port they departed from. But they were both young men with a sense of history. What they were embarking upon was something historic in itself: the first pilgrimage by Anglo-Saxon Christians to Rome. To acknowledge that history, and because it was a good place to find a ship sailing to France, a likely site for their embarkation was Richborough, the old Roman port and fortress of Rutupiae. It stands at the origin of Watling Street – in itself a plausible route to the coast – and at the mouth of the Wantsum Channel, which cut off the Isle of Thanet from the mainland, and where the River Stour drained into the Channel. There was a good harbour near the fort and although the fort had been abandoned following the Roman withdrawal, there's no reason to suppose that the harbour was no longer in use, since it follows maritime logic to anchor there while waiting for the tide to help push the boat out into the Channel.[3]

Having crossed the Channel, Biscop and Wilfrid made their way south, eventually meeting the king of this new country, Clovis II. The king proved to be a man of like years to the two travellers and, to Wilfrid's eventual dismay, a man much influenced by his wife, Queen Balthild.[4]

The distrust Wilfrid felt for the queen was all the stranger because she was a countryman to the two pilgrims. Queen Balthild came from the kingdom of the East Angles. Sold into slavery as a girl, she had been bought in 641 for, as she told Biscop, 'little money', but on account of her beauty and wit she soon found herself in service to Erchinoald, the mayor of the Merovingian palace. Among the duties she had to perform was washing the feet of travel-stained lords arriving at the royal court.

As Balthild grew, her beauty became apparent to all, not least Erchinoald. A widower, Erchinoald decided that he would marry Balthild even though she was of low birth. But despite his power, Balthild had no wish to marry Erchinoald and, being a shrewd girl as well as a pious one, she managed to fend off his advances – only to find that she had come to the attention of the young king, Clovis. He had succeeded to the throne at the age of five when his father, Dagobert I, had died. As five was a bit young to actually rule, Clovis's mother, Nanthild, acted as regent for the first years of his reign. But Nanthild died in 642 when Clovis was still only nine. From that point onwards, Erchinoald became the effective ruler of the kingdom.

With Erchinoald being his chief advisor, Clovis had come to know the mayor's young cup-bearer, a girl only a few years older than him, and he fell in love with Balthild. Despite Erchinoald's arguments that it was the duty of a king to marry for the kingdom by taking to bed the princess of an allied realm, Clovis would not listen and, as soon as he came of age at fifteen, he married Balthild, making her his queen.

It was an astonishing rise for a slave girl but one not entirely without precedent in Frankish history. Later chroniclers of Queen Balthild's life wrote in a noble ancestry to make her appear more legitimate, but the earliest history of her life states that she was of low birth. Her elevation was thus due to her beauty, wit and personality.

Clovis II married Balthild in 648. His queen had been in Francia, in the kingdom of Neustria, for seven years. She did her royal duty, providing three sons to Clovis in quick succession. But Balthild did not forget her origins, nor what she had endured in her early life. She became known for the generosity of her almsgiving, such that Clovis assigned Balthild her own almoner. In a move that indicated how difficult her early life had been, she outlawed the practice of slavery in the kingdom and, to make sure that slave traders could not export their way to riches, she also forbade the export of slaves, while also ransoming many slaves herself, especially young girls.

In 653, when Biscop and Wilfrid arrived in Francia, the royal couple had been married for five years. Clovis was twenty, Balthild a little older. Mayor Erchinoald retained his power. (The mayors of the Merovingian kings grew steadily more powerful, until their office became hereditary, with the mayor wielding the real power in the kingdom and the Merovingian king acting as a ceremonial figurehead. This continued under such notable figures as Charles Martel until, in the end, the mayors decided to make themselves kings in name as well as power, putting aside the Merovingians and becoming the Carolingian dynasty.)

While the travellers from Britain were well received by Clovis and Balthild, it's clear from our sources that they had very different views of Queen Balthild. Following their departure from the royal court, Biscop and Wilfrid continued south, stopping in Lyon. There, they parted company, with Biscop continuing on to Rome and Wilfrid staying in Lyon as the guest of Bishop Aunemund. According to the biography of Wilfrid written after his death by Stephen, a monk at Ripon Abbey which Wilfrid later founded, Bishop Aunemund was so taken with Wilfrid that he wanted to marry his niece to the young man. As a bride price, Aunemund wanted to give the governorship of a nearby province to Wilfrid. Perhaps after some hesitation, Wilfrid refused. However, in Stephen of Ripon's *Life*, the biographer goes on to accuse Balthild of ridding herself of Bishop Aunemund by murdering him and installing her own man. This she did, according to Stephen, to eight other bishops as well.

As a result of Stephen's portrait of Balthild, this Anglo-Saxon queen of Francia developed a reputation as a cross-Channel Jezebel. But the only source for these claims is Stephen's biography of Wilfrid: there's nothing in the French sources to suggest she went around ordering the deaths of bishops. Instead, in her adopted country, Balthild was revered as a saint following her death. So Wilfrid appears to have had some issues with Queen Balthild that were not shared by Biscop or, indeed, the people she ruled in Francia.

There was a thread running through Anglo-Saxon writing, beginning with Balthild and continuing right through to the Norman Conquest, of dread of the machinations of queens behind the throne. It seems to begin in Stephen's biography of Wilfrid, but it continues with the story of Oswiu's daughter, Ealhflæd, who poisoned her husband, the king of Mercia, and Offa's daughter, Eadburh, who married the king of the West Saxons and poisoned him too.

Then there was the royal marriage career of Judith, the daughter of Charles the Bald, king of the Franks. Judith was betrothed to the 50-something Æthelwulf, king of Wessex, when she was only twelve and married him when she was thirteen. Because of the notoriety of Eadburh, the West Saxons did not allow the king's wife to reign as queen; she was merely the king's wife. However, a Carolingian monarch such as Charles the Bald was not about to have his daughter serve merely as consort to a king: Judith was anointed Æthelwulf's queen when she married him. However, returning to Britain, the mismatched couple found that Æthelwulf's son, Æthelbald, had rebelled against his father. In the end, Æthelwulf and Æthelbald negotiated a compromise, where each took half the kingdom. But then, in 858, after two years of marriage, Æthelwulf died, leaving Judith a widow at fifteen.

However, rather than returning to her father's court, Judith decided to stay put and marry the new king, Æthelbald, the son of her late husband. This marriage caused dismay among the clerics in Wessex, but there was little they could do about it. However, two and a half years later, Judith's second husband also died. Although still childless, she had been married and widowed twice by the time she was seventeen. This time, Judith did return home but, as further evidence of what a remarkably independent young woman she was, rather than remaining in the convent into which her father placed her, she eloped with a young nobleman named Baldwin and married him. Outraged, Charles the Bald had his daughter and her husband excommunicated. However, Judith and Baldwin travelled to Rome and pleaded their case together before the pope, winning him round. In the end, Charles relented, and the excommunication was lifted. Possibly still hoping to rid himself of his son-in-law, Charles charged Baldwin with defending Flanders against Viking attacks – a dangerous position to hold. However, Baldwin proved a capable warrior, repelling Norse raids and consolidating his position as the king's faithful retainer. Judith and Baldwin went on to have four children together.

Perhaps it was this thread of independent Anglo-Saxon queens, first excoriated by Wilfrid's biographer, that produced a reaction from the clergy. It may also have been a reaction to the high status of women in Anglo-Saxon society. Under Anglo-Saxon law, women could inherit, they had status under law, and the *weregild* for a woman was the same as that for a man of the same status. The status of women remained high throughout the medieval period, with laws and customs protecting their rights independently of husbands and sons, while the later spread of the ideals of courtly love gave noble women further areas in which to exercise power and influence. It was only later, following the Renaissance, that these rights were eroded. Perhaps it was precisely this relative independence and power that produced this recurring fear of powerful queens among some of the Anglo-Saxons that first found expression in Wilfrid's biographer.

To sum up: Balthild was an Anglo-Saxon, sold into slavery in Francia who avoided the instant temptation of marrying a powerful older man but still ended up marrying the king. She sponsored the Church and did good works, produced three sons, all three of whom ended up as kings themselves; she founded a convent and, giving up her worldly wealth, retired there and, after her death, was revered as a saint in her adopted country. It sounds like a perfect Christian life. So why did Wilfrid dislike her so much?

It's tempting but simplistic to chalk it down to Wilfrid being a misogynist. But in his later career, Wilfrid struck up close relationships with powerful women, most notably Æthelthryth, queen of Northumbria (a relationship that caused considerable friction with Æthelthryth's husband, King Ecgfrith, as Wilfrid supported the queen in her determination to maintain her vow of perpetual virginity despite her marriage to the king). It may be that Wilfrid saw first-hand the effect of some of the queen's political machinations in the death of his friend and sponsor, Bishop Aunemund, and never forgave her for this. If so, it was a successful calumny as Queen Balthild, despite her origin, retained a reputation for treachery among her own people, the Anglo-Saxons.

Their different relationships with the queen may also explain why Biscop and Wilfrid parted company in Lyon, with Wilfrid remaining in the city and Biscop continuing on to Rome alone (apart from the retainers he took with him for protection and company on the journey).

*

Lyon is already quite far south, but Biscop had to make his way through the Alps and down the spine of Italy to get to Rome. Travelling along the old roads that had once united the empire to its capital, the remains of the Imperial past grew steadily more impressive as he journeyed south. Not all the old roads were navigable. Via Julia Augusta, which would have been one possible route, was found unnavigable by a late Imperial poet two centuries earlier. But there were roads that were still in use. Or Biscop, being comfortable on water, might have embarked on a ship from southern France and sailed along the coast to Ostia.

Whatever his route, Biscop arrived in Rome in 653. He had done the journey within the year – no mean feat considering that there were lengthy stops along the way, particularly in Kent and then in Francia.

In the mid seventh century there were no cities in Britain. There weren't even any towns. The population was dispersed, living in small farming and herding communities. It's likely that Biscop, in his travels, had seen ruins of cities, not least York and London, but these had been largely deserted. Canterbury, as the centre of the Church in Britain, had probably the greatest settled population of anywhere in the country, but it would only have been a few hundred souls.

Crossing the Channel, Biscop and Wilfrid saw, with increasing wonder, the scale of the old Roman civilisation. Much more had been preserved and was still in use there. This was the first time either of them saw men and women living in houses made of stone, and worshipping in stone churches, too, with glass windows to let in the light. In places, aqueducts still brought water from distant hills to cities that hummed with life. And while some of the roads had fallen into disrepair, others were still in use, marching across the land as if giants had lain them down.

But all that he had seen along the way could not have prepared Biscop for Rome itself.[5] Although the city was a shadow of its Imperial glory, with a population of maybe 50,000 as compared to the million or so people who had lived there in its pomp, it was still the most populous city that Biscop had ever seen. The buildings left by the emperors still mostly stood, although many were abandoned.

From the sightseeing point of view, it was as well that Biscop arrived when he did. Ten years later, the Byzantine Emperor Constans II visited Rome (one of only two Byzantine emperors to set foot in the old capital of the empire). While professing good relations with the pope, Constans nevertheless stripped the city's buildings of their ornaments and statues and removed all the bronze. But on Biscop's first visit he had the chance to see the Pantheon still gleaming in the morning sun, and the hundreds, if not thousands, of statues that decorated the old Imperial buildings.

But splendid though these ruins were, they were not the reason that Biscop had travelled over a thousand miles. Indeed, it's interesting reading the accounts of travellers to Rome at this time. They pay almost no attention to the old Imperial city. What they have come to visit is the new city of martyrs and saints and churches. Their itineraries read as a programme of church visits, inspections of relics and marvelling at the Christian sites.

The nature of Roman power had changed. Ruins were all that was left of its long-gone political power – and there are few things more bathetic than the lost traces of a once dominant power. Instead, the visitors came to see the new power that had grown up in the heart of Babylon, outlasting it and subsuming the old city into its own growth: this was a spiritual power, a place where the Apostles had walked, preached and met their end. And not just Peter and Paul but a whole line of saints and martyrs. There are some places where the wall between worlds becomes thin, almost transparent, and Rome, at this time, was one of those places, particularly for the pilgrims.

So, on reflection, it's little surprise that the pilgrim visitors of the medieval era coming to Rome saw it in a very different light to the English nobility of the eighteenth century. The new pilgrims were like Real Madrid fans visiting Madrid: that city might have the Prado and the Palacio Real, but all they want to do is visit the Bernabeu and see a match there. This was true of Biscop. He had gone all that way to stand in the presence of the Apostles, Peter and Paul, and to pay his respects to the successor of Pope Gregory, who had sent the first mission to the Anglo-Saxons 56 years earlier.

But while Biscop must have been hoping to pay his respects in person to the successor of Peter, he was disappointed. Pope Martin I was not there. On 17 July 653, Martin had been arrested by soldiers of the Byzantine Emperor Constans II and taken to Constantinople, arriving there on 17 September 653.

Constantinople considered itself the New Rome, and the emperor considered himself ruler of the Old Rome. Much of Italy had been reconquered by the Emperor Justinian in the sixth century. However, the Lombards, a Germanic people, had conquered a large tranche of Italy by the middle of the seventh century. The Lombards quickly integrated with the native population, but their name endures to this day in Lombardy, one of the Italian provinces. When Biscop made his way through Italy to Rome, he found the Lombards in control of northern Italy and the plain of the River Po. If he had made his way further south, he would have found that the Lombards also ruled the shin and ankle of Italy's boot. The Byzantines still controlled Rome, however. The Byzantine exarchate (the name for a Byzantine province) was ruled from Ravenna, on the east coast of Italy, where the Byzantine governor, the exarch, had his seat. From Ravenna, the exarch's writ ran along the coast from roughly Venice south to where Rimini is today, then took in a strip running across the Apennines and the area around Rome, as well as the toe and the heel of Italy's boot.

Although Constantinople had its own patriarch, the unfortunate fact that the emperor shared the city with the patriarch meant that Byzantine emperors took personal interest in Church matters. The emperor generally appointed the patriarch of Constantinople, as well as presiding over Church councils. Some emperors even promulgated ecclesiastical edicts under their own authority. To make matters worse for Pope Martin, Constantinople had been deeply shaken in the previous decades by the sudden explosion of Arab armies from the desert. The Byzantine and the Persian Sassanid Empires had exhausted themselves during a century-long conflict, leaving both exposed to this eruption of nomadic tribes espousing a new religion. In a few years, the Arabs had overthrown Byzantine control of the Near East, taking Syria, Egypt and North Africa, not to mention Jerusalem itself.

Faced with this new threat, the Byzantines sought explanation for why they were being tested in this way. Being a fundamentally religious empire, one response to this new threat was to seek a religious explanation, which became a profound dispute over the nature of Christ. The debate was over whether Christ had two wills, human and divine, or one, with the Monothelites holding that Christ had only one will. This went against the formulation of the Council of Chalcedon in 451 that Christ is fully human and fully divine. However, for various reasons, the patriarch of Constantinople espoused the one-will view, and the emperor backed him up.

For a while it looked like their arguments would carry the day but while the Eastern Church mostly backed the new ideas, the Church in the West was opposed, and in particular the bishops of Rome set their mitres against it. In 649, Pope Martin I convened the Lateran Council, which formally condemned Monothelitism.

Emperor Constans was enraged. Not only was the pope meddling in matters that he considered his own province but also, among the condemnations issued by the Lateran Council, was one against an edict that he himself had promulgated, the *Typos*, which forbade the discussion of the whole topic on pain of severe punishment. The dispute had seriously split the Byzantine Empire and, with Muslim armies pushing hard against overstretched Byzantine forces, Constans needed to draw a line under the argument and unite his empire against the new threat.

Martin I would have none of this. Not only did he convene a council and condemn the emperor's edict, he also zealously promulgated the results of the council. Not used to having a prelate defy him in such manner, Constans ordered the exarch of Ravenna to arrest Martin.

In July, troops of the exarch carried out that command, bundling Martin from the Lateran Palace and shipping him to Constantinople. Constans would have executed Martin on the spot, but the patriarch pleaded for the life of his fellow bishop. Nonetheless, Constans had Martin tortured and imprisoned. In the meantime, Constans put pressure on the Church in Rome to elect a new pope and, on 10 August 654, it did so, proclaiming Eugene I the bishop of Rome. To ensure that there would be no question of two popes in one Rome, Constans sent Martin into exile, to the city of Cherson on the Crimean peninsula, as far away from Rome as it was possible for a Byzantine emperor to banish a man. The now ex-Pope Martin died there, four months after his arrival, the last pope to be recognised as a martyr for the faith.

While the Monothelitic controversy is not mentioned in the primary sources about Biscop (Bede's *Lives of the Abbots of Wearmouth and Jarrow*, and his *Ecclesiastical History* and the anonymous *History of Abbot Ceolfrith*), the organisation of the monasteries that Biscop went on to found twenty years after this first trip to Rome suggests that the dispute had a profound impact upon the young Anglian. For the very structure of the twin monasteries – two separate houses united under the rule of a single abbot – suggests an institutional refutation of the heresy of Monothelitism and an affirmation of the dogmas declared by the Council of Chalcedon.

According to Chalcedon, Christ was fully human and fully divine. Within him there was a normal human will, albeit uncorrupted by sin, and the divine will. However, being incorrupt, Christ's human will aligned perfectly with the divine will, although the two remained distinct, as shown most clearly when Jesus prayed in the garden of Gethsemane on the night before his arrest that this cup should pass from him so that he would not have to undergo the torment of crucifixion. The Monothelites argued that Christ possessed only one will, his human will being subsumed into the divine will. As Christian theology, this fails because it makes Jesus other than human: he becomes an avatar of divinity, clothed in flesh but still essentially divine, a god play-acting as a human being.

Benedict Biscop went on to found a monastery with two houses under one abbot: two separate institutions representing two separate wills but united under the rule of a single abbot: God as one person but also fully human and completely divine. It was a telling statement of Benedict Biscop's attitude to the Monothelite heresy.

Although Biscop arrived in Rome when the city was in turmoil following the pope's abduction, the new Christian sites and sights were still open to him. He lodged in the monastery of St Andrew on the Caelian Hill. This was a very convenient location as the basilica of St John Lateran, the church of the bishop of Rome, was just a few hundred yards north-east of the monastery. The adjacent palace was the main residence of the pope at the time and the centre of the Church. It was only in the fourteenth century, after the papacy returned from its exile in Avignon, that the popes moved their main residence to the Vatican, the Lateran Palace having suffered a disastrous fire in their absence.

Of course, Biscop visited the Vatican area, for the basilica of St Peter had been built there over the tomb holding the remains of Peter. He also went to the basilica of St Paul Outside the Walls, erected over the grave of Paul, and the basilica of Santa Maria Maggiore, a particularly magnificent church erected in the fifth century, being consecrated on 5 August 434.

The churches we see today are very different from the buildings Biscop saw in 653. St Peter's is, of course, an entirely new building, the old basilica having been torn down and rebuilt (the money required for its rebuilding becoming one of the triggers of the Reformation). St John Lateran was largely rebuilt in the sixteenth century. St Paul Outside the Walls endured for 1,435 years, largely as first built, until a workman working on the gutters caused a fire which burnt the church down to the ground on 15 July 1823. The original intention was to rebuild the church as it had been, but that proved impossible, although the final church is in the style of the original. Only Santa Maria Maggiore survives intact at its core, with the original fifth-century mosaics still adorning the nave and triumphal arch.

Walking into Santa Maria Maggiore, seeing the light fracture upon the glittering mosaics, looking up at the ceiling, seemingly as high as the heavens but giving taste of the heaven to come, one can imagine the overwhelming effect these great churches at the heart of Christendom must have had on the young man who had travelled so far to see them.

They had a similar effect on Wilfrid when he too finally made it to Rome. Biscop and Wilfrid were, so far as we know, the first Anglo-Saxons to visit Rome on pilgrimage and of their own volition. We do know that some of their countrymen had made it to the city two generations earlier, for Bede records the famous occasion when Pope Gregory saw some youths for sale in Rome's slave market and, asking who they were, was told that they were Angles from

Britain. In one of the very few cases where a pun works across languages, Gregory reportedly replied, '*Non Angli sed angeli.*' However, the Angles in question were not willing visitors but victims of the Anglo-Saxon trade in slaves, a trade that continued long after the rest of Christendom had outlawed it.

Biscop and Wilfrid both became committed to the Roman style of Christianity, seeking to import its practices, its architecture and its spirituality to their own land. But while Wilfrid was a straight-down-the-line advocate for how they did things abroad – it was Rome's way or the highway, so far as he was concerned – Biscop would become nuanced in his importation of European practices into his homeland.

*

Returning home full of enthusiasm for what he had seen on his travels, Biscop remained in Britain for a little over a decade. We don't know what he did during this decade. However, Biscop's time in Britain coincided with the victory of Oswiu, king of Northumbria, over Penda, king of Mercia, at the Battle of Winwæd in 665. The victory turned Oswiu into the most powerful, and richest, king in the country. With Oswiu ascribing his survival to the new god, the servants of the new god present in Northumbria would have been well placed to harvest kingly gratitude. One of those who did so was Wilfrid, becoming abbot of the monastery in Ripon sometime before the Synod of Whitby, in which Wilfrid played a major part.

There is no mention in the records of what Biscop was doing during this time, although he seems to have struck up a friendship with one of Oswiu's sons, Ahlfrith, who was ruler of Deira, which more or less covers the same area as modern-day Yorkshire. When Biscop decided to journey to Rome again around 665, Ahlfrith wanted to accompany him, but his father would not give him leave to go. Which is pretty much the last record we have of Ahlfrith, although Bede notes that Ahlfrith attacked his father. If so, the attack failed and Ahlfrith disappears – whether into death or a monastery, we don't know.

In the end, Biscop set off without Ahlfrith. This trip would prove to be particularly significant for Biscop and his future monasteries. Arriving in Rome, Biscop could see first-hand what had happened when Pope Vitalian, attempting to improve relations with Emperor Constans II, invited him to Rome. Constans arrived on 5 July 663 and spent twelve days in the city, attending papal masses and gladhanding Church prelates. However, after an apparently fruitful stay, Constans ordered his men to pillage bronze statues from the city and strip the bronze tiles from the roof of the Pantheon. Two years later, when Biscop arrived, he saw the consequence of attempting to placate the secular power.

While this experience probably cemented Biscop's dislike of Monothelitism, even more significant was the route he chose for his return home. Rather than travelling overland, Biscop crossed the Ligurian Sea, arriving at the abbey of Lérins in 666. It was founded by St Honoratus in c.410 and lies on an island about three miles south of modern-day Cannes. Despite vicissitudes over the years, including Saracen raids that left most of the monks dead, an unwitting part in Franco-Spanish wars and suppression following the French Revolution, the monastery has kept bouncing back. It was refounded in the nineteenth century and the Cistercians established a community there that continues to this day.

Biscop spent two years at Lérins and by the end of those two years he had become a monk and taken the new name of Benedict. He left the island a different man to the one who had arrived there.

Biscop's choice for his name in religion was significant for everything he was to accomplish during the rest of his life. Benedict of Nursia (480–547), or St Benedict, was in many ways the father of Western monasticism, his influence spread by the adoption of his Rule by many different orders. At this point, in the middle of the seventh century, his influence was not so ubiquitous as it became later in the Middle Ages, but his precepts clearly had a profound influence on Benedict Biscop. However, he did not limit himself to his namesake's Rule. According to his own testimony to his monks, Benedict Biscop had lived in seventeen monasteries, observing the rules by which each regulated its corporate life, and when he established his own monasteries, he wrote a Rule that took what he regarded as the best of all those rules as the Rule for his own houses. Unfortunately, Benedict Biscop's Rule has not survived, so we don't know how it differed from Benedict of Nursia's, but the consensus among scholars is that it followed its pattern reasonably closely.

Perhaps just as significant was Benedict Biscop's destination when he left Lérins in 667. Rather than returning to Britain, he made his third visit to Rome. But, unbeknown to him, he arrived in the city at a particularly opportune moment. For Benedict Biscop was not the only visitor from Britain to arrive in Rome in 667.

Three years earlier, Deusdedit, the archbishop of Canterbury, had died, most likely from plague. In his place another Saxon, Wighard, was appointed to the archbishopric with the support of both Oswiu and Ecgberht, king of Kent. To confirm his elevation to the archbishopric and to receive the pallium that marked his office, Wighard travelled to Rome to be consecrated by Pope Vitalian. Wighard made it to the city but never returned to Britain; he died in Rome. That left the Church in Britain without a head.

With the party that had accompanied Wighard to Rome still in the city, Pope Vitalian decided to supply this new and distant diocese with an archbishop from among his own clerics. He initially asked a friend, Hadrian, the abbot of a monastery in Naples, to take the chair but Hadrian demurred. As an alternative, Hadrian suggested another candidate for the vacant archbishopric, a Greek named Theodore.[6] On the face of it, Theodore seemed like an unlikely choice since he was already 65. Even today, it would be asking a lot of a 65-year-old to move to a new country, with an entirely different culture and a strange language, to begin a completely new career there. What was more, the journey to Britain would be arduous, and the tasks falling upon the new archbishop were likely to be just as difficult.

Up until recently, almost all we knew about Theodore derived from Bede's *Ecclesiastical History*. But over the last few decades, some deep and subtle scholarship has unlocked much new information about this crucial figure in the history of the Church in Britain. The painstaking analysis of the Biblical commentaries produced by the school in Canterbury that Theodore founded has revealed all manner of unexpected details about Theodore's life before he was dispatched to Britain and indicate why Pope Vitalian chose him for the role.

Theodore was born in 602 in Tarsus, the modern-day city of Gözlü Kule, Türkiye. While a sizeable city in the seventh century, Tarsus was a satellite of the great city of Antioch, which lay a hundred miles to the east, the journey possible by a well-maintained Roman road. We can now say that Theodore laid the foundations of his knowledge in the schools of Antioch, for the exegesis of the Canterbury school he founded bear all the hallmarks of Antioch, in particular its focus upon understanding the literal meaning of the Bible. To do this, the Greek-speaking schools of Antioch often used the Septuagint (the Greek version of the Bible) as keys to unlock the meaning of the Vulgate (the Latin Bible). There were also many Syriac speakers in Antioch, which helped with untangling knotty problems of etymology. Many of the Church Fathers were Syriac speakers and there was a deep Syriac theological literature. The centre of Syriac-speaking Christianity was the city of Edessa (now Sanliurfa in Türkiye), 150 miles further east of Antioch, which Theodore probably visited, too.

So, in his youth and young adulthood, Theodore had breathed the air and thought of a profoundly different experience of Christianity among peoples and places that were very different to seventh-century Britain – but much closer to the world of the New Testament.

While Theodore was studying in Antioch in the early decades of the seventh century, the Byzantine and Persian Empires were continuing with the long-drawn out struggle that had occupied both empires for the last two centuries. Neither side was strong enough to decisively and permanently defeat the other; both were strong enough to continue the struggle. The Persians conquered Antioch and Tarsus in 612 and Damascus and Jerusalem in 613. Theodore was ten when the Persians conquered Tarsus, and asides in the

Biblical Commentaries reveal a degree of familiarity with Persian customs, including the remark that the cups in Exodus 25:31 were long and pointed, like Persian drinking vessels. One can only wonder how the young Theodore got to see the Persian conquerors drinking at a feast.

The Byzantines reconquered Tarsus and Antioch, then Damascus and Jerusalem, finally inflicting a heavy defeat on the Persians at the Battle of Nineveh in 627. But both sides were left exhausted by the decades-long conflict and vulnerable when, a few years later, Arab armies espousing a new religion rode from the desert. The Persian Empire, which had endured since the days of Cyrus the Great, collapsed utterly. The Byzantine Empire reeled before the Islamic conquest, losing the Holy Land and Syria in 637, as well as Antioch and Tarsus. The surging Arab armies were only turned back from the walls of Constantinople by the Byzantines employing Greek fire to burn the Arab ships.

The Muslim conquest of the Near East sent a wave of refugees west, and among them was Theodore. If he left as Tarsus fell, then Theodore was 35 years old when he became a refugee. Where else to go but the city safe behind the most secure fortifications of the age: Constantinople itself. But not only was the capital of the empire a safe refuge, it was also home to a university, housed in the Imperial Basilica, next to the Octagon, where the professors lived, all in close proximity to the public library and the Hagia Sophia, the greatest church of the city. Already a great centre of learning, the Arab conquests brought a new wave of scholarly refugees to the city. Among them, Theodore found like minds and teachers, from whom he learnt law, philosophy and natural science, medicine, astronomy and *computus*, the science of determining the date of Easter.

From Constantinople, Theodore went on to Rome. We do not know how long he spent in Constantinople or when he arrived in Rome, but he lived in his new home as a monk, tonsured in the oriental manner (that is, he shaved his head completely). A quirk of his consecration to the See of Canterbury was that Theodore had to let his hair grow before he could receive the Western style of tonsure, with the crown shaved and a torus of hair growing around the head (to suggest the Crown of Thorns).

The Eastern monks living in Rome were important actors in the Monothelite controversy. Following the Lateran Council convened by Pope Martin to deal with the controversy, the decision of the council was published with a list of the scholars who had taken part in the council. Among the list of names, coming after the abbots and priests but above the deacons, was 'Theodorus monachus'. It's likely, verging on probable, that this was Theodore himself. That he had particular expertise in these complex philosophical and theological matters was confirmed some years later, in 680, when Pope Agatho wrote to the Byzantine emperor that there was only one man qualified to write about them, and that was Archbishop Theodore.

This was the man that Pope Vitalian asked to accept the chair of Augustine in Canterbury. Theodore had already had a varied and distinguished career. Now, when most other men would be thinking about retiring, he agreed to journey to the furthermost edge of the world – for the British Isles were girdled by the Great Ocean that had no end – and become the bishop for a people who only a generation or two before had been pagans, and illiterate pagans at that. That Theodore accepted the request says much about him. But, in a gentle revenge, he agreed to the request on condition that the man who had nominated him, Abbot Hadrian, came too.

Hadrian was a considerable scholar in his own right. A Berber, coming originally from North Africa, he brought his own learning as well as experience of another part of the Christian world with him to Britain.

Although the two men had agreed to the pope's request, there remained the task of getting them to Britain safely. Which was where Benedict Biscop came in. He had arrived in Rome from Lérins at the same time as these matters were being settled, so it must have been quite natural for Pope Vitalian to ask him to accompany Theodore and Hadrian on their journey to Britain, acting as their guide and interpreter where necessary.

The party of prelates took its time returning to Britain, stopping in Paris for six months where Theodore, Hadrian and Benedict were guests of the bishop of Paris, Agilbert, who had previously been bishop of the West Saxons (this fact alone indicating how the conversion of the Anglo-Saxons to Christianity was opening them up to greater contact with the rest of Europe). Agilbert's abbey followed a Rule that blended Benedictine and Columban elements (St Columba founded the monastery on Iona, which had played a crucial role in the conversion of the Northumbrians), providing Benedict with further examples of different monastic practices. After their stay in Paris, Theodore continued to Britain with Benedict, leaving Hadrian behind. We don't know why he stayed, but the North African did eventually follow two years later.

Theodore arrived in Kent on 27 May 669 and set about familiarising himself with his new archdiocese with all the urgency of a 67-year-old man unsure how many more years God would grant him. One of his first actions was to appoint his young guide, Benedict Biscop, as abbot of the monastery of Ss Peter and Paul (later St Augustine's) in Canterbury itself. Benedict remained the abbot there for two years, until Hadrian finally arrived in Britain.

During their travels and then for the two years he was abbot of the monastery of Ss Peter and Paul, Benedict had ample opportunity to learn from Theodore, particularly as the old man, alone at first and then with Hadrian's help, set up a school at Canterbury to teach their knowledge to these people at the edge of the world. Such was its breadth and depth, the Canterbury school probably produced the finest Biblical scholarship in the Latin West between the decline of the Roman Empire in the West and the establishment of the medieval universities.

When Hadrian arrived in Canterbury and took over as abbot of Ss Peter and Paul, Benedict had to find a new role. From what he did next, it's clear that he had decided to establish his own monastery, taking its curriculum from what he had learnt from Theodore and Hadrian.

As the key feature of the Canterbury school was teaching, the first thing Benedict did was make another trip to Rome – his fourth – to collect the books necessary for his establishment. Unfortunately, we don't have a catalogue of the library that was established at Wearmouth and Jarrow, but looking at Bede's work, scholars have worked out that it must have included at least 200 books.

The most essential texts for a monastery, which Benedict must have obtained on this visit, were copies of the psalms (the psalter being the basis of monastic prayer life), the Gospels and, if possible, a copy of the complete Bible. This last would not have been so easy to obtain as complete copies of the Bible were expensive and rare. However, we do know that the library at Wearmouth/Jarrow did contain such a book, a pandect – or complete text in a single volume – of the Bible in the Old Latin translation (that is, a version that predated Jerome's authoritative translation, which became known as the Vulgate). On the way back from Rome, Benedict stopped off in Vienne, a city in south-east France which had been a major early Christian centre, to add further books to his growing collection before returning to Britain.

Benedict arrived back in Britain in 672 and travelled to Wessex. He had become a friend to Cenwalh, king of the West Saxons. The bishop there was the nephew of Agilbert, bishop of Paris, with whom Benedict had stayed previously, and there was already a Benedictine presence in the kingdom. But Cenwalh's death in 672 put paid to Benedict's plan for establishing a monastery in Wessex – the political situation there becoming uncertain – and he decided to return to his native Northumbria.

\*

In Northumbria, Benedict Biscop found a new king on the throne. King Oswiu had died of natural causes in his late 50s, no mean achievement for a king at this time, and had been succeeded by his son, Ecgfrith.[7] Ecgfrith's mother was Eanflæd, the daughter of Edwin, who later became abbess of Whitby. Ecgfrith, inheriting from a father who had reigned for an impressive 28 years, with the last fifteen as the most powerful king in the land, found himself in a very strong position.

As such, Ecgfrith had wealth, and to spare. Arriving in Northumbria, Benedict Biscop must have been a man of wonder. This native son had travelled all over the world, including four trips to Rome itself, a city over whose name hung a cloud of numinous power, spiritual and temporal. We can only imagine the tales Benedict must have been prevailed upon to tell the king and his court during the long nights in his great halls, scattered throughout the kingdom: stories of wonder and travel, travellers' tales from the greatest traveller of his time.

Such a man, and his monastery, would have been an ornament to any kingdom. To ensure Benedict remained in Northumbria, Ecgfrith offered him 70 hides of land near the mouth of the River Wear. A hide was a unit of land large enough to support a family from its produce; its exact area depending upon the quality of the land (better land would need a smaller area to feed a family than poorer land).

It was a rich, in fact a kingly, gift and in 674 Benedict laid the foundations for the monastery of St Peter at Wearmouth. One of his most significant early decisions was to appoint a prior of the monastery. The man he chose was named Ceolfrith. He came from the same social class as Benedict, being the son of one of Oswiu's thegns. Born in 642, Ceolfrith was fourteen years younger than Benedict, who was 42 when he founded St Peter's, and he had become a monk in 660, first at Gilling and then, from 664, at Ripon, Wilfrid's monastery. As such, Benedict had to ask Wilfrid's permission for Ceolfrith's move to St Peter's, which Wilfrid duly gave. Ceolfrith would become perhaps the single most important influence on Bede as he grew up.

There had been monasteries in Britain before but most of these, following the Irish pattern, were simple affairs, with churches built of wood and thatch. Benedict, however, had been to Rome. He had seen glorious buildings raised in stone, gilded within by mosaics that glowed as if the sun shone inside, illuminated by light flooding through windows of coloured glass. For his foundation, Benedict wanted to make something similar.

The problem was, none of his people had the skills necessary to build such buildings. The Anglo-Saxons were wonderful carpenters and extraordinary smiths. Unfortunately, wood does not survive the centuries well, so we don't have any surviving examples of their wooden halls. But metal does endure, and their ability as sword smiths and metalworkers is revealed in the pattern-welded swords forged for kings and their favoured warriors, and the buckles, brooches and hilt fittings revealed at Sutton Hoo and by the Staffordshire Hoard.

But they didn't do stone.

To build a stone church like those he had seen on his travels, Benedict had to import skilled labour. This was where the huge range of contacts that Benedict had made during his travels came in particularly useful. One of these was an abbot in Francia, named Torthelm. The relationship between the two men may have been stronger than normal because the name Torthelm is closer to Old English than Old French, suggesting that Torthelm might have been an Anglo-Saxon who had moved to Francia. It was from Torthelm that Benedict recruited stonemasons to build his church. But not just masons. Glass-making was another skill that was foreign to the Anglo-Saxons, so Benedict recruited glaziers, not only to make the windows for his church but also to teach their skills to local craftsmen, so that there would be men to repair and replace the windows when necessary.

Having overseen the foundation of his monastery and the completion of most of the buildings, Benedict set off to Rome once again, taking Ceolfrith with him this time. In his absence, Benedict put a relative, Eosterwine, in charge of the monastery.

Benedict had given careful thought to what he wanted for his monastery, and this journey to Rome proved particularly significant. Learning was obviously going to play a key role at the monastery, so he returned with further books to add to the already considerable library he had amassed. But knowing full well that the majority of the rustic people who would come to his church for mass were illiterate, Benedict also brought back a selection of pictures, illustrating scenes from the life of Jesus and from the final book of the Bible, the Apocalypse, so that the people attending his church could see and understand aspects of the new religion on the walls around them. Another important aspect of Christian worship of the time was relics, the physical remains of earlier holy men and women and their associated objects, which carried with them a cloud of numinous power as a result of their contact with the sacred. So Benedict and Ceolfrith brought back to Northumbria a selection of relics, although we don't know what they were. To help with the practical running of the monastery through the liturgical year, they also returned with calendars, psalters and service books.

While in Rome, Benedict had an audience with Pope Agatho. During his stays in various monasteries, Benedict had seen examples of conflict between local bishops and monasteries, with bishops exerting their authority over monasteries within their diocese. Benedict clearly wanted his own monastery to have a degree of independence from episcopal control, so he petitioned Pope Agatho for a privilege guaranteeing that freedom and also ensuring that the local bishop could not impose an abbot on the monastery against the result of the election of the monks. Because of his previous service to the Holy See, Benedict must have been held in high regard in Rome. Pope Agatho granted Benedict's monastery the privileges he asked for, setting it out in a formal document that Benedict brought back with him to Britain.

But not only that. Pope Agatho granted Benedict a great honour. When Benedict and Ceolfrith set out to return to Britain, the pope sent with them his own arch-cantor, John, the man responsible for overseeing the liturgical chant and song at St Peter's in Rome. Musical notation had not yet been developed, so the only way to learn new music was to hear it. By sending the chief musician of Rome all the way to Northumbria, Pope Agatho was sending the music at the heart of Christendom all the way to its furthest reaches.

John the arch-cantor carried more than music with him: he brought the acts of the Lateran Council of 649 with him, too, the council that had condemned Monothelitism. Pope Agatho's reign saw the final healing, and final condemnation, of this heresy. After Constantinople survived the long Muslim siege of 674–678, Emperor Constantine IV wrote to the pope, seeking reconciliation. Pope Agatho convened councils throughout Europe, then sent representatives to Constantinople to attend the Sixth Ecumenical Council in Constantinople from 680 to 681. The pope's representatives read a letter to the assembled council affirming the settled belief of the Western Church that Jesus had two wills, human and divine, with his human will perfectly in accord with His divine will. The council heard the arguments of the Monothelites, with Constantine himself attending many of the sessions. In an effort to turn the council in their favour, one of the Monothelites proposed to prove their case by raising a dead man through his prayers. A corpse was duly brought into the council and the priest attempted to raise him to life again, whispering prayers into the cold ear of the body. This was not a particularly credulous age, but people did believe in miracles, although these were frustratingly unpredictable. If the prayers had succeeded, the Monothelites might well have prevailed. One can imagine silence falling upon the council while the assembled bishops watched, tensely, as the Monothelite priest whispered urgently into the dead man's ear. Perhaps the prelates present who were most opposed to Monothelitism whispered prayers of their own that the man stay dead.

He did. Monothelitism was formally condemned. And the breach between the Eastern and Western Church was healed for the next few centuries.

Having returned from Rome with such riches, Benedict, Ceolfrith and John set about training the monks at St Peter's in monastic chant as well as adorning the church with the pictures they had brought back.

It was also around this time, in 679 or 680, that a young boy, only seven years old, was brought to the monastery. The little lad must have been wide-eyed at the wonders he saw and heard: a building made of stone, like the hills themselves; this was something no one had been able to do in this land since the works left by the giants of old, such as the Wall that spanned the country from sea to sea. Within, the church was lit by light passing through glassed windows, illuminating the glowing pictures upon the wall. And the sound . . . it was the sound of heaven itself, as the monks chanted the psalms during the Offices of the day.

While it's quite likely the young Bede saw the king when he visited St Peter's, it's unlikely that he ever spoke to him in any meaningful way, for Ecgfrith died in 685, when Bede was still only twelve or thirteen. However, Ecgfrith must have visited the new monastic establishment that he had so handsomely endowed, for he decided that he liked it so much he wanted to have another. In 681, King Ecgfrith gave Benedict another 40 hides of land, some seven miles north of St Peter's, along the bank of the River Tyne near to where it flows into the North Sea, in modern-day Jarrow.[8]

Here, Benedict established a new monastery, dedicating it to St Paul. The dedication was significant. Saints Peter and Paul were both martyred in Rome. Their relics were there in the city, underneath the churches raised over their tombs. That Rome was where the two greatest of the Apostles were martyred did much to secure its primacy among the various apostolic patriarchies. By dedicating his monasteries to Ss Peter and Paul, Benedict was also dedicating them to the Roman Church – but Rome in its most universal, most catholic sense, as being the local embodiment of the Church's universality. It was also a statement of fidelity to the successors of the Apostles, namely the popes, and an expression of gratitude for the way that they, from Gregory onwards, had turned their attention towards a pagan land at the end of the world.

We don't know when John left Northumbria and returned to Rome, although to effectively train the next generation of monks in the art of monastic chant would have taken at least a few months. The greater likelihood is that John spent a year or two at Wearmouth before returning to Rome. Winter was not a time to travel, except under grave necessity, and spring and autumn storms presented dangers to sea crossings, so he most probably waited for the calmer weather of summer before taking passage south.

John did not just bring tunes with him; he also brought the acts of the Lateran Council – the very council that had condemned Monothelitism. For Benedict, this must have seemed divine confirmation of his own memories of the conflict between Pope Martin and Emperor Constans II. So when he established St Paul's, Benedict decided that the two monasteries should act as one, united under the rule of a single abbot, as Jesus had two wills, human and divine, united because of the perfect accord of his human will with His divine will. It was also a proclamation of how the bishop of Rome united the apostleships of Ss Peter and Paul through the years up to their own time.

It was a statement in stone and institutions, realised through the lives of the monks living at St Peter's and St Paul's.

\*

Having overseen the establishment of St Paul's, Benedict left to make what would prove to be his final visit to Rome in 685, to procure further necessaries for his monastery. He returned with more books (naturally), pictures to decorate the new church, vestments and some silk cloaks, apparently intended as gifts and trade items.

Benedict came back to find his royal patron, Ecgfrith, dead. Against the advice of St Cuthbert, Ecgfrith had continued to pursue an aggressive policy of expansion northwards against the Picts.

We can trace the last months of Ecgfrith's life with quite unusual precision for a king who reigned so long ago. In autumn of 684 he was at a Church council on the River Aln where Cuthbert was appointed as a bishop. The consecration took place in York on 26 March 685, with the king almost certainly in attendance along with Cuthbert's brother bishops.

Then, on 23 April 685, we have an extraordinary physical record of Ecgfrith's presence in Jarrow. For in the church of St Paul that still stands there is a dedication stone, with an inscription carved in Latin, that records the church's dedication by King Ecgfrith and Abbot Ceolfrith on the ninth day before the kalends of May in the fifteenth year of King Ecgfrith: 23 April 685.

Ecgfrith would die less than a month after taking part in the dedication of the church of St Paul at Jarrow. The king had sponsored the community there, so it was natural that he should want to be present for the dedication. But Ecgfrith also knew that he was about to set out on a military expedition that, for all his confidence, carried risks. Being there when the church was dedicated was a good way to remind God that he had given the monks this land so that they might do God's work. It surely wasn't too much to ask God to support him in his work? But God's favour was not so easily bought.

There was also a practical reason for Ecgfrith coming to Jarrow shortly before heading north on his punitive expedition against the Picts: the Tyne was probably the site for one of the king's naval bases. From there, it was an easy and quick voyage north into Pictish territory.

Having done all that he could do to ensure God was on his side, Ecgfrith set out with his army at the beginning of May, travelling north to Bamburgh and gathering his warband as he went. His intention was to bring ruin down upon Bridei, the ungrateful king of the Picts. Success must have seemed certain. Ecgfrith had ensured divine favour by supporting the foundation of a new monastery. His warband was composed of trained and experienced warriors, armed with the finest weapons of the time. The law code promulgated by the king of Kent a couple of decades later defined an army as a group of more than 35 men: this was a time of small, highly trained armies, not the mass levies of the later Viking Age. Ecgfrith likely travelled north with no more than a few hundred warriors.

What a sight they would have been. Riding on horses, wearing brightly dyed clothes with their round, painted shields and weapons glittering with gold and garnets, they were an army designed to draw attention. Armed with spears and swords, they rode north, laying waste to the possessions of the king of Fortriu as they went.

The kings of Northumbria had extended their control northwards over the previous decades until they controlled the central belt of Scotland, including the stronghold at Edinburgh and probably

Stirling too. Defeating Bridei would establish Ecgfrith's control over all the region north of the central belt, something not even the Romans had achieved. The English would have established political control over a Scotland that did not yet exist.

But it all went horribly, disastrously wrong.

Overconfidence probably did for Ecgfrith. Thinking Bridei's forces no match for his own, he pursued the Picts as they apparently routed – only to find himself caught in a prepared trap. On 20 May 685, Ecgfrith was lured into battle at a place known as Nechtansmere. He was killed, along with the greater part of his warband. Their bodies were despoiled, the rich weapons and armour they wore stripped from their bodies by the victorious Picts.

The Battle of Nechtansmere[9] might be the most decisive little-known battle in British history. It put a halt to Northumbrian attempts to push their kingdom further north for three-quarters of a century. It took until 750 before King Eadberht felt that he had strength sufficient to hazard a further venture north. He had initial success, conquering the plain of Kyle in 750 but a later attack, in 756, saw Eadberht's army all but wiped out. The boundary thereafter fluctuated somewhat, before settling down to roughly following the line of the River Tweed, after the Battle of Carham in 1018. But it was the Battle of Nechtansmere that put a halt to what had seemed the inevitable northern expansion of Northumbrian power. The battle was a turning point: from it, we can trace the future course of Scotland and its boundary with the new country of England forming to its south.

If Ecgfrith had won, and continued the Northumbrian push north, then it's quite possible that any boundary between the two different countries would have lain much further north, or even that Scotland would have been subsumed into a larger northern state (although the later arrival of the Vikings would have placed huge strain on such a kingdom).

Although forty years old when he was killed, Ecgfrith had no children. His first wife, Æthelthryth, had remained steadfast in her vow to perpetual virginity. Wilfrid, now bishop of Ripon, had supported the queen's oath which, not entirely surprisingly, led to a breakdown in relations between Ecgfrith and him. In the end, Ecgfrith released Æthelthryth from her marriage vows – she went on to found the abbey at Ely – while he married again. However, his second marriage also did not produce an heir.

The next in line to the Northumbrian throne would have been Ecgfrith's brothers, but one of them, Ahlfrith, apparently rebelled against their father, Oswiu, and subsequently disappears from the historical record while the other, Ælfwine, died at the Battle of Trent in 679.

With no children or brothers available to take the throne of Northumbria, the net was thrown wider, settling upon the unlikely figure of a scholarly exile from Northumbria, one Aldfrith. He was a half-brother to Ecgfrith, the product of an early alliance of Oswiu with Fin, an Irish princess. As such, Aldfrith spent his childhood and early adult life in Ireland and the islands of the west coast; his mother tongue was Gallic rather than Old English, and Iona was the source of his faith. However, following the model of Irish monks, Aldfrith appears to have travelled widely through the monasteries of Ireland and north-west Scotland to pursue his studies.

It's notable that the king chosen to succeed to the throne of Northumbria following this devastating defeat by the Picts was a man who would have been very well known to Bridei, king of the Picts. Although the Northumbrian sources pass discreetly over the matter, it seems likely that a key factor in Aldfrith's accession to the throne was precisely his close relationship with the Picts and the Irish (Ecgfrith had earnt the enmity of the Irish after his devastating raid on the island in 684).

As king, Aldfrith abandoned the expansionism of his half-brother, being content to rule Northumbria within the boundaries that had been established; the kings of the Picts and the Dal Riadans were no doubt relieved to be freed from the aggression of their neighbour. While Aldfrith eschewed military adventures, he supported the pursuits that had occupied his previous life, sponsoring the work and learning of the Church within his kingdom. While Aldfrith's reign saw a decline in Northumbria's political power, it laid the foundations for Northumbria's cultural golden age.

So although Ecgfrith's death removed a powerful protector, Aldfrith's relatively peaceful reign produced stable conditions that allowed Benedict's fledgling monasteries to flourish.

However, during Benedict's final trip to Rome the monasteries had been stricken with an illness which the chroniclers labelled plague, although this was probably not the bubonic plague that would devastate the medieval world. The disease killed many of the monks including Benedict's kinsman, Eosterwine, who had been left in charge while Benedict was away. Ceolfrith and the community had chosen Sigfrid, a deacon, to replace Eosterwine, and Benedict approved the decision. To further secure the future of his monasteries, Benedict bought three more hides of land from King Aldfrith, paying for the land with two of the silk cloaks he had obtained in Rome. But not long afterwards, Benedict's health began to break. Over three years he became progressively more paralysed, until he was only able to move his upper body. Sigfrid was also stricken with illness, leaving the government of the monasteries in abeyance.

Although so weak that he could barely move, Benedict was able to choose Ceolfrith as the new abbot of the joint monastery of St Peter and St Paul. The choice, Bede tells us, was welcomed by the monks.

Knowing that his death was approaching, Benedict set before his brethren his final wishes as to the governance and future of their monastery. He urged the monks to keep the Rule that he had devised for their lives. When selecting future abbots of the monastery, he emphasised repeatedly that the community should not be persuaded to follow the cultural temptation of appointing a man to the office because of rank or family. Indeed, Benedict went so far as to say that he would rather everything he had built up by the rivers Wear and Tyne should return to wilderness than that they should appoint his birth brother as abbot in his place. This is the only mention of Benedict having a brother. It suggests that, during his three years of infirmity, relatives of Benedict might have been putting pressure on the community to accept the Baducinga family as hereditary rulers of the establishment. Had they done so, the Baducinga would have been set to inherit the very substantial land holding that supported the monasteries. Benedict was absolutely emphatic that the monks must not allow this; instead, they should select the man from among the community whom they judged best suited to the office.

Using the Biblical example of how Israel had endured while ruled by a single king but had slowly perished when divided between the kingdoms of Israel and Judah, Benedict enjoined his monks, of both houses, to follow the rule of their single abbot.

As for the library he had so painstakingly assembled, Benedict exhorted his community to keep the collection intact, not allowing it to be split up, and to look after the books (which would mean regularly recopying the most used volumes). The library was to educate the monks and the wider community they served.

By the end, Benedict was left so weak that he was unable to move his head without help. On 12 January 689 he died at St Peter's, the first monastery he had founded. He was buried in the church. Bede was sixteen or seventeen by then, so he would have been a witness to Benedict's final illness and death.

Despite the vicissitudes of the centuries, the two churches that Benedict founded all those years ago still stand, although much extended over the centuries. The monasteries themselves were attacked by Vikings in 794, a year after the seismic attack on Lindisfarne. With their exposed positions by the coast and next to rivers, the monasteries were ideal targets for raiding Vikings. The community hung on for a while but by the mid ninth century the monasteries were abandoned. There was an attempt to refound the monasteries in the 1070s but after initial enthusiasm, the monks who moved there were ordered back to Durham. The monasteries were restored, but in much reduced fashion, in the fourteenth century as outposts of Durham Abbey. Both houses continued until Henry VIII suppressed monasticism in England, dissolving them in 1537.

Parts of both churches date to their original building. As to what the monasteries looked like in their heyday when Bede and hundreds of other monks laboured there in prayer, teaching and writing, we now have a far better idea of the sites' appearance through the painstaking excavations undertaken at Wearmouth and Jarrow by Dame Rosemary Cramp from 1963 to 1978.

In the case of the monastery of St Peter, it was built on slightly raised ground on the northern shore of the River Wear at its junction with the sea. In Bede's time it was known as Æt Wiuraemutha in Old English, or Ad Uiuraemuda in Latin. The buildings were largely made from limestone quarried locally. The seaside location allowed for good communication by boat but crossing the river required a ferry, and the community quickly acquired some land on the south bank of the river to ensure that they had a safe mooring place there for their boats.

Dame Rosemary's excavations found that the path running from the church to the river predates the establishment of the monastery, suggesting that there was something at the site that was frequented enough to produce a path. What that was, we don't know, although scholars have speculated it might have been a Roman watch tower or a pagan shrine.

The church itself may originally have had two storeys, the normal nave and a second storey above that. The archaeology is not definitive, and Bede's Latin description allows for either a second storey or a separate refectory. The interior of the church was plastered and painted, probably with red stripes, while the exterior was whitewashed, making the building gleam whenever the sun shone. There was also what appears to have been a covered walkway, rather like the later medieval ambulatories, extending at right angles from the church down towards the river.

Apart from the main church there were two other chapels on the site, one dedicated to Mary and the other to St Lawrence, although the archaeologists were not able to ascertain their locations. As well as the churches, there was also the dormitory where the brethren slept, a kitchen and a bakery, as well as sheds and stables.

The monastery of St Paul in Jarrow was built to the south of the River Tyne, in the crook of a bend of a tributary, the River Don.

It was set on marshy ground, the local topography having given a name to the original inhabitants of the region, the Gyrwe, the marsh dwellers. The site for the monastery was slightly raised but then fell sharply to the east, to the mud flats leading to the tidal Don. This was a good anchorage, known as 'The Slake', which lay away from the dangerous waters at the head of the River Tyne. Although the two monasteries are only six miles apart by land, there were, so far as we know, no existing roads linking the two monasteries, although presumably the monks must have created a good footpath linking the two establishments while the monasteries endured, since there would have been times when the weather precluded travel by boat between them.

Unlike St Peter's, which is right at the mouth of the Wear, St Paul's is set two and a half miles inland from the mouth of the Tyne. Apart from any other reasons, the mouth of the Tyne is a notoriously rough passage of water, so founding a monastery there would have made for difficult communications across the rivermouth. The Don itself had a bridge or causeway across it, allowing for easier communications to the south of the monastery.

The church of St Paul was built from sandstone blocks. As at Wearmouth, the building was plastered within and whitewashed without. Apart from the main church there was a second church, built in line with St Paul's but somewhat smaller at roughly half the length. The dormitory and kitchens were built parallel to the two churches and closer to the river, with steeply shelved gardens leading down to the shore, where there were workshops.

Both monasteries were glazed; their coloured glass windows, although small, were unique in Britain at the time.

The two monasteries – their churches and some of their other buildings made of stone and whitewashed to stand out in the sun and set on raised ground by major rivers – would have been visible from many miles around. Their interiors were just as striking: the walls plastered and painted while the paintings that Benedict had imported ran up the walls where the nave met the sanctuary. Although not on the same scale as the basilicas Benedict had seen in Rome, his churches of St Peter and St Paul successfully brought a sense of Romanitas, its dignity and its weight of history, to the shores of the North Sea. And it was among these buildings, outposts of stone in a largely wooden world, that Bede grew up and lived his life.

## CHAPTER 3

# The Making of a Monk

Qui natus in territorio eiusdem monasterii, cum essem annorum septem, cura propinquorum datus sum educandus reuerentissimo abbati Benedicto, ac deinde Ceolfrido. ('I was born on the lands of this monastery, and on reaching seven years of age I was entrusted by my family first to the most reverend Abbot Biscop and later to Abbot Ceolfrith for my education.'[1])

This is all Bede tells us about his background. It comes at the end of his *Ecclesiastical History*, after he has presented a condensed chronological overview of the history he covered in more detail earlier in the book and after the list of his own books. A few sentences later he goes on to say, *Nono decimo autem uitae meae anno diaconatum, tricesimo gradum presbyteratus* ('I was ordained deacon in my nineteenth year and priest in my 30th'), and that's pretty much it for autobiographical information. This does make the task of subsequent biographers quite difficult. However, in one sense, Bede's reticence about the events of his life was proper for a monk who, by entering the monastery, was stepping outside the flow of time and entering into eternity. Monastic life, at its core, escapes the direction of history: rather than being shaped by events, as history is, it is moulded by rhythms – long, stately rhythms – which are the closest we can come to the experience of eternity when still held within time's bounds.

As he tells us himself, Bede was seven years old when he stepped outside time and was presented to St Peter's monastery at Wearmouth.

The year was 679 or 680. The monastery had been founded in 674. Monasteries in our present-day imagination are time-encrusted institutions or picturesque ruins of even greater antiquity. This was not what the young boy saw when he arrived. The buildings were newly erected, the stone of the church freshly quarried or recently recycled from nearby Roman buildings; even the paint was fresh and gleaming. The institution itself was young and dynamic, staffed by young men of great energy and greater earnestness.

Seven might seem a young age to become a monk, or anything else for that matter, but it was by no means unusual among the Anglo-Saxons for boys of that age to be sent away from home. Among the warrior aristocracy, it was common practice for a boy to go to an allied family at about this age to be fostered there, learning the arts of war and making contacts and alliances that would serve him, and his family, well in later life. Children were sometimes sent as hostages and pledges of good behaviour to kings who won victory in battle but did not wipe out their enemy. No less a child than King Oswiu's son, Ecgfrith, was given as a hostage to King Penda at some point during the long conflict between the two kings. But hostage children were imposed by the victors. Fostering sons was done freely, in another example of the sort of mutual exchange that was fundamental to this society. A boy going from one family to another would, in most cases, be matched by another son going in the opposite direction, tying the knot of mutual obligation tighter.

While this was the main reason for giving sons into the foster care of other high-ranking families, there may have been another unspoken factor at work. At a time when sudden death, through war or pestilence, could remove everyone from a location, having spread your bloodline out more widely meant that the likelihood of family survival increased. If plague struck, wiping out all the local family, having a son or two quartered elsewhere meant that there was some-one still alive to carry on the family and claim its land. When Bede entered the monastery, land ownership among the Anglo-Saxons was either loanland (*lænland*) or folkland (*folcland*). Loanland was, as the name implies, land given, usually by the king to one of his servants, where ownership was retained by the giver. Loanland was normally given for a number of years or for the life of the recipient. Folkland was essentially family land held in ownership through long custom and, as such, ownership could not normally be transferred outside the family, not even by sale.

Benedict, Wilfrid and the other founders of early Anglo-Saxon monasteries were faced with a dilemma when trying to secure the future of their establishments. The land upon which their monasteries depended could not be preserved under the ancient laws of folkland, for the simple reason that monks were not blood relatives and their heirs were heirs in the spirit, not the blood. However, taking the land as loanland necessarily left the future of the monasteries at risk should a later king decide to revoke the loan.

So the Church developed a new concept of ownership, bookland, whereby land was granted to Church establishments in perpetuity through a written and witnessed charter. Over the centuries, the idea of bookland evolved into the concept of land ownership that we now hold as self-evident, where people are free to keep or sell their land, and other possessions, as they see fit. But if we still lived under the law of folkland, then your house would have been in your family for generations and you would have to pass it on to your children, and they to theirs, essentially forever.

Bede tells us nothing at all about his family or why he was brought to the monastery when he was seven. However, it was not uncommon for young boys, particularly in Ireland, to be given to the monks at about this age so that they could receive an education before returning to the family later.

Christianity had made conversions among the Northumbrian Angles from the late 620s onwards but it was only really established during the reigns of Oswald and Oswiu, from 633 to 670. Bede was born in 672 or 673, so his parents, assuming they were in their twenties when he was born, were either first- or, more likely, second-generation converts to the new religion.

In Bede's later work, he writes of vows made by kings, when asking their new God for his favour, that they would give to him a child if the favour was granted. So perhaps Bede's parents made a similar vow with respect to their own child. Or maybe he was given to the monks for education but his aptitude and eagerness to remain at the monastery was enough to keep him there. Could he have been orphaned, either before or after entering the monastery? With Bede's testimony of the close proximity of his family home to the monastery and their complete absence from any part of his work, one wonders if he lost them to disease. After all, a pestilence did strike the monasteries, wiping out many of the monks, so perhaps Bede lost his family to the same disease. That might explain the complete lack of even veiled references to his family anywhere in his work. But then again, Bede wrote eloquently of Benedict Biscop's charge to his monks that rule of the monastery should go to the man best fitted to the role and not be allotted because of blood relationship to the founder. For Benedict, and Bede too, brotherhood in Christ was more important than blood relationships, so perhaps he simply chose to remain silent about his family as being irrelevant to his readers.

Despite this lack of explicit information about Bede's family, most scholars think that he came from the same elite that produced Benedict Biscop. Evidence for this is circumstantial but reasonable. Almost all the early monastic figures whose names have come down to us were originally sons or daughters of the nobility, from Cuthbert through Hild to Benedict Biscop and Wilfrid. As children of the nobility, they had the social advantages that allowed a natural progression within Church hierarchies, as well as the necessary connections to royal figures who could provide patronage for monasteries and churches.

Furthermore, the name Bede, in the alternative spelling Beda, appears in the king list of the neighbouring kingdom of Lindsey, as does Biscop, suggesting these names were used in the higher reaches of Anglo-Saxon society. Although against this must be set the disinclination among Anglo-Saxon parents, even royal parents, to repeat names of ancestors when naming their own children. The practice was more often to take a prefix, such as 'Os', and construct novel names for children by appending a different suffix. Unlike the post-Conquest kings, there's no need to distinguish Anglo-Saxon kings by numerals because they almost all have unique names.

Nevertheless, on balance Bede probably did come from a prominent family. However, it is clear from his subsequent life that the men of the monastery became his true family, and, in particular, Abbot Ceolfrith became a new father to him.

The name with which Bede was christened would have been Bǣda, in the Northumbrian dialect of Old English. The name is derived from the verb *beódan,* which means to bid or command. The name Bede is also recorded twice in the *Book of Life* (*Liber Vitae*) preserved at Durham Cathedral, one of the instances presumably being our own Bede and the other the Bede who served as priest to Cuthbert. *Liber Vitae* are also known as confraternity books. They record the names of people who have entered into spiritual brotherhood with a church or monastery, often by visiting as a pilgrim. The list is kept so that the monks and priests of the institution can continue to remember these spiritual brothers and sisters in their prayers long after everyone who knew them personally is dead. The *Liber Vitae* at Durham Cathedral records the names of visitors to Lindisfarne, Chester-le-Street, where the monks repaired after being driven from Holy Island by Viking attacks, and Durham, where they finally settled.

\*

It's likely that Bede arrived at Wearmouth when Ceolfrith and Benedict were both travelling to and from Rome, on Benedict's fifth trip there and Ceolfrith's only journey to the city. But soon after they returned. This was the trip on which Benedict's prizes included John, the arch-cantor of St Peter's, travelling to Britain to teach these new Christians how to sing a new song.

For a boy who had never been further than a few miles from his home, the arrival of these exotic figures must have been a marvel. The church itself was something extraordinary, a building of stone and glass, as opposed to the wood and shutters of the buildings he had known before. But then Benedict, Ceolfrith, John and their party of far travellers arrived, with the tales of their journey and the cargo of their treasures. Therefore, at a young age, Bede realised that he did not have to travel to see the world, for the world would come to him, at Wearmouth.

His principal reason to be there, however, was work – and the work of a monk is prayer. The essential function of a priest is active: he has to perform the sacraments, giving them to those who need them. But the monk's role is passive: prayer in its purest form is being still with God. But as creatures in time, that's not easy to do. So prayer is channelled through song and, in particular, the chanting of the psalms. Bede would probably have been aware of this even before his arrival. Being born in the vicinity of the monastery to parents who were sufficiently devout to place their boy into the care of Benedict Biscop, he had probably attended mass at St Peter's – although he was born before the monastery was founded so he could not have been christened there.

As a boy freshly arrived in the monastery, the first task was to learn this work. With Latin being a foreign language, the learning was first done by rote repetition, in particular through committing the responses that accompanied the prayers to memory.

In most monasteries it is quite likely that a large proportion of the monks, perhaps even the majority, did not become fluent in Latin. So long as they could chant accurately from memory, they did not need to know how to conjugate verbs or decline nouns, they just had to sing them. Given the time and effort Benedict went to in order to equip his monastery with a library, it's likely that St Peter's and St Paul's required higher levels of learning from its monks. As an adult, Bede was a committed teacher, and that commitment to teaching must reflect the teaching that he himself received.

The early Irish model of monastic education had the boys learn from an older, more experienced monk, with much rote learning and chanting out loud, followed by writing lessons using wax-covered slate tablets and metal styli. The arrival of Theodore and Hadrian in Canterbury had brought a new model of learning to Britain, based in part upon the old Classical modes of learning, as well as greatly expanded content – and Benedict must have brought some of that curriculum with him when he came home to Northumbria.

Not long after Bede's arrival at Wearmouth, in 681, Benedict was given new land at Jarrow and he dispatched Ceolfrith there to found the monastery of St Paul. Bede was eight or nine. We don't know if he accompanied Ceolfrith from the start of the new venture, but his testimony suggests that if he was not at Jarrow from the start, he was there soon afterwards. Ceolfrith was undoubtedly the man who had the greatest influence on the young Bede, moulding and pruning a mind that was avid for learning.

The prerequisite for deeper and wider learning was Latin. The books in the library at the monastery were in Latin but, much more important than that, the Bible was in Latin too. Bede's life as a scholar was steeped in Biblical analysis and exegesis. His written Latin conveys a complete mastery of the language worthy of the Classical masters of the language who wrote when Latin was still a living tongue. This was by no means a given for religious Latinists of the time: many of them affected a rather florid style or wrote prose that was peppered with an idiosyncratic grammar to be found nowhere in Cicero.

No baby in Britain heard their parents babbling *amo, amas, amat* at them, still less *hic, haec, hoc*. Latin had to be learnt and for that you needed teachers, there being no textbooks. So Bede's facility with Latin was a product of the men (and it was men, in his case) who taught him.

In his short autobiographical note, Bede says that his family gave him to Benedict Biscop and then Ceolfrith to be educated. So the most likely sources of his knowledge of Latin were these two men. During his many journeys and his long stay at the monastery at Lérins, Benedict had plenty of opportunity to learn Latin from people who knew the language well, and his commitment to learning suggests strongly that he had the motive to learn the language as well. In the fractured world of the time, Latin was the lingua franca of the Church, the only truly international organisation there was.

What's more, Benedict had much time with Theodore, escorting him back from Rome and then acting as abbot for two years, in which to hone his Latin and to learn Greek to a reasonable level. However, Benedict could not have been Bede's principal teacher. His responsibilities were such that he would not have had much time to teach boys. Furthermore, in 685 Benedict made his final trip to Rome and then, not long after his return, he was afflicted with the creeping paralysis that would eventually kill him.

So while Benedict was not Bede's principal teacher, he set the framework of Latin teaching that came to fruition in Bede's apt mind. However, there was another way in which Benedict was a formative influence on Bede.

The decline of the Roman Empire in the West was, in some ways, a shift in loyalty from the international to the local. It's likely that the Britonnic elites who took control of the country following the withdrawal of Roman power still saw themselves as Romans, but Romans withdrawing from the increasingly rapacious tax demands of the empire. In fact, even as the empire dissolved in the West, the last part of its control that it relinquished was its tax-gathering rights and abilities. The ability to raise funds to pay for the army was crucial to Roman endurance, and its failure was key to the Roman collapse.

The Romano-Britonnic elite in Britain, having freed themselves from Roman political control, were able to continue their Roman lifestyle while no longer being burdened by the tax demands of an empire that had never paid too much attention to their needs. It was something of a win-win situation at first. Among that elite, their identity remained Roman but their loyalty had shifted to something and somewhere closer to home.

However, as Britain dissolved into smaller and smaller kingdoms with the breakdown that accompanied the arrival of the Anglo-Saxons in large numbers, ideas of loyalty and identity continued to shift. By the sixth century, loyalty had become personal and local, tied to a particular warlord who provided protection to his peasants and gold to his warriors, and identity had fractured down to the tribal, even the familial, level. This remained true for most people into the seventh century, but the arrival of the Church, with its explicitly international dimension, began to provide alternative routes to loyalty and identity.

With no one is this better exemplified than Benedict Biscop. As we saw in the previous chapter, he was born into the Northumbrian elite but renounced the life of war and embarked upon his travels in his early twenties, to explore and broaden his religion. When Biscop left Rome in 665 he did not return home but went to Lérins, where he spent two years and where he intended to spend the rest of his life. So already by 667, when he was in his late thirties, Biscop had exchanged local and familial loyalty for a commitment to the Church, a commitment that was not bound to any particular place but rather one in which he sought the place where he might best pursue his monastic vocation.

When Benedict eventually returned to Britain, he saw no particular reason to return to his native Northumbria, instead trying to found a new monastery in Wessex. As the name indicates, the people of Wessex were of Saxon descent, while the Northumbrians were Angles; the two dialects were quite distinct and the kingdoms, while not direct rivals, were only nominal allies. It was only after the death of Cenwalh, the king of Wessex, that Benedict decided to engage his remaining high-level contacts, returning to Northumbria and seeking the patronage of the king there – this was clearly a decision born more from expedience than any deep desire to return to his native country. King Ecgfrith's enthusiastic sponsorship ensured that Benedict founded his monastery in Northumbria but having done so, Benedict made three further trips to Rome, as well as a journey to Francia to recruit the stonemasons and glaziers able to build the sort of church he wanted – a church built according to a very different, continental model of building.

So Benedict had clearly abandoned the local and tribal roots of identity that gave most people of the time a profound sense of who they were. Benedict was first and foremost a Christian and a monk, but his Christianity and his monasticism were moulded on

European patterns. For a native of Britain at this time, it was a very unusual set of loyalties.

But not only had Benedict exchanged local and tribal loyalties for religious and international ones; he also put aside the familial ties that were the most fundamental bonds of belonging for almost everyone else. As he was dying, Benedict gave a final address to his monks in which he placed bonds of spiritual brotherhood and affinity to the truth above any ties of blood:

> I tell you in all sincerity that as a choice of evils I would far rather have this whole place where I have built the monastery revert forever, should God so decide, to the wilderness it once was, rather than have my brother in the flesh, who has not entered upon the way of truth, succeed me as abbot. Take the greatest care, brothers, never to appoint a man as father over you because of his birth.

With almost his dying words, Benedict put himself in firm opposition to the customs of inheritance that would mean a blood relative of his own being installed as the next abbot. The monks of his monastery were to ignore the ties of blood, or indeed the pressure of kings and bishops, for he goes on to say: '[A]lways appoint from among yourselves, never from outside the monastery . . . you are to meet as a body and take common counsel to discover who has proved himself fittest and most worthy by the probity of his life and the wisdom of his teaching to carry out the duties of this office . . . Then you are to summon the bishop and ask him to confirm your candidate in office with the customary blessing.'

The model of loyalty that Benedict bequeathed to his monastery was institutional and international, rather than familial and local. It was a model that Bede absorbed but did not entirely replicate, as we shall see later.

But while Benedict was a key influence on Bede through the monastery that he founded and the attitudes he inculcated, he was not Bede's principal teacher. That role fell to Abbot Ceolfrith. The monk who oversaw the building of the monastery at Jarrow was the key influence on the young Bede, particularly if he took Bede to Jarrow to help with the building of the monastery of St Paul's. Ceolfrith had also travelled to Rome with Benedict, so he had had the opportunity to hone his Latin there. His long association with Benedict also allowed Ceolfrith to learn from him.

However, another and earlier source of Ceolfrith's knowledge of Latin was Wilfrid. Ceolfrith spent some of the formative years of his monastic career, when he was in his early twenties, at Ripon with Wilfrid. As the self-proclaimed foremost proponent of Roman practices, Wilfrid was fluent in Latin and committed to ensuring his monks were proficient in the sacred language. So Ceolfrith's understanding of Latin was shaped by Wilfrid, Benedict and his own journey to Rome.

Around the time he arrived at the monastery, Bede was exposed to another opportunity for profound learning in the person of John, the arch-cantor from St Peter's in Rome, who probably would have stayed in Northumbria for at least a year and possibly two. John's principal task was to teach the monks to sing but since the chant was in Latin, that would have involved some instruction in the language too. With the air of far-off sanctity and power that cloaked John as the result of his provenance, he would have been a significant influence on the young Bede.

As well as these men, it's possible that Bede received further training in Latin during his novitiate. At this time, the purest form of Latin taught in Europe was that taught in Spain. The monastery library had a relatively large number of works derived from Spain, particularly those by Isidore of Seville, so some scholars have speculated that among the monks there was a Spanish native who, through the purity of his Latin, was given particular responsibility for the teaching of the language. While plausible, it's a circumstantial theory with no other supporting evidence.

Bede was clearly an outstanding pupil. As a young novice, he and his brethren began their education by scratching the letters on wax-covered tablets, learning the sounds that accompanied each letter and then progressing to syllables. With the sounds of Latin committed to memory, instruction moved to grammar, spelling, the way to order words in Latin and how to write them properly – one of the key skills necessary for monks was the ability to copy books. Rather than dedicated books of grammar, Bede likely learnt his Latin from the psalter, the collection of psalms that form the basis of monastic prayer.

Bede's family gave him into the monastery as a *puer oblatus* – a boy dedicated to God but not yet a professed monk. The oblate made a personal promise to follow the Rule of the order to which he had been given, which was usually renewed annually, until either he should decide to make a formal profession of vows to the order, or to leave it.

Giving children as oblates was popular in the early medieval period throughout Europe but was subject to abuse, leading the Council of Toledo in 656 to propose reforms including that children younger than ten should not be accepted as oblates and that any oblate should be free to leave the monastery at puberty should he wish to do so, although the reform obviously hadn't yet filtered through to Northumbria when Bede was offered as a seven-year-old oblate.

Bede never left the monastery. Although he does not say so, at some point he must have made the first set of vows, entering the novitiate at his monastery. This is a period when the prospective monk lives as a monk, under all the rules and discipline of the monastery, while he ascertains if the monastic life is his calling, before making permanent vows. But just as important during this period is the reaction of the monks among whom the novice is living: they are deciding if the novice is right for them. In the most basic sense, the senior monks are deciding if they will be able to bear having this young man living with them for the rest of their lives. It's like auditioning for a family rather than being born into it.

*

Bede was with Ceolfrith at St Paul's, Jarrow, from early in its history, possibly even from when its first stone was laid. As labour is part of the Benedictine Rule, we can expect that it formed part of Benedict Biscop's Rule, too: the monks had to do physical work. In the early days, that work was building the monastery. Bede was about nine, but he had to put in his shift with the other monks, hauling stone from where it was quarried or recycled. The monks worked hard. The monastery was founded in 681 and the dedication stone for the completed church still survives, now cemented into the north porch (there is a helpful replica of it at ground level). It reads:

DEDICATIO BASILICAE
SCI PAUL VIIII KL MAI
ANNO XV EFRIDI REG
CEOLFRIDI ABB EIUSDEM
Q ECCLES DO AVCTORE
CONDITORIS ANNO IIII

'The dedication of the church of St Paul on [23rd April] in the fifteenth year of King Ecgfrith and the fourth year of Ceolfrith Abbot and under God's guidance founder of this same church.' The fifteenth year of Ecgfrith's reign was 685, so the monks and masons built the church in four years. By the time of its dedication, Bede was about thirteen. His formative years had been spent building the monastery; not just the churches (there were in fact two churches on the site, a larger one that presumably served the local people and a smaller chapel that was probably reserved for the monks – it is this chapel that survives in part in the church of St Paul today as its chancel) but also the other buildings that made up the monastery, as well as working in the gardens and looking after the livestock. A young novice monk did a bit of everything.

In 686, a year after the dedication of the church, plague struck the monastery at Jarrow. After Abbot Ceolfrith's death, one of the monks of Wearmouth and Jarrow wrote a biography of their late abbot (in this case, the author was not Bede). The anonymous monk wrote:

. . . a sudden outbreak of plague struck Britain and devastated it far and wide. This carried away to God many
monks from each of his [Benedict's] monasteries . . . But in
the monastery which Ceolfrith ruled, all those who could
read or preach or were able to sing the antiphons and the
responsories were carried off by the plague except the abbot
himself and one small boy, who had been brought up and
taught by him and who until the present day holds the rank
of a priest in the same monastery . . . Because of the plague
the abbot was very sorrowful and ordered the previous custom to be interrupted and that the whole psalter except at
Lauds and Vespers should be recited without antiphons.
But when this was done for the space of only one week
with many tears and laments, he felt unable to bear it any
longer so he decided that the psalms with antiphons should
be resumed as before. With everyone trying their best, he
completed this by himself but with the help of the boy
mentioned above, with no small labour, until he trained
sufficient companions in the work of God or else obtained
them from elsewhere.

The boy was Bede. He was about fourteen when the plague carried away everyone but himself and the abbot. No doubt Ceolfrith
had already formed a high opinion of the boy beforehand but his
response to the crisis that had struck the monastery served to confirm his judgement about the boy, as well as forcing him to give
Bede a crash course in the singing of antiphons and the reading
of Latin. We don't know how advanced a student Bede was at this
point, but having to sing the Office with one other monk meant a
rapid advance in his knowledge of Latin – and a further deepening
of the already deep bonds between the boy and the abbot.

For those who have not spent many days in a monastery, what
exactly Ceolfrith and Bede were doing will be somewhat obscure.
The work of a monk is prayer, and the main form of those prayers
are the psalms from the Old Testament. These are poems and songs

of praise, lamentation, exultation and, almost, despair that are traditionally ascribed to King David. The psalms develop ideas and emotions particularly through a device called parallelism – a drily mathematical term for some of the most heartfelt poetry ever composed. Better to see and hear it than to force an explanation upon it, so let's pick a psalm at random: Psalm 29.

> Give unto the Lord, O ye mighty, give unto the Lord glory
> and strength.
> Give unto the Lord the glory due unto his name; worship
> the Lord in the beauty of holiness.
> The voice of the Lord is upon the waters: the God of glory
> thundereth: the Lord is upon many waters.
> The voice of the Lord is powerful; the voice of the Lord is
> full of majesty.

In each of these couplets, the second line repeats the idea stated in the first line in different words, inflecting and, sometimes, expanding upon it but not changing it. It's a device that was characteristic of Hebrew poetry and song.

The early Church adopted the use of psalms in its liturgy from Jewish practice (unsurprisingly, as the earliest Christians were almost all Jews), which featured a call-and-response style of singing, where a cantor sang alternating parts of the psalm with a choir. However, for both musical and practical reasons, this developed into the singing of psalms with an antiphon, where the antiphon was a short repeating phrase interspersing the longer psalm verses – essentially, a chorus.

The practical reasons were that the congregation in a synagogue, who sang the antiphon, were not necessarily good enough singers to navigate singing the psalm, and nor would they know the psalm off by heart to recite it, while not all would be able to read it and nor would there be enough copies of the psalms for them to read it. Whereas a short antiphonal phrase, that could be sung and memorised on the spot, served much better as a chorus to the psalm text.

The practice of antiphonal singing transferred early to Christian practice. According to a fifth-century writer, it was Ignatius of Antioch (who died in 107 having written a series of letters to the churches as he made his way to Rome to be executed) who introduced the practice after experiencing a vision of two choirs of angels singing in call and response. Scholars of music generally attribute the incorporation of antiphonal singing as coming from the Jewish synagogues in Syria and Egypt and then entering the early Christian monastic communities in the deserts of Syria, Palestine and Egypt.

Pope Gregory the Great, the man who dispatched Augustine on his mission to Britain in 597, put together a collection of texts suitable for singing as antiphons, and Augustine brought a copy of this antiphonary with him when he arrived in Kent, teaching its contents to the religious trained in Canterbury.

Benedict Biscop, of course, went one step further and brought the pope's own cantor back with him to Northumbria to teach his monks how to sing. So it's clear that the monasteries of St Peter and St Paul saw the correct singing of the Office as the fundamental aspect of their duties.

So when disease carried away all his monks, leaving Ceolfrith with just Bede in his monastery, he was clearly devastated. Not only had he lost many men that were dear to him, but it seemed that he would not be able to carry on with the work of prayer – a work rendered more urgent by the fact that their prayers were needed to help carry the souls of their brethren to God. However, singing the psalter without the customary antiphons served to emphasise their loss, for each sung verse was asking to be answered by its antiphon, and the response was only silence. After a week Ceolfrith could bear the silence no longer. The two of them, man and boy, embarked upon the work of monks together, singing the psalms with the antiphons, presumably with Ceolfrith singing the psalm and Bede, his voice still unbroken, adding the antiphon in a high counterpoint.

By taking on the role of an entire choir of monks, the young Bede demonstrated to his abbot his ability and his commitment. With just the two of them there, Ceolfrith had ample opportunity, as well as a pressing need, to teach Bede as much as he could and as quickly as Bede was able to learn it: the speed with which the boy absorbed the knowledge must have gratified the abbot. For as Ceolfrith gradually restaffed the monastery, he kept the young lad in mind.

Six years later, in 692, Bede was ordained as a deacon at the age of nineteen. This was unusually young. The canonical minimum age for ordination to the diaconate was 25. We don't know why Bede was ordained at such a young age. It may simply be that while the canons (laws) of the Church officially gave a minimum age for the diaconate, in practice this was generally ignored. On the other hand, Bede's early ordination may reflect a recognition of his exceptional ability.

The order of deacons can be traced back to the group of seven men whom the Apostles chose to help them in distributing alms and looking after the poor in the very early days of the Church; the Stephen whose martyrdom is marked on 26 December was one of them. The charitable role of deacons was gradually subsumed into other Church offices and the diaconate became a step on the road towards ordination as a priest, although recent reforms have seen moves to restore it to a distinctive role in the structure of the Church.

The exceptional ability that may have been the reason for Bede's early ordination to the diaconate lay first in his ability as a teacher. We can tell, from the list of Bede's works and various bits of internal and external evidence, that the first books he wrote were, essentially, textbooks for the training of monks. He mainly wrote these books in the decade between his ordination as a deacon in 692 and his ordination as a priest in 702. These books, which include a Latin primer, more advanced works on Latin prose and poetry, and the knowledge necessary to calculate the date of Easter correctly (*computus*), comprised a basic syllabus of the things necessary for a monk to know outside the fundamental skill of learning how to sing the Office.

By 702, when Bede was ordained as a priest, the boy had become a man of 30 years, respected by his peers at the monastery and with a growing network of contacts across the country and even abroad. Benedict Biscop and Ceolfrith had taken the boy who had been put into their care at the age of seven and moulded him into a monk – a monk formed according to the principles of learning and study, as well as rigorous devotion to prayer, that was the bedrock of the monastery at Wearmouth and Jarrow.

Although we remember Bede now for his scholarship, his was a life and a scholarship firmly built upon the great work of a monk: prayer.

## CHAPTER 4

# The Life of a Priest

In uttermost silence, Bede lay prostrate before the altar in the church of St Paul. His face rested on the stone upon which he lay but, despite the silence, he was aware of the presence of the whole community around him in the church. Their breath and their prayers filled the space, holding him up.

The stone was cold beneath his forehead. Bede tried to pull his mind back to the prayers he should be saying at this moment, but odd thoughts and memories kept intruding: burying the last of the brethren at St Paul's when the plague took all save he and Abbot Ceolfrith; the sound of his voice, still high and unbroken, singing the antiphon alone while Ceolfrith sang the psalm in his bass; waving farewell to his parents when he left them to come to the monastery – although while he could remember waving, he could no longer clearly recall their faces; the thrill that passed through him the first time he realised that he understood what he was hearing when the psalm of the daily Office rose in many voices through the church; sitting in the circle of monks listening to Abbot Adomnán, come all the way from Iona, telling them the tale of the Holy Places that he had heard directly from Bishop Arculf, who had walked the streets of Jerusalem and Nazareth, sailed upon the Sea of Galilee and bathed in the River Jordan; the realisation that the marks on the slate were not just marks, they were words – and he could read them; all these memories and more swirled through his mind. He strove to put them aside, to concentrate on why he lay upon the cold stone in the church of St Paul, before the bishop and the abbot.

*

It was the 702nd year since the incarnation of Our Lord, and Bede was 30 – the same age at which Jesus had begun his public ministry. At nineteen, Bede had been ordained a deacon, taking on the responsibility of reading from the Gospel during mass (only a bishop, priest or deacon may read from the Gospel during religious services). The eleven years between his ordination to the diaconate and his ordination to the priesthood were filled with learning and teaching.

As a priest, Bede was now able to carry out the sacramental functions of his vocation. Given that he was in a monastery he probably wasn't called upon to carry out many weddings or baptisms, but he could now celebrate the mass, consecrating the bread and wine so that they became the body and blood of Christ. He was able to feed his brethren divine food and give them holy drink. Then, when they were dying, he could give them the last rites, preparing his brothers for their final journey.

It was an incredibly intimate vocation, one that brought him into direct contact with all the members of the community. Normally, a monastery would only have a small number of ordained priests – a monk had to pray rather than preach – so Bede's raising to that office was further sign of the high regard he was held in by his brethren. But Bede's priestly duties were private to the monastery and his brethren; he hardly mentions them in his writing.

In the afterword to his *Ecclesiastical History*, Bede lists the books he had written up to that point. There were 44 in his list (which actually misses out a couple, namely his non-travelling travel guide to Israel, *On the Holy Places*, a book of miscellaneous answers, *On Eight Questions*, and two letters). While Bede doesn't usually give dates for when he wrote his books, through internal evidence, external references and general detective work scholars have established a reasonably robust order for the writing of his books.

From that, we can see that Bede started his writing career not long after his ordination as a deacon. His early works were closely tied to his teaching, being essentially textbooks for the teaching of novices. The first lesson necessary for novices was Latin, and Bede spent his twenties thinking carefully about the teaching of Latin to boys with no knowledge of the language – as had been true for him, too. The library had some of the standard grammars for learning Latin, written when the language was still heard in everyday speech, but to these Bede added *On Orthography*, a volume designed to help the Latin learner by listing the pitfalls that, no doubt, he had stumbled into on his own journey to knowledge.

But monks also required practical knowledge of the world, both because they had to live in that world, raising animals, harvesting fields and catching fish, but also because the world was essentially a second book written by God, a mute scripture to complement the written scripture of the Bible. To that end, Bede wrote *On Times* and *On the Nature of Things*. Time, and its intimate relationship to the calendar and thus to that point in time when history and eternity met and fused in the crucifixion and resurrection of Jesus Christ, was of especial concern to Bede. So, unlike his other practical textbooks, he returned to the subject after his ordination to the priesthood, writing a much-expanded version of *On Times*, *The Reckoning of Time*.

There is a particular problem when writing the life of a monk like Bede: nothing happened. There are virtually no events in his life to write about. His life was his work, and it ran, for the most part smoothly and without interruption, all the way to his death. And indeed, for a monk, this was how it should be. To be a monk is to live by the rhythms of eternity in time.

However, while Bede's life probably followed the regular pattern for a monk following a Benedictine-style Rule at the time, it was not a pattern that all his brethren followed. Most notably, Benedict, the monastery's founder, had led a remarkably peripatetic life, and Ceolfrith, Bede's beloved abbot, had moved around too, starting his monastic career at Gilling Abbey before going to Ripon and finally ending up in Jarrow, where he managed to fit in a trip to Rome. Some of Bede's religious pen friends, such as Bishop Nothhelm, also moved a lot: when Nothhelm visited Rome, Bede asked him to do some research in the papal archives for him.

But Bede himself did not move. Given the esteem he was clearly held in by his brethren, he could surely have requested permission to travel to Canterbury or even to Rome. But there's nothing to indicate that Bede ever asked to make such a trip.

That's not to say that Bede only walked the few miles from Wearmouth to Jarrow and back again. He did make some short journeys apart from this monkish commute, but we can find traces of only three trips further than the twin monastery. First, having been commissioned by the monks of Lindisfarne to write a life of their beloved St Cuthbert, Bede made the journey north to the Holy Island. We don't know what route he took, but the quickest and, in good weather, the safest way was by boat. It's 50 miles in a direct line from St Paul's in Jarrow to Lindisfarne and around 75 by sea. The sea journey, in good weather, could be easily done in two days, especially with favourable winds – although that does beg the still-open question of whether or not Anglo-Saxon ships had sails. No clearly masted ship has been excavated from this era, although not many boats at all have been found from this time. The exception, of course, is the Sutton Hoo ship but that was rowed rather than sailed. However, even supposing the Anglo-Saxons only rowed and never sailed, the trip was still practical in two days in gentle weather. By comparison, it might well have taken six days by land.[1]

As well as visiting Lindisfarne (which would also have been useful for making monastic contacts who would later help in his research for his *Ecclesiastical History*), Bede paid a visit to an Abbot Wictred to talk about *computus* and, towards the end of his life, he went to York where he discussed the life of the Church with his erstwhile pupil, Egbert.

And that's it as far as travel was concerned. Bede was clearly content with his life as a monk and a scholar, with his teaching and his reading and his learning. Knowing that he had at his monastery the greatest library in Christendom, Bede did not have much cause to wander: most of what he wanted or needed was in Wearmouth and Jarrow.

But of course, a scholar never knows enough. Bede always sought for new knowledge. He was one of the most assiduous listeners when Adomnán visited, committing to what must have been a prodigious memory the abbot's stories of the Holy Land, and then supplementing it with Adomnán's book so that he was able to write his own guide to the Holy Places.

It's a curious fact in itself that Bede chose to write his own book about the Holy Places. Comparing his text to Adomnán's, it's clear that the latter provides most of the content for his own book, although Bede's work is significantly shorter than Adomnán's. In the afterword to his book, Bede states that he compared Adomnán's account of the geography of the Holy Places to those he had read in other books, using both to distil his own account. Perhaps part of the reason for Bede's decision to write himself lies in his description of Adomnán's prose, which he calls 'jagged'. For as accomplished a Latinist as Bede, that might have been reason enough to write his own version of the book.

However, there were also tensions between the Church in Northumbria and on Iona. Bede wrote *On the Holy Places* before 709 and probably in 702 or 703. Iona did not adopt the Roman method of calculating Easter until 716. Knowing that many monasteries would be fascinated to have a book enabling the monks to imagine themselves into the Holy Land, Bede may have decided to provide it himself rather than having Adomnán's work copied. Bede took a particular, forensic delight in working out the exact dimensions of places and buildings from their descriptions in scripture. He worked out that there were 90 side chambers to the Temple in Jerusalem, 30 on each floor.[2] His reckoning of the length and breadth of the Dead Sea – 67 by 17 miles – compares well to its actual dimensions of 53 by 10 miles.[3] This was the geographical complement to his love of pinning down historical sequences.

However, despite Bede's ability to extract information from his sources, there were times when the books he had at his disposal simply did not contain the information he required. When this became apparent, Bede had another resource available: a wide, and geographically dispersed, circle of ecclesiastical friends who had access to different books and further records. Should his friends not have the information themselves, they might still be able to find it for him. For someone who travelled so little, Bede had a broad range of clerical acquaintances. Foremost among these were the men of his own community. Abbot Ceolfrith was a close friend, a father figure and Bede's principal teacher when he was young. But Bede was also close to Ceolfrith's successor, Abbot Hwætberht, who like his predecessor had also visited Rome (it begins to seem that Bede was the only monk there who didn't!).

Outside his own community, Bede corresponded with other religious, and some of these letters have survived, having been copied and disseminated by their recipients. Among Bede's correspondents were Plegwin of Hexham, who wrote to tell him about the feast held by Bishop Wilfrid where one of the priests, David by name, had laid a charge of heresy against him. An important correspondent was Albinus, abbot of Canterbury and a main source for Bede's information on the Augustinian mission. Acca, bishop of Hexham, corresponded with Bede on scriptural matters and was another major source of historical knowledge.

Perhaps Bede's most important researcher was the London priest Nothhelm, who became the archbishop of Canterbury. Albinus conveyed his information about the Augustinian mission and its relations with the kings of Kent to Bede via Nothhelm and, when Nothhelm told Bede of his plan to visit Rome, Bede asked him to transcribe the letters in the papal archives concerning Augustine's mission. Further correspondents included the bishops of Winchester and Lindsey, while Bede was able to ask Bishop Wilfrid some questions one-to-one when Wilfrid visited the monastery. Although Wilfrid was not Bede's episcopal ideal, the two men were on sufficiently good terms for Bede to ask him about the delicate matter of whether Wilfrid's spiritual charge, Queen Æthelthryth, really had preserved her virginity through not one but two marriages (he confirmed that she had).

While Bede writes at some length in his history about religious sisters, he appears to have had little personal contact with them, although the abbesses of Whitby and Ely were among his correspondents.

Although Bede's correspondents were mainly fellow religious, he had friends and contacts among the secular elite. He dedicated the *Ecclesiastical History* to King Ceolwulf having already sent the king his first draft to read. Although we don't have the names of any other friends among the men with swords, many visited the monastery and, because they were well travelled and with information aplenty, Bede plied them with questions. At the same time Bede's own reputation for learning meant that many of the men with bloodied hands sought him out, too.

So while Bede's personal orbit was largely restricted to the round between St Peter's and St Paul's, he was able to travel widely through the tales and letters of his friends and correspondents. Indeed, he was able to travel from the world's edge – the northern island where he lived, with his monastery situated less than two and a half miles east from Segedunum, the easternmost fort of Hadrian's Wall – to its very centre, Rome. He was not so isolated, after all. And the regular rhythm of the monastic life served to reduce further any sense of isolation.

*

Bede's daily rhythm followed the same beats as his brethren, punctuated as it was by seven prayers during the day and another during the watches of the night. Benedict Biscop's Rule shared with the more famous Rule of his namesake a concern that monks should not be idle, but after his novitiate Bede probably did not spend much of his time in manual labour outside the scriptorium. His talents were so obviously directed towards teaching and learning that he spent his time of labour working with the novices, teaching them Latin and the other things necessary for monks to know. Bede had a high view of the calling to teach. In his *30 Questions*, he wrote of no lesser figures than the Apostles and Church Fathers as teachers.

While Bede regarded teaching as a high calling, he had the practical teacher's experience of the difficulties involved in drumming knowledge into minds less avid for learning than he had been himself. In *The Reckoning of Time*, Bede accepts the fact that, despite his best efforts, the book he was writing would never be as effective a teacher as he was in person. However, the *Reckoning* does provide us with a fascinating insight into how Bede taught his students. His standard method was to begin with a simple example, showing his workings, before moving on to a more difficult example, again with the steps laid out for the student, before finally starting with the answer and working backwards to the formula that produced the answer, both to show that the method is correct and to cement it more completely into his pupil's memories. Bede also took account of the background knowledge of his students, writing 'streamed' methods for determining the Moon's zodiacal sign according to whether the student already knew the names and order of the zodiac, and his degree of mathematical knowledge. In another classic teacher move, Bede also asked his more able pupils to explain a problem to their less advanced classmates: teachers throughout history have employed this method and it's a standard technique in today's classrooms.

As a teacher,[4] Bede sought to anchor his teaching in the lived experience of his students. Like himself, they were insular, with little knowledge of places and peoples far away. So he employed what they knew to teach them of things far away: a hand-held torch coming closer at night mimicked the light of a star in the far heavens while he asked his students to imagine people sitting around a winter fire pit, close enough to be comfortable, far enough not to be burnt, not so far that they shivered, as an image for the earth's climatic zones.

However, Bede did not neglect the necessary manual labour involved in the production of the books that was such an activity at Wearmouth and Jarrow; it's highly likely that Bede was one of the hands that wrote the huge pandect of the Bible, the *Codex*

*Amiatinus*, which is the sole survivor of the three pandects produced there during his time.

The special gifts that Bede brought to teaching and learning were recognised and encouraged by his community. In the list of his books that Bede appended to the *Ecclesiastical History*, he begins with the twenty works of Biblical commentary that first won him recognition, both from his community and the wider Church. These works he mostly wrote after his ordination to the priesthood. They are characterised by a meticulous attention to the exact sense of the words in front of him, followed by an expansive search for the allegorical meaning of these words fuelled by Bede's comprehensive knowledge of the commentaries of the Church Fathers and an eye for pragmatic detail.

Bede's commentaries were extremely popular in the centuries following his death. The great efflorescence of Anglo-Saxon missionaries, that saw young men from Britain set off back across the North Sea to evangelise the people they still regarded as cousins, saw many requests sent back to the scriptoria at Wearmouth and Jarrow for copies of Bede's commentaries, so much so that the monks there struggled to keep up with the demand.

Leading the rhythmic life of a monk, there were relatively few 'events' in Bede's life: for the most part, it was a constant cycle of teaching, learning and writing set to the daily routine of singing the Divine Office. There was his arrival at the monastery as a boy, the plague that killed everyone save himself and Ceolfrith at Jarrow, and his ordinations to the diaconate and the priesthood. And that is almost it. Almost, but not quite.

In 716, the outward serenity of Bede's life was disrupted in a manner that left him so upset that he was unable to work for a couple of weeks. For a man whose life was his work, it shows the depth of his distress.

The reason for Bede's unhappiness was Abbot Ceolfrith's unexpected departure from the monastery, fourteen years after his pupil's ordination to the priesthood and when Bede was 44 years old. Ceolfrith had, to all intents and purposes, been his father during most of his childhood and all his youth, as well as being his principal teacher. The two men shared a deep intellectual and spiritual communion. They had worked closely together in the years following Bede's ordination on the great work that the twin monastery had embarked upon, its production of three complete pandects of the Bible. The decision to undertake this work was taken by Ceolfrith, as abbot, but it was based upon his knowledge of the abilities of his community and Bede in particular. For the production of a complete Bible text was not simply a matter of gathering sufficient vellum and starting writing: it was a huge work of scholarship.

What they embarked upon was the production of what we would call today a critical edition: a copy of the Bible where every word and sentence was carefully scrutinised and assessed so that it accorded as closely as possible with the text of the Bible as first written. Given that the Old Testament was originally written in Hebrew before being translated into the Greek Septuagint, and the New Testament was written in Greek, while the version they proposed to produce was to be in Latin, there were huge questions of translation that required solving.

The whole community engaged in the enterprise, but Bede was the key scholar involved: Ceolfrith was no mean scholar himself but being abbot was time-consuming. The two men nevertheless collaborated closely in this, the greatest enterprise of the twin monastery, and after many years labour they had produced three wonderful editions of the complete Bible. The survivor, the *Codex Amiatinus*, lends weighty witness to the scale of the enterprise, coming in at 75 pounds (34 kilograms), with dimensions to match (20 inches by 13 inches, or 50.5 centimetres by 34 centimetres) and 2,060 pages.

It must have been something of a triumph for the community. One copy of the pandect was placed in St Peter's, another in St Paul's, and the third was to be a gift. A gift for the pope in Rome. For the community regarded its faith as a gift from the successor of St Peter. They drew a line from their day back to the mission dispatched to Britain by Pope Gregory in 597, a mission of which they saw themselves as the fruit. The gift of the complete text of the Bible was in recognition and gratitude for the part that the successors of Peter had played in fostering the faith among the Anglo-Saxons.

But what Bede had not reckoned upon was Ceolfrith deciding to take the gift personally. Knowing the likely reaction of both his community and his friends, Ceolfrith had kept his intention secret until almost the eve of his departure. By 716, Ceolfrith had been abbot of St Paul's, Jarrow, for 34 years. He had assumed the abbacy of the twin monastery around 690, so he had been in charge of everything for 26 years. He was 74 years old – and he knew, although he may not have let on, that his health was beginning to fail.

Ceolfrith decided that, before he died, he wanted to return to the tombs of the Apostles in Rome, to spend his final days near the mortal remains of Peter and Paul, the two saints for whom the two monasteries he had looked after for so long were named. Ceolfrith had visited Rome before, in 679, when he was 37, so he was not travelling under false ideas of the glory of Rome: the city in the seventh century was a pale, unpopulated shadow of its Imperial heyday. No, he was going because he wanted to be near Peter and Paul when he died.

The previous abbots of Wearmouth/Jarrow had all died in office. Presumably few of the brethren even considered that Ceolfrith, who had been the constant presence through the lives of probably everyone living in the monastery by this point, would abdicate. For while he was going on a journey, there was no prospect of his return and almost as little possibility of any communication from him.

This is something difficult for us to understand today, when modern communications make it possible to talk to someone face to face wherever they are. This is a recent development, however. My own parents arrived in Britain, separately, in 1960. They could write letters home but news of the sudden death of my grandfather in 1967 arrived via a two-line telegram. My father, coming from Sri Lanka, was only able to return once to see his own father. And this was when we had reliable post. For most of history, to travel far away from home was to be removed as completely from your family and friends as if you had died.

Ceolfrith's proposed departure was, in effect, his death to his brethren – and Bede was stricken with grief. He gives no indication as to whether he tried to talk to Ceolfrith, to get the old man to change his mind, but no doubt some among the brethren would have done so. But it was to no effect. Ceolfrith's purpose was set. He would leave as part of the party from the monastery taking the Bible to Rome. If God spared him, he would present it to the pope in person.

In his report of Ceolfrith's leavetaking,[5] Bede tells how many of the monks begged their abbot to stay. One suspects he was among those reduced to tears. Ceolfrith, not wishing to prolong the agony of departure, did not delay, setting off just three days after telling his brethren that he was leaving. Refusing all gifts of money, having heard mass in the church of St Peter at Wearmouth, Ceolfrith departed on the morning of 5 June, which Bede tells us was a Thursday, taking a boat across the River Wear before mounting a horse and riding away. He left behind, Bede reports, about 600 men split between the two monasteries.

Left without an abbot, the monks met to select a replacement for Ceolfrith. Although clearly held in high regard by his brethren, there's no indication that Bede was ever considered as a possible candidate for the abbacy. While it's clear that Bede had no ambitions towards clerical advancement – his temptations were those of the scholar, not the religious bureaucrat – that needn't necessarily have meant that he was safe from advancement: a very reluctant Cuthbert had been inveigled into becoming bishop despite hiding in a hermitage on Inner Farne in his effort to avoid the post. If Bede's brethren had considered him a suitable abbot, they would have prevailed upon him to accept the post. But it appears that Bede's brethren concurred with his own view of himself: his ministry was teaching, not leading.

Following Ceolfrith's departure the monks of the twin monastery moved quickly, convening a meeting three days later on Pentecost Sunday. All the monks of St Peter's, Wearmouth, were present and most of the senior monks from St Paul's, Jarrow. They chose Hwætberht as the new abbot, a monk who, like Bede, had been at the monastery since childhood. Having been elected abbot,

Hwætberht went after Ceolfrith with a few companions – was Bede among them? – to inform him of the decision. They found Ceolfrith waiting for a suitable ship to carry him south.

Ceolfrith's intimation of his own mortality proved all too accurate. After he finally boarded a ship and sailed to France, he and his travelling party had only reached Langres, 150 miles south-east of Paris, before Ceolfrith was taken ill and died. There were 80 men in the party accompanying Ceolfrith. Not all of these were monks: some were servants, others were travellers sharing the costs and reducing the dangers of travel by moving in convoy. Some of Ceolfrith's companions returned to Northumbria to convey the news of his death to his brethren, but others continued on to Rome, bearing the precious pandect that they had laboured so long over.

It took Bede a long time to return to his labours after Ceolfrith's departure. He was so upset that he was unable to work, although of course he took his usual place in the church to sing the Office. It took time and thought for Bede to come to terms with Ceolfrith's departure and, characteristically, he sought to understand what had happened through meditating upon the Bible.

He found the key in the life of the prophet Samuel, as recounted in the books of Samuel in the Old Testament. According to the First Book of Samuel, the prophet was the son of Elkanah and Hannah. Elkanah had two wives, but Hannah had been unable to bear any children while Elkanah's other wife had produced children, taunting Hannah for being barren. Nevertheless, Elkanah continued to favour Hannah, despite her childlessness. In despair at her inability to conceive, during one of the family pilgrimages to the holy site at Shiloh (this was before the Temple had been built in Jerusalem), Hannah went to the sanctuary and offered up prayers and tears to God, begging for a child and vowing that, if she were granted a baby, then she would dedicate him to God.

But Hannah's prayer was not only heard by God, but by a priest, Eli, who was also in the sanctuary. At first, Eli thought Hannah's prayers were drunken mumblings, but he soon realised that they were prayers, and Eli blessed Hannah. Eli was important as he was one of the very last of the Judges who had ruled Israel before it became a monarchy.

When Hannah returned home, she fell pregnant and gave birth to a son, whom she named Samuel. When the boy was weaned, she brought Samuel to Eli and, in accordance with her vow, gave Samuel to Eli to raise, occasionally visiting the boy as he grew. As an adult, Samuel played a key role in the transformation of Israel from a collection of tribes who recognised the temporary authority of a Judge in times of military crisis to a monarchy under a single king. Samuel anointed the first king of Israel, Saul, and then, when Saul proved unworthy of the role, he anointed David in secret as his successor.

It's not difficult to see why Bede should identify himself with Samuel and Ceolfrith with Eli: given into the care of an older man to raise and teach, his life had in its structure been similar to that of the Biblical prophet. Therefore, Bede looked to the lessons in the life of Samuel for a path through the shock he had received from Ceolfrith's leaving – and he found it. For Samuel had played the crucial role in the transition of Israel from a loose confederation of tribes to a kingdom under the rule of a king. Samuel had anointed Saul, conferring God's blessing upon him. The prophet had proclaimed the king who had made Israel one. There was a lesson there for Bede but, typically, he did not let it lie. For a similar role had been performed by the fourth-century historian of the Church, Eusebius of Caesarea, who had told the story of the Church and Emperor Constantine, who had pulled the religion into the heart of the empire. That Bede was thinking along these lines is suggested by his calling the new abbot of the twin monastery, Hwætberht, Eusebius. But the real Eusebius was Bede himself, and he found a renewed sense of purpose following Ceolfrith's departure by taking on the mantle of historian prophet for his own people. Like the ancient Israelites, they weren't one people but were split into tribes with little overarching sense of unity. The call to unity was a prophetic function.

Bede was going to be the prophet of his people.

## CHAPTER 5

# The Great Work

It was dark. Lying on his back, staring upwards, Bede could see only the shadows that lived under the roof. Without turning his head, he could hear the breath of the monks lying alongside him in the dormitory. Some slept quietly, others more noisily; Brother Cuthbert had been snoring, off and on, since Compline.

While his brethren slept, Bede was waiting. He was waiting for the bell to sound from the church of St Paul, summoning them from sleep to work. Since the age of seven, Bede had lived by the bell's rhythm, rising from sleep, or work, or study, at its call. He had become so familiar with its tempo that now his body waited upon it rather than the other way round, pushing him from sleep in readiness.

The bell rang. Its bright metal summons sounded even brighter in the night's quiet. To either side Bede heard the breath catch of men summoned from dream into waking, but his own breathing continued smooth and untroubled as he sat and then stood. Sparks, bright as shooting stars in the dark of the dormitory, told of one of the novices striking steel on flint to light a taper for the torch. But Bede was already moving towards the door, his feet picking a clear path between the waking monks.

Reaching the door to the dormitory, Bede lifted the wooden bar holding it shut and pulled it open. By God's mercy, the night was clear, calm and still, although cold. His feet had walked the path from the dormitory to the church so often that he could find his way even when the sea mist, the haar, flowed in from the east and left every man alone in a world no wider than the stretch of his arms.

Looking up, Bede marked the great constellation in the sky to the south. He found its old pagan name, Frig's distaff, coming to mind. His ancestors, looking into the sky, had seen the three stars as the place upon which the goddess wound the wool for her spinning. But the constellation had a new name now: Orion.

The Milky Way cast its net of light up to the highest heaven. The sky was fiercely cold on this February night, dark but studded with innumerable lights. Bede had tried to count them before, when he was still barely more than a boy, but he had stopped when he realised that stars he could not see when looking straight at them would appear when he looked away. As such, it truly was impossible to count the stars in the sky, for they multiplied with the slightest turn of the head. It seemed that God had made some things to be beyond counting.

The stars cast sufficient light for him to see the way. Behind Bede, the rest of the fraternity followed, the sound of step and cloth and breath the only noises in the still night. Breath mist rose above the column of men, the incense of their intent on this cold night. Ahead, Bede saw the outline of the church standing above him. The monastery at Jarrow stood on ground sloping down to the River Don, with the church set higher than the dormitory. Its roof cut the starline: above star points, below darkness.

But then, through a window, a pale, yellow light flickered, died back, then gleamed forth once more. Within the church of St Paul, the tapers were being lit in preparation for the monks' arrival and the singing of the night Office: Nocturns.

With the lighting of the tapers, Bede lost some of his night vision. Behind him, he heard the customary stumbling as monks, similarly losing sight, stumbled on stone or fellow. That was an advantage of lying awake when the bell rang and being the first out of the dormitory: there was no one in front for him to walk into.

But the greater advantage was to be the first to enter the church.

They had built the church of St Paul in the Roman manner rather than from wood, as was the custom with his people. They had constructed it from sandstone blocks that they had taken from an old building left by the Romans, binding the blocks together with yellow lime mortar. Bede had helped in the building as a boy, labouring to pull the carts of stone to the site of the church. Now St Paul's stood on the ridge proud of the River Don. The wide Tyne into which the Don emptied was visible from the upper windows of the church. The door at the west end of the church was sheltered by a porch, but light was spilling out: the door was already open.

Leading the way, Bede entered the church, breathing in its familiar smell of candle wax and incense. He walked up the nave and took his place in the choir. The brethren filed in behind him, each man going to the place he knew. The abbot, Ceolfrith, following behind his brethren, walked between the waiting monks and took his place.

'*In nomine Patris . . .*'

In a movement that had become nigh as familiar as breathing, Bede and the monks crowded in alongside him did the same. Forehead, breast, left shoulder, right shoulder.

'. . . *et Filii, et Spiritus Sancti.*'

Abbot Ceolfrith turned to the great psalm book open before him and began to sing. The brothers raised their voices in response, the sound of their prayer going forth from the church into the dark of the night.

While the world slept, men prayed.

For Bede, one among the brethren, this was the heart and matter of his vocation, the work that, above everything else, he had dedicated himself to since he had arrived at the monastery as a boy.

Prayer was the Great Work of monks. Standing together as a community in the middle of the night, they prayed in song, their chant filling the church of St Paul, defying the dark without.

\*

Today, we view Bede through the lens of his work as a historian and a scholar. But, by his own lights and testimony, he was a monk before and above everything else.[1]

Since relatively few people today have met a monk, and even fewer have any experience of monastic life, we need to understand the nature and purpose of the Great Work that Bede embarked upon every day of his life from the age of seven in order to understand anything else about him.

A monk is a man who prays. Within Christianity, the monastic life has its roots set deep. Jesus himself frequently withdrew to pray. Sometimes he took disciples with him – on the night before his crucifixion, he took Peter, James and John – and sometimes he went alone, withdrawing into the desert wildernesses that pushed deep into the Holy Land.

But perhaps the best place to start an account of monasticism is with the incident recounted in St Luke's Gospel when Jesus went to visit his dear friends, the sisters Martha and Mary and their brother Lazarus. Delighted to have Jesus staying with them, Martha rushed about, preparing food, sweeping, cleaning, doing all the many things a hostess does to make the visit of her guest comfortable. But Martha could not help noticing that while she was doing all this work to make Jesus comfortable, her sister, Mary, was sitting at Jesus's feet, not doing anything helpful or useful, but simply sitting there, looking and listening.

In the end, irritated out of forbearance by the lack of help, Martha remonstrated with Jesus, asking him to tell Mary to lift a finger or two and help with the preparations. But Jesus gently rebuked her, saying that Mary was doing the greater work by simply sitting at his feet, and looking and listening to him.

That is what monks do. Taking their cue from Mary, they sit or kneel at the feet of the Lord, looking and listening. Since they do not have Jesus bodily present, they do this by prayer. That prayer can be vocal or silent, raised up in chant and softly spoken, or uttered silently in the hidden room of the heart.

For the Gospels are full of stories and examples of prayer: how to pray and what to pray and the effect of prayer. These examples of prayer are amplified and extended by the many examples of prayer in the wider Bible, of which the most important to the monastic life are the psalms. Traditionally said to be largely composed by David, the psalms are, precisely, prayers, but prayers of every stripe and character: prayers of praise and supplication, of lamentation and despair, of triumph and exaltation. The psalms encompass the whole range of human thought, emotion and situations and, as such, are a veritable book for the life of prayer.

The particular character of the monastic life takes its direction, however, from an injunction in St Paul's first letter to the Thessalonians where he says, 'Rejoice evermore. Pray without ceasing. In every thing give thanks: for this is the will of God in Christ Jesus for you' (1 Thessalonians 5:16–18).

The early Christians, faced with intermittent Imperial persecution and the incomprehension and ridicule of the wider population, strove to live this as much as possible, but monastic communities would have been impossible for the early Church: they would have been all too visible targets.

While historians have generally concluded that Roman persecution was usually local and intermittent, graffiti confirms the derisory attitude of the general population to its Christian minority. The earliest physical representation we have of a crucifixion is a crudely inscribed graffito of a man with a donkey's head being crucified and, scratched underneath it in Greek, the words 'Alexamenos worships [his] god'. This was not meant as a compliment.

It was only with the official toleration of Christianity signed into law by the Edict of Milan in 313 that Christianity could advance fully into the Imperial daylight. By this time, however, the monastic movement had already begun. There are hints of solitaries, both men and women, from as early as the second century, although these solitaries generally lived on the edges of civilisation rather than withdrawing completely into the wilderness. However, in the third century men started going into the desert to be alone with God. Indeed, 'eremitic', from which we derive the word hermit, comes from the Greek word *eremos* – desert. While St Anthony of Egypt was not the first of these desert-dwelling hermits, he was the first to become widely known. As his fame spread, people were drawn to the mountain where he was living in the remains of an old Roman fort. These would-be disciples set up dwellings around Anthony and, in the end, he emerged from the solitude of the fort to oversee them. Anthony set about organising his disciples for the next few years but then withdrew further into the desert. Indeed, one of the marks of the solitary life has always been the way the world has chased after those who seek to withdraw from it.

It was St Pachomius who established the first organised cenobitic monastery ('cenobitic' comes from the Greek word κοινόβιον, or *koinóbion*, which means community life) in the first half of the fourth century in Egypt. By no means everyone had the physical capacity or the skills to live alone in the desert. The community that Pachomius organised brought men into a community where they lived in their own cells but came together to work and worship. Pachomius devised a Rule and also organised separate communities for women. Living in community, obedience – seen as the death to self in following without demur the commands of another – became an integral part of the monastic way.

Cenobitic monasticism rapidly spread. By the end of the fourth century the deserts of Egypt, Palestine and Syria, and the Judaean Desert, were studded with monastic communities.

However, monasticism remained largely a phenomenon of the Eastern Church until a young Roman of a wealthy family, John Cassian, arrived in Palestine in the late fourth century. John Cassian became a monk, visiting many of the monasteries of the region, until an early theological controversy made it necessary for him to flee. One major disadvantage of Christianity having become the state religion of the Roman Empire was that the emperor in Constantinople became involved in disputes, with all the power the state could bring to bear to suppress those espousing ideas the emperor did not favour.

Cassian was sent to Rome to plead with the pope and, while there, he was asked to found a monastery like those of the East near Marseille. The Abbey of St Victor became the model for many later Western monasteries.

However, while John Cassian brought monasticism to the Western Church the most important figure in its future development was an Italian, Benedict, from Nursia in Perugia. Benedict (c.480–547) was born into an aristocratic Roman family and, as such, would have been expected to direct his family's fortunes when he came of age. But when he was twenty years old Benedict abandoned his studies and withdrew into the Simbruini Mountains, living there as a hermit for the next three years. As so often happened with hermits, the more Benedict fled the world, the more it pursued him. When the abbot of a local monastery died, its brethren came to Benedict to ask him to be their abbot. All too aware that these monks were not of the same stripe as he, Benedict initially refused but, ground down by their entreaties, eventually agreed. It did not go well. They tried to poison him. Benedict escaped, only for another local priest to try to poison him, too.

Faced with an array of people wanting to kill him – apparently for the crime of highlighting their failures by his holiness – Benedict left the area and founded the great monastery at Monte Cassino. The monastery was still there in 1944, atop its hill overlooking the Valle Latina, when the Allied advance ground to a halt before the German Gustav Line. Although the German commander, General Kesselring, did not commandeer the monastery as part of his defences, many Allied officers became convinced that the Germans were using it as an observation post and on 15 February 1944 it was subjected to a bombing attack that left it in ruins. The only casualties of the raid were 230 Italian civilians who had taken shelter in the monastery. However, the abbey was rebuilt after the war and remains a Benedictine monastery to this day.

In order to regulate the lives of his monks, Benedict wrote a Rule of life for them. His Rule was greatly influenced by John Cassian, but it bore, most of all, the mark of Benedict's own practical moderation. *Ora et labora*, prayer and work, was at the heart of Benedict's Rule, which mandated one third of the day to prayer, one third to sleep and one third to manual labour, works of charity and sacred reading. Monks were to be bound by vows of obedience, poverty and chastity, as well as swearing constancy to the monastery that the supplicant joined, and the humility to be spiritually formed there.

The Rule sets out practical guidance for how this is to be done, from advice on being obedient and humble to chapters on monastery management. As such, it became the Rule for thousands of monasteries that were founded in Europe over the next 500 years. Not all of them followed Benedict's Rule to the letter, but his influence was pervasive.

Pope Gregory the Great was an enthusiastic sponsor of Benedictine monasticism. Indeed, most of what we know of Benedict's life comes from his *Dialogues*. With papal support, Benedictine style houses spread throughout Western and northern Europe, usually working in reasonable harmony with the local bishop.

However, as Christianity spread northward in Europe it advanced into areas that were wilder and less cultivated. Less Romanised. The human geography became sparser, with fewer towns and no cities. It was not a landscape that suited the episcopal organisation of the Church. But it was a landscape that suited men who wanted to escape the suffocating presence of their fellows to be alone with God. Monasticism's original eremitic temper was reinforced by the very terrain in which it was now operating. When Christianity reached Ireland in the fifth century, Patrick and his fellow missionaries found a country that had none of the urban infrastructure of the empire. There were no cities, no towns, no real concentrations of population at all. The Church structure that had developed amid the decline of empire, where a city-based bishop had charge of the surrounding area, simply could not work where there were no cities to support a bishop and his clergy.

Instead, the Church in Ireland developed a monastic organisation. With monasteries becoming self-supporting centres of activity, they could support the necessary clergy to minister to the surrounding area in a way that no other locations could in Ireland. So when King Oswald of Northumbria invited monks from Iona to evangelise his people, they brought this clerical structure with them.

However, in Britain, there were two competing systems of Church organisation. The Augustinian mission that had been dispatched by Pope Gregory the Great and which had arrived in Kent in 597 naturally divided the country into bishoprics. Pope Gregory's original instruction was for there to be two bishoprics, in London and York, corresponding to the old southern and northern dioceses of Britannia when it had been part of the Roman Empire. However, arriving in Kent, Augustine had quickly realised both that he needed the support of the king of Kent, who was not going to be happy with him moving to London, which was under the control of a rival Anglo-Saxon kingdom, Essex. Adapting to circumstances on the ground, Augustine took Canterbury as his episcopal see – which is why the archbishop of Canterbury remains the leading cleric in the country to this day. The two ecclesiastical systems, the Roman and the Irish, existed in parallel during the rule of King Oswald, but under his brother and successor, King Oswiu, the Church began to adopt the Roman system throughout the land.

*

Northumbria in the seventh century stood on the very edges of the world. The kingdom was bisected by the still largely intact remains of the Wall by which the Romans had delimited the boundaries of their rule (although their influence extended far north of the Wall). It was a world of petty kingdoms, some no bigger than shires, and local warlords who amassed gangs of warriors to stake their claims to rule, defending their gains by the sword and, usually, dying by the sword, too.

It was into this world that Benedict Biscop was born.

While the Rule of St Benedict was the most widespread and influential in later centuries, in the seventh century there were many monasteries that lived under different rules. By visiting and staying for extended periods of time at many different monasteries, Benedict was able to experience and evaluate the strengths and weaknesses of these different rules. When it came time to propound a Rule for his monastery, Benedict took elements from what he had learnt and crafted his own Rule for his foundation at Wearmouth.

While we would wish that that Rule had come down to us, it has not. Neither Bede nor any of the other monks at Wearmouth and Jarrow recorded it – perhaps because, being a lived reality, they did not need to – and then, when the monastery fell victim to the depredations of the Vikings in the ninth century, the monks that escaped did so in haste, leaving behind any written account of the Rule of their life.

The lack of a record of Benedict Biscop's Rule means that we cannot say for certain what the details of a typical monastic day was for Bede and the other monks of Wearmouth and Jarrow. What we can say for certain, however, was that it revolved around the public prayer of the psalms, the Divine Office that John, the arch-cantor from Rome, had been brought to Britain to teach the native monks. We can also say that it would have included times set aside for physical labour, for intellectual and scholarly labours such as teaching and copying books, time for eating, rest and a little time for recreation.

There was good reason for these early monastic communities becoming centres of learning and economic activity. By their Rules, monasteries sought to be self-sufficient. Their quest for self-sufficiency was helped considerably by gifts of land from the king and the nobility, but the land still had to be farmed and managed. Indeed, monasteries would prove to be centres of innovation and research and, being nodes in a communication network, these innovations spread rapidly around the monasteries of Britain and Ireland.

One recently uncovered example is the tidal mill excavated by Thomas McErlean and Norman Crothers in 1999 at Nendrum Monastery in Northern Ireland. Nendrum sits on the shore of Strangford Lough which, while appearing landlocked, is actually connected to the Irish Sea via the narrow Strangford channel. The 150-square kilometre (58 square miles) lough is therefore tidal, and the monks made use of the regular rise and fall of the water in the lough by building an ingenious tidal mill to power horizontal grinding stones.

McErlean and Crothers found the remains of two tidal mills, dating from 619 and 787. The 619 mill is the oldest yet found. To power it, the monks built a tidal pool 120 metres long and 20 metres wide that filled as the tide rose. Then, when the pool was full, the monk charged with operating the mill closed the sluice gate, trapping the water in the mill pool as the tide receded. Once the water level had fallen far enough, the monks pulled out the plug sealing a hole in the side of the tidal pool. A jet of water promptly gushed out, hitting the horizontal water wheel set below the outflow and turning it. The water wheel turned the wooden shaft stuck into it, which in turn rotated the millstone set in the mill house above the water wheel, grinding the wheat poured into the central hole via a hopper.

The Nendrum tidal mill is an elegant piece of engineering and a fine example of the many technical innovations that were developed or adopted in Europe after the collapse of the Western Roman Empire.

We remember the Romans as excellent engineers. After all, the evidence is still standing: buildings, aqueducts and colosseums intact two millennia after they were built. But the truth of the matter is that, apart from these works of civil architecture, the Romans were not good engineers. For example, Roman iron was poor quality, for neither smelters nor smiths had a deep understanding of the processes involved. Nor did the Romans make much in the way of technological progress. There was no need to. With a slave-based economy, any problem could be solved quickly and cheaply by throwing people at it. There was no need to develop more efficient methods of doing the job.

However, the rise of Christianity meant the end of slavery. With labour much more expensive, there was an incentive for people to look for, and to put into place, more efficient ways of doing things. During the next few centuries, Christian kingdoms invented or adopted the heavy plough, the horse collar and the three-field rotation system. These all had a measurable impact. Early medieval peasants were appreciably bigger and heavier than their Roman era counterparts as a result of eating better diets. A little-known side effect of access to a better diet is that the general intelligence of the population improved. A growing child who suffers from malnutrition will have their physical and mental development stunted. So the removal of slave labour produced incentives for more efficient working, which produced increased crop yields, which led to a better-fed population, which produced more intelligent children, which led to further improvements in technology. It was a virtuous circle that would have produced even more results if not for the chronic instability produced by the depredations of the Vikings from the ninth century.

Water mills, such as the one at Nendrum, are one example of this renewed search for more efficient ways of doing things. With monasteries aspiring to be self-supporting, monks had strong incentives to find new ways of doing the labour-intensive tasks necessary for daily life.

Nendrum is the earliest water mill yet discovered in the British Isles. Further mills have been discovered around the Irish coast dating from the seventh century. Given the proximity of many British monasteries to suitable tidal streams, it seems quite likely that more ancient tidal mills await discovery. Wearmouth and Jarrow both lie beside tidal river estuaries so it would not be at all surprising if the monasteries also had water mills in their heyday. However, later building on the river shore means that it's unlikely we will be able to turn up the evidence for this.

Early medieval technology spread because monasteries had good channels of communication. Indeed, Bede's work, and in particular his *Ecclesiastical History*, depended upon him being able to communicate with other monasteries in Britain. The connections were both personal – monks visiting other monasteries – and epistolary: Bede quotes at length from a number of letters sent to the Church in Britain. While monasteries shared new productive technologies, the knowledge that was most useful, most eagerly communicated and most earnestly received was knowledge of God as contained in scripture. Books.

Larry Hurtado's work on the very earliest Christians has demonstrated that right from the very start Christians were a particularly bookish sect, even amid the widespread literacy of the Roman Empire. What set them apart, bibliographically, from rival sects was not just their bibliophilia but the form it took: where the scroll was the most common form of book in the empire, Christians from the outset preferred the codex. For example, of all the manuscripts surviving from the second century, 95 per cent are scrolls and just five per cent are codices. But if we look at surviving Christian manuscripts from the second century, 75 per cent are codices and only a quarter are scrolls. This Christian preference for reading from a codex was even more marked for scripture: over 90 per cent of identifiably Christian scriptures from the second and third centuries are codices.[2]

Various practical reasons have been put forward for why early Christians so favoured books over scrolls, including that they could contain more text and that finding proof texts was easier with a book than a scroll. However, early codices were all short books while the Jews, who were just as committed to close Biblical reading as the Christians, continued to prefer scrolls and do so to this day in synagogues.

Some modern-day scholars have argued that these early Christians used codices because they were simply better and more convenient ways of storing and reading text. However, there is nothing in the historical record to suggest that this was the case, and if codices were so self-evidently better, why didn't the wider literary culture of the empire adopt them?

Since there is no record of why early Christians preferred using books to scrolls, particularly for scripture, we can only speculate. One idea that fits the available facts is that Christians chose the codex as the vessel for their sacred texts precisely because it was different from how the rest of the world around them kept their texts. After all, this was a wider world that still fitfully persecuted Christians for their religion as well as deriding them. By putting their sacred texts into a different form to the rest of the Roman world, the early Christians were separating them physically from the domain of the prince of this world.

As the main readers of codices, early Christians worked hard on the best way of constructing books. Surviving manuscripts show how they experimented with different ways of folding and binding the leaves until, in the third century, they hit upon making a book of several gatherings made of sheets sewn together to form a quire which was then bound together. The book you hold in your hand today is made in essentially the same way, a direct descendant of these early Christian codices.

Codices rapidly grew more popular when Christianity became the official religion of the empire. As monasticism developed, the knowledge and techniques of making books became vital to the new monasteries as they depended upon books to do their work of prayer. This was even more the case in monasteries, such as those at Wearmouth and Jarrow, that were committed to learning and teaching.

Books, their making, reading and writing, were the knowledge at the heart of the monastic revolution that spread throughout Europe. Monks laboured at making and copying books, working in stinking tanneries to prepare the parchment or hunched in scriptoria painstakingly copying texts. It was hard and difficult work, but it was work worth doing. For it was in these books that the words of God were found.

It was also those words that formed the basis of the monastic day – and its night. While we don't know the details of the Rule that Benedict Biscop gave to his monasteries, we are reasonably confident that it followed the Rule of St Benedict for the times of prayer. Developing the injunction to pray always, and placing it within a practical framework, Benedict had adopted two key phrases from the psalms: 'Seven times a day I praise you' (Psalm 119:164) and 'At midnight I rise to give you thanks' (Psalm 119:62). With the authority of the psalmist behind him, Benedict enjoined his monks to pray seven times during the day and once in the middle of the night. The day-time Offices were called Matins (later known as Lauds) at dawn, Prime during the first hour of light, Terce at the third hour (around 9 a.m.), Sext at the sixth hour (around noon), Nones at the ninth hour in the mid-afternoon, Vespers at sunset and Compline before retiring to bed. The night-time Office was called Nocturns (becoming Vigils in later terminology).

As the practice developed and became codified, with particular readings and psalms set for each day of the year, monasteries had to develop the resources to enable them to carry out this work: psalters, Bibles and Gospels.

A typical prayer offered during one of the Offices consists of an introduction entreating God's aid, a hymn, a psalm, a canticle (a song usually taken from scripture such as the song of Hannah in 1 Samuel 2:1–10), another psalm, a reading from scripture, a responsory (a psalm or canticle sung by a solo cantor with the monks answering), another canticle, final prayers and intercessions. Most of this is sung or chanted and it will typically take around an hour. With seven day-time Offices, that would be about seven hours of the day devoted to prayer.

But monks did not only pray during the day; they got up in the middle of the night to pray as well. However, praying Nocturns might have been a little easier for Bede and his brethren than we would find it today. There is growing evidence that people in the Middle Ages typically divided their sleep into two parts, waking in the early hours for a while before going back to sleep. Accustomed as we are to thinking that a good night's sleep requires eight uninterrupted hours, this might seem strange. But our current sleeping arrangements are the consequence of us pushing back the empire of night.

Today, we live in light. We live in bright spheres of illumination, spheres of diameter sufficient to push the dark away. Living in a city, the night sky is no longer dark: a few scattered stars struggle to be seen against the general mattress of grey unlight that suffocates the sky. To have any understanding of what it was like for the greater part of human history, you must visit a country where electric lights are rare, or venture far away from human habitation in a richer country.

For Bede and his fellow monks living in Northumbria, summer was a time of light, but winter was different. At the winter solstice in this northern latitude, the sun sets before 4 p.m. and does not rise again until half past eight the next morning. The day is just over seven hours. That leaves seventeen hours of night. While twilight will extend the period of sight somewhat, that will still leave more than fifteen hours of darkness. That's a long time to sleep.

Too long. According to Roger Ekirch, the practice in the Middle Ages was to go to sleep not long after sundown but then, in the middle of the night, to wake and generally potter round, do chores, talk, check the fire and, for married couples, have sex.[3] Far from being a practice limited to the early medieval period, biphasic sleep appears to have been common practice throughout human history. Indeed, a 1995 experiment by sleep scientist Thomas Wehr suggests that, absent of artificial lighting, it is our natural sleep rhythm. In the experiment, fifteen men were isolated from artificial light and put into a day of ten hours of light and fourteen hours of darkness – with the darkness being true darkness. During the night hours they were not allowed to exercise or play music: there was not much else for them to do but sleep.

At the start of the experiment, the subjects slept uninterruptedly through the night but after four weeks their sleep patterns changed: the men slept for two roughly equal stretches, waking for one to three hours in between their sleeps. The sleep hormone melatonin had changed to match their new sleep pattern, indicating that this was a change at the biological level.

There are mentions of first and second sleeps in many letters, court records and other literatures of the medieval and early modern period, with other records going back to Antiquity. The casual way it is mentioned indicates something so normal as not to be remarked upon. It is a sleep pattern found in other animals, too, suggesting that it is a normal response to the day/night cycle.

If Roger Ekirch is right, then it may not have been so unusual for Bede and his companions to wake in the middle of the night. However, it was one thing to sleepily drift awake and then gently potter around in the warmth and quite another to get up and struggle out the door into whatever weather the night had in store, stumble through the dark to the church, and stand there singing and chanting. Not a few monks found this part of their Rule a sore trial. The eleventh-century Benedictine monk Raoul Glaber was tempted by an interior demon to stay asleep, the demon whispering to him, 'I wonder why you are so eager to jump so quickly out of bed, as soon as you've heard the signal, and to interrupt the sweet rest of sleep, while you could give yourself up to rest until the third signal.'[4]

But other than the injunction of the psalmist, why should monks shuffle wearily from their beds to a cold and dark church in the middle of the night? The reason was that they were engaged in a war against a dreadful foe, and prayer was their weapon.

*

Early medieval society, at least in its upper echelons, was fundamentally martial in character. Before the advent of Christianity in Britain there was very little option for a young nobleman other than a life dedicated to the practice of war. The men who founded and inhabited the early monasteries of Britain and Ireland were largely drawn from the warrior class, and they brought the attitudes of their class into the cloister with them. The enemy was the devil, and his army the powers of darkness. Jesus was their gift-giving lord, to whom they owed loyalty to death.

In the night, stumbling to the church, the wind howling and rain lashing, the powers of darkness were all too physically real, trying to prevent them doing God's work. In the enclosed, sacred ground of the monastery, its limits delimited by a ditch and raised boundary to separate it from the realm of the prince of this world, the monks had their stronghold. But it was a stronghold under constant assault, spiritually as well as physically.

Chaos, violence and palpable evil were all too common in early medieval Britain. In his *Ecclesiastical History*, Bede remembers the reign of King Edwin of Northumbria as a time of surpassing peace and, as proof of this, he states that it was a period when a woman with babe at breast could safely go forth. But for a woman and child to be safe going outside alone does not appear a particularly high bar to clear. For this to be the proof of a golden age of peace suggests how dangerous ordinary life was for most people when straying from familiar precincts.

As discussed previously, it's most likely that Bede himself came from the warrior aristocracy. However, even if his background was humbler – a possibility – his lifelong immersion in the monastic culture of Wearmouth and Jarrow would have left the circumstances of his family as a minor influence upon the grown man. We know that Benedict Biscop had been a warrior in his previous life: the skills he learnt from this probably helped give him the confidence to undertake so many long and dangerous journeys.

As understanding and appreciation for the monastic life grew among the Anglo-Saxon warrior elite, they quickly came to recognise that there were significant parallels between the life of a warrior and the life of a monk.

The gesiths of the king's warband swore oaths of loyalty to him. Allegiances were personal. While a soldier today serves the Crown, in Bede's day a warrior served the man who wore the crown. According to the ideals of this warrior society, that pledge was to the death: the warrior should die alongside his sworn king, defending him to the end. The fact that this was held up as the ideal suggests that it was by no means always observed in actuality: many warriors might well have held themselves freed from their oath at the death of the man to whom they had made their pledge. Indeed, some accounts do tell of warriors switching sides or abandoning the battle at the death of their lord. Nevertheless, the ideal remained service unto death.

While alive, that service entailed the king's warrior band travelling with the king as he made his way around his kingdom, consuming the food renders that constituted the main form of taxation, hearing cases and dispensing justice, and generally maintaining the complex web of personal relationships that held the kingdom together. As part of the king's comitatus, a warrior lived a communal life with his peers. They ate together, they drank together, they travelled, fought and lived together. Indeed, it's difficult for us to realise just how communal this life was: in the king's halls, there might be a separate room into which the king and his wife could withdraw at night, but his men slept in the hall, laying down together on the floor. Having to sleep close up to other people meant that there would have been strict, if unwritten, rules of etiquette. We know from later times that the sexes slept separately and that there were appropriate sleeping positions.

Further separating them from the ordinary run of humanity, warriors did not normally marry for as long as they continued in service to the king as part of his warband. It was generally only when a warrior had been released from immediate service and given land that he could marry and start a family. In the early Anglo-Saxon period, this land was not an outright gift but remained under the ownership of the king, reverting to him upon the death of the man to whom the land had first been gifted. In practice, the land usually passed on to his children, but the principle remained: it was a gift from the king and, if the son did not serve in the same way his father had, then the land returned to the king.

It was only with the rise of the Church, and its insistence that the land given to its use be bookland, rendered over in perpetuity, that the expectations of the warrior aristocracy changed too, so that the land became their land, to have and to hold, rather than the king's land given in gift and as easily taken away.

It's not hard to see the parallels between the life of one of the king's retainers and the life of a monk in a monastery. With most of the men in both walks of life coming from the same social class, the demands of communal living would have been familiar to them. While the warrior pledged his oath to the king, serving him to death, the monk made his vows to God, serving Him to death, too. In terms of living arrangements, the main difference was that warriors travelled around the kingdom whereas monks generally lived settled lives, not least Bede, who rarely left the twin monasteries.

But there were other parallels between the two ways of living, too, and these at the sharp end of their vocations.

The key battle formation of Anglo-Saxon warriors was the shieldwall. Anglo-Saxon warriors carried round shields with a heavy central boss. Shields were normally between one and three feet in diameter and held in the left hand. (But not invariably. From the wear patterns on its hilt, the sword buried at Sutton Hoo was apparently wielded by a left-hander, meaning that its bearer carried his shield in his right hand.) Moving into the battle line, the warriors raised their shields, overlapping with the men on either side of them, to make a single, flexible, mobile barrier: it was a bit like taking a moving wall into battle.

The battle normally resolved into an effort to break the enemy's shieldwall while maintaining the integrity of your own. As such, it became a scrum of exhausted, sweat-dripping men trying to poke their spears into openings while keeping tight with the men on either side. The shieldwall breaking would allow the enemy to force their way through and roll up your line, with fatal results. Being able to rely on the men standing to the left and right was vital: they held your life in their hands.

The prayer life of early medieval monks was the spiritual equivalent of these exhausting, shoving, scrummaging battles, with less swearing and blood but more weariness and persistence. Seven times a day and again in the middle of the night, Bede and his brethren put aside whatever task they were employed upon – as a warrior might be summoned from the hall when the alarm went up – and they trooped into the church, lining up there, side by side. Side by side, united in prayer, the monks of early medieval Britain did combat with the powers of darkness, raising their voices and hearts against the chaos and evil that swept around daily life. This was true spiritual combat, the close companion to the work of their warrior brethren accompanying the king.

In fact, the parallels went even deeper, extending to the division among warriors between the ordinary fighters who held the line and the elite warriors who were tasked with breaking the enemy line or facing, in single combat, the champion of the foe.

Monks, too, knew this division, between the ordinary, cenobitic monks who lived in community and contended with the enemy in the company of their fellows, and the eremite, the solitary hermit who went out from the monastery to the wild and lonely places to wage single combat against the devil and his demons.

The Irish were the main practitioners of this solitary monasticism. After the abortive mission of Paulinus failed with the death of King Edwin in 632, the monastic tradition in Northumbria drew from Irish sources for its models. With the conversion of the Irish having been a peaceful affair, there was little opportunity to win the red crown of a martyr's death: no one there was putting Christians to death. To make up for this, Irish monks became deeply committed to the white martyrdom of exile. Given the climate in Ireland, it was not possible to go into the desert, and so the early Irish monks instead sought out the most bleak and lonely places they could find. The isolated rock peaks of Skellig Michael, jutting from the great ocean seven miles west of the Iveragh Peninsula, give some indication of how far they were prepared to go in seeking wild and remote places. Others took ship in little currachs – skin-covered boats – allowing God, the wind and the sea to take them where they would, be that to a new land or a wet grave.

All these expressions of heroic spiritual endeavours were supported by the martial culture from which the Irish monks sprang, where tales of heroic daring and wild boasting followed by even wilder actions were the norm.

Coming to Britain and founding monasteries at Lindisfarne and elsewhere in Northumbria, Aidan, the monk Iona dispatched to King Oswald to convert his people, and his brethren found a warrior culture among the Anglo-Saxons that was not so different to their own. That similarity was reflected in their monastic cultures. Boys, such as Bede, generally joined the monastery at tender ages. There, they were trained into the community of monks, carrying out tasks while being taught how to chant and pray and, ideally, how to read and write Latin as well as English. As young men, they became professed monks, joining the brotherhood, just as one of their warrior brethren joined the warband of the king. Like the king's warriors, they engaged in battle in company with their brethren.

But also like their warrior brethren, there were champions among them. In any warband, there were elite warriors, the fiercest, bravest and most skilled. To these men, the king gave the best weapons and armour and perhaps even a helmet. Armed with the finest weapons, skilled through practice and combat, these warriors took the key places in the shieldwall. To them was given the job of piercing the enemy's line and hunting down the enemy leader. In the battles of the high and late medieval periods, kings and high-ranking nobles were generally captured and ransomed rather than killed. It was not so at this time. Killing the king ended the battle. It was the job of the king's champion warriors to end the battle.

But sometimes, they might stop a battle taking place. On occasions, the king's top warrior would meet the enemy's elite warrior in single combat, the battle decided by one man dying rather than many. From the company of his brethren, the champion stepped forth, girt with the finest armour his lord could provide for him, wielding a pattern-welded sword, its hilt studded with garnets and wrapped in gold, shield in the other hand. There were rules for duelling, ranging from the training duels fought among the king's own warband through three-shield battles to fights to the death. As the armies watched, the two champions fought.

There was a similar division among monks. While most monks lived in community, there were a small number who, having been accepted and trained into community life, left the monastery to wage personal combat with the powers of darkness. Even those who were bound to their communities because they led them, such as Aidan and Cuthbert, would withdraw from their brethren and go away to pray alone. In this they were following both Jesus's own practice and the logic of their culture.

Other monks left their brethren to become full-time hermits. In 698 a young man named Guthlac joined the double monastery at Repton in Derbyshire. But after two years living as a monk there, Guthlac petitioned the abbess for permission to become a hermit and, permission being granted, he went and lived the rest of his life on the island of Crowland in the Fens. Living a life of noteworthy privation, Guthlac soon attracted people to him for spiritual council – the best hermits always found that no matter where they went, the world pursued them. Guthlac's biographer also wrote of how demons attacked Guthlac, appearing to him in hideous guises and screaming and squawking. However, Guthlac endured their attacks, fought them off with prayer and fasting, and after his death his body was found to be incorrupt – a sure sign of sanctity.

Hermit monks such as Guthlac were the champions of their communities and their societies, celebrated in hagiography and legend as were their warrior counterparts. And it's this interweaving of local and Christian culture that helps to explain why the Anglo-Saxon warrior elite embraced Christianity so thoroughly and completely. It fitted into their world view while also extending and broadening it. It provided possibilities and lives that were impossible before.

While Bede admired and venerated the solitary monk going out into the wilderness to fight the devil on his own, it was never his choice. He was devoted to the Opus Dei, to singing the Office in company with his brethren. Faced with the choice of Martha and Mary, Bede chose Martha and working with others for the kingdom of the Lord. In that work, the daily Office became part of his very being.

Monks today have retreated to the margins of society. Of course, in Britain this decline was first driven by the deliberate suppression of monasticism by Henry VIII. However, the nineteenth century saw a vigorous resurgence of monasticism in Britain, with many monasteries, Anglican as well as Catholic, being established. But the number of monks and monasteries declined during the second half of the twentieth century, and today there are only a few thousand monks in the UK. For most people they have become an irrelevance dwindling towards extinction.

But that is premature. Monasticism has been a feature of human societies for thousands of years, appearing in different guises but with shared features in cultures around the world. It has undergone periods of expansion and periods of decline. These periods mimic the life cycle of religious orders, which are established in a fever of fervour, grow rapidly, expand and reach a plateau, then become adulterated and decline, only for that decline to be reversed for a while by a fresh impetus of reform and renewal until that spends itself and decline begins again. It is a spiked cycle of slow decline, until an entirely new order is founded to repeat the pattern.

As to predictions that monks will become extinct, that seems unlikely, too. Monasticism flourishes most when people grow disgusted and disillusioned with human society. The initial explosion in Christian monasticism occurred against the backdrop of the chaos and violence that marked the fall of the Western Roman Empire. The thirteenth-century renewal via mendicant orders such as the Franciscans and Dominicans took place amid a febrile atmosphere of failed crusades (the Fourth Crusade had disastrously ended up sacking Constantinople rather than aiding the Crusader kingdoms, the Children's Crusades ended in disaster and there were internal crusades against the Albigensians and the Cathars).

With disillusionment and disappointment spreading among all sectors of society today, but particularly among the young, and values being proposed via fleeting images across social media, I predict that, contrary to all expectations, the 21st century will see a renewal of monasticism, although it's likely to take some new and unexpected forms. But in a time and a culture where little is authentic and less worth living for, the option to call a plague down on all the houses of conflict and withdraw to a place apart will appear as the only possible option for more and more people. If so, they will follow along the same sort of path that Bede did during his lifetime in the monastery. For there are patterns to monastic life, patterns formed by the great overarching rhythm of sung prayer.

As part of a choir of monks singing the Office, Bede was formed by this rhythm. The pace of the chant is such that, even if the monk's mind wanders, the rhythm continues to control the underlying mental contours. The Office is communal and inexorable: it continues at its own pace, its sheer unrelenting onwards movement imprinting itself into the soul of the monk. In this respect it is like the repeated mantra of Eastern religious traditions: the words transcend and undercut their own meaning, dissolving into the music that carries them.

Because the Office is prescribed and repetitive, and because it relentlessly flows on at a pace that makes it impossible for the monk chanting it to continually and fully reflect on the meaning of all he is saying, then the prayer becomes, on its surface, mechanical: sung almost without thought. The inexperienced monk may reach this point and fret that he is not praying properly, that he is not paying sufficient attention, and attempt to redouble his concentration.

But often this is not a dereliction of prayer but a deepening of it: by the paradox of music and rhythm, the chanting of the words of the psalms deepens to wordless prayer, the prayer of the heart raised to God without the mediation of limiting thoughts and words. The mystery at the heart of the prayer of monks is that the chanting of words becomes, after many years, a form of contemplative prayer. Repeated throughout the day and again in the night, this prayer seeps into the soul of the monk. Ideally, it should reorder his mind and his soul, slowly untwisting the knots that distort the character and deform the heart, until the monk is able to keep some part of his mind always looking towards God while he continues with his other tasks.

There is another story of Mary and Martha in the Bible, in John's Gospel. This time, their brother, Lazarus, is gravely ill. The sisters send for Jesus, but he is too late: their brother, Lazarus, dies before he arrives. In their grief, the sisters are being comforted by relatives when they hear that Jesus is on his way. Mary stays in the house in the company of the other mourners, but Martha rushes out to meet Jesus. Seeing him, Martha says to Jesus that if only he had arrived sooner, her brother would not have died. So it was to Martha, not Mary, that Jesus delivered the great statement of his nature, telling her, 'I am the resurrection and the life: he that believeth in me, though he were dead, yet shall he live: and whosoever liveth and believeth in me shall never die' (John 11:25–26).

Both sisters, Martha and Mary, the active and the contemplative, saw and heard Jesus's message and followed it. Bede's devotion to the monastic life was Marthan: he was a doer. A scholar, a priest, a teacher, a singer. He embodied the active monastic life and, by the prestige attached to his name and example, Bede helped make the way of Martha as important as the way of Mary. And these monks, working in scattered communities throughout Europe, set about rebuilding the world.

My Beloved is the mountains,
The solitary wooded valleys,
Strange islands . . .
Silent music.[5]

## CHAPTER 6

# Student and Teacher

Monastic life had two poles: the communal life and, rising out from the mass of monks, the solitary, eremitic life of the warriors of the spirit. These were the poles of Martha and Mary, of St Peter and St John, the practical organiser of the early Church and the disciple whom Jesus loved, to whom Jesus entrusted care of his mother while dying upon the Cross. Thus, through the early centuries of monasticism, the higher ideal was the contemplative life as exemplified by Mary and John, rather than the practical ministries of Martha and Peter, ministries that inevitably entailed dealing as much with the matters of the world and money, that tainted thing, as with the matters of God.

In his sermon on St John the Evangelist, Bede explicitly sets up St Peter as the model for the active life and St John as the model for the contemplative life. The active life was open to every Christian, religious or secular, but it still required maintaining the soul free from stain of sin, while devoting one's energies to the practical tasks Jesus had enjoined upon his disciples: visiting the sick, feeding the hungry, burying the dead, clothing the naked and showing the lost the way to the Truth.

In contrast, the contemplative life was open only to a few Christians, chiefly monks, who by following the precepts of the active life had cleansed their souls and freed themselves from the snares of the world. Then, through ardent prayer and meditation, these champions of the religious life might ascend, in this world, heavenwards in mind and spirit, gaining 'a foretaste of the joy of the perpetual blessedness . . . by ardently desiring it, and even sometimes . . . by contemplating it sublimely in mental ecstasy' [Homilies on the Gospels, I.9, p.91]

Many of the monastic heroes of Bede's *Ecclesiastical History* lived lives that spanned both poles, the active and the contemplative. Aidan and Cuthbert, the two religious that Bede holds up as the highest examples of the monastic life, combined leading monasteries and, in Cuthbert's case, being a bishop as well, with regular retreats into solitude where they could contemplate the divine away from the distractions of the world and their fellow men. Both men, in their final days, withdrew from the world to be alone with God. Cuthbert died alone in his cell on the Farne Islands, Aidan leaning against a wall of the building that later became St Aidan's Church in Bamburgh.

In his works, Bede held these men up as the template for the Christian life and the good death. But this was not how Bede lived nor how he died. The *Letter on the Death of Bede*, written by one of Bede's students who was also called Cuthbert and who later became abbot, records the manner of the master's death. The letter indicates that Bede had been ailing for a while, his health and strength slowly failing him. It was clear to Bede and his brethren that he was dying. However, despite knowing this, Bede did not follow the lead of his monastic hero, Cuthbert. He did not seek isolation. He did not go off to a small cell far away from other people. He did not even withdraw from his fellow monks. Instead, he remained where he was, teaching, learning, reading and writing to his very dying moments. Almost his last recorded actions were to finish his translation of St John's Gospel into English.

Bede was a teacher and a scholar. In the short account of his life that he puts into his *Ecclesiastical History*, he tells how the monastic life of praying the Office sat alongside his delight in teaching and learning, reading and writing. Like the monastery in which he lived his life, Bede's own life had twin foundations: monastic prayer and scholarship. And by remaining a scholar to his dying day, Bede gave his contemporaries and his successors a new and fresh model of the Christian life. Teaching, learning and scholarship became not simply the means to an end but the very point of his earthly life. A monk, or any serious Christian, might therefore live a life of learning and scholarship for its own sake, and that life would be pleasing to God.

This credo resonated through the centuries. There is a direct line from Bede to the foundation of the first European universities in the eleventh and twelfth centuries. The Schoolmen who taught and disputed at Bologna, Paris, Oxford, Cambridge were the disciples and successors of a man who had lived 400 years before them on the shores of the North Sea. As such, Bede's importance can scarcely be overstated. He made a new approach to the Christian life possible. The whole apparatus of intellectual inquiry and the life of the mind as worthy ends in themselves can be traced back to him.

So the question arises of how Bede acquired the knowledge he spent a lifetime deepening and disseminating. The first necessity was Latin, the language of learning as well as the Bible. It also had the immeasurable advantage of being an international language, spoken and read by learned men and women throughout Europe. The status of Latin was in part because of the Roman Empire. Latin was the language of Virgil and Cicero, of Augustus and Julius Caesar. It carried a weight of history, prestige and power built up through a thousand years of Imperial history – and the sense, among the various peoples of the early medieval period, that they were the unworthy successors to something greater.

The ideal of European political unity is far older than the European Union. Indeed, in its various iterations – the Carolingian Empire, the Holy Roman Empire, the Napoleonic Empire – the idea harks back to the lost unity of the Roman Empire. Many people in medieval Europe harkened back to the Roman example of one empire under one emperor. But now, the thinking went, it would be one empire under one emperor under one God.

In the fractured world of medieval Christendom, unity was an ideal that forever lay tantalisingly just out of reach. Not least among the thinkers fascinated by it was Dante, who consistently supported the Holy Roman Emperor over the pope in the political sphere precisely because he hoped for a unified Christendom. Nostalgia for the empire was all the greater in a Europe in which war was endemic between its constituent countries and their brawling martial classes. Of course, that nostalgia overlooked the carnage wrought by the civil wars that broke out between rivals for the Roman purple, but then nostalgia derives some of its charm from the ability to overlook the less favourable parts of the past.

For Bede, however, the idea of European political unity was moot as he was living in a country that had only recently managed to organise kingdoms into units bigger than shires. Most of the petty Anglo-Saxon and Britonnic kingdoms of the fifth and sixth centuries had been subsumed into larger polities, leaving the big four Anglo-Saxon kingdoms of Wessex, Mercia, East Anglia and Northumbria, with Kent, Sussex and Essex just about hanging on as independent political entities. The Britonnic kingdoms, under pressure from the expanding Anglo-Saxon kingdoms but consistently hampered by the custom of partible inheritance that saw kingdoms split between the king's sons, had nevertheless also consolidated to the kingdoms of Strathclyde and the Pictish lands of what would become Scotland in the north, Dumnonia in the West Country, and Gwynedd, Powys and smaller kingdoms in Wales.

But if Britain was still fractured, it had recently seen the arrival of a number of highly educated and far-travelled clerics who put in place the foundations of the educational system that nurtured Bede.

The old school system of the Roman Empire that prepared men for public life disappeared from Britain and Gaul during the fifth and sixth centuries. There were probably still some remnants of it in Britain in the fifth century when the Britonnic priest Gildas wrote his polemic against the corrupt rulers of his time, *On the Ruin and Conquest of Britain*. It is primarily a diatribe against corrupt kings, the outpouring of a latter-day Jeremiah and possibly the most frustrating historical document ever written. Luckily, for our purposes what is important is not what Gildas wrote but how he wrote it: in flawless literary Latin. Therefore, in the Britain of Gildas's youth there still existed institutions or people capable of teaching a young religious how to read, write and think in grammatically and stylistically correct Latin.

However, under the pressure of the many wars of fifth and sixth century Britain, it became less and less possible to sustain knowledge and the teachers to teach it. Outside Britain, the old Classical educational system had diminished to a few outposts in Italy and Iberia. But there arose, in the most unlikely place imaginable, a new centre of European learning, a land that was so far from the centre as to be off the edge of the world: Ireland.[1] Never conquered by the Roman Empire, the Irish lived in a non-urban society organised into little, clan-based kingdoms. It was into this world of perpetually warring statelets that Patrick appeared, bearing a new message that struck so deep into the Irish soul it was as if a fissure had opened up, unveiling a ladder to heaven.

The first, heroic, generations of Irish monasticism merged acts of spectacular self-mortification with voluntary exile, self-abnegation for Christ and the scholarly efflorescence of a pre-literate society suddenly drunk on the power and beauty of the written word.

Irish monks needed to learn and to teach and, standing completely outside the old structures of the Roman Empire, they had to come up with ways of doing this on their own. Details are thin but they seem to have approached this by setting an older monk to teach younger ones in a manner analogous to a master with his apprentices. To start with, the teaching was mainly rote learning, the monk teacher reading and the boys memorising. For a people that were still steeped in oral culture, such a learning style would probably not have been so tedious, or so long-winded, as it would be for us.

The first necessity for these novice monks was to learn sufficient Latin to be able to say and sing the Office. For many monks, not much more was necessary, but Bede was no average monk. He was given to the monastery at Wearmouth when he was seven and, we must suspect, quickly showed exceptional ability. Bede affirms that his first teacher was Benedict Biscop himself, the founder of the monastery, but then he came under the care of Ceolfrith, to whom Benedict had given the task of building and establishing the monastery at Jarrow. So it seems highly likely that Bede moved to Jarrow too while still quite young.

With Benedict absent so often, and then slowly incapacitated for his final three years by a creeping paralysis, most of Bede's day-to-day teaching must have come from Ceolfrith. Some scholars suspect that Bede may also have been taught by a monk or monks originating from Iberia, where the most classically correct form of Latin was spoken in the seventh century. Indirect evidence for there being a connection between Iberia and Britain at the time was the wide circulation of the works of Isidore of Seville in Anglo-Saxon England: only the works of Pope Gregory the Great were more widespread.

\*

While Bede is generally reticent about the details of his own life, we can discern something about the pedagogy employed at Wearmouth and Jarrow from what he says about other alumni of the monastery. Notably, in his *History of the Abbots*, Bede writes of his near contemporary, Hwætberht, who became abbot in 716. Bede writes that Hwætberht had received his formation at Wearmouth where he had learnt 'the arts of writing, chanting, reading and teaching'.

These four are very different from the seven liberal arts – grammar, rhetoric, logic, music, geometry, arithmetic and astronomy – of Classical civilisation. For a monk, reading, writing and chanting were the foundations of his work as a monk. But what is notable for our investigation is that alongside these three, Bede includes 'teaching'. Hwætberht was taught how to teach. That Hwætberht had been taught how to teach shows that the teaching monks at Wearmouth and Jarrow had given considerable thought to how to do their job.

Remember that Bede, in his aside as to what had afforded him the greatest delight in life, includes teaching alongside learning and writing. These were men who were committed to teaching for reasons both of necessity but also of joy: and there are few things better done than necessary tasks completed with true enjoyment.

Bede was ordained as a deacon at the uncanonically young age of nineteen, in about 691. We might suppose that one reason for his early ordination was that, through his outstanding ability, he was already teaching the younger monks, and the additional authority of holy orders would be helpful in dealing with a class of young boys. Whether they were being trained to join the other monks at Wearmouth and Jarrow or were the sons of the nobility being given a sound basic education, they were still boys, with all the energy and capacity for pranks that young boys have always had. A teacher still in his teens might not have commanded the sort of attention required in classes in which rote learning was a vital component. Giving Bede the prestige of holy orders might have helped him in calling his charges to attention.

Much of Bede's time in the decade and a half following his ordination as a deacon was devoted to teaching. We know that because of what Bede wrote during these years: a succession of practical textbooks covering the basics of monastic education. *On Orthography* is a textbook of elementary Latin. *The Art of Poetry* and *The Figures of Rhetoric* take the student further towards mastering Latin, reaching the fluency necessary to compose technically correct Latin verse and to understand the language in the depth required for the study of scripture. *On Time* and *On the Nature of Things* are textbooks on nature, in particular astronomical cycles, and the calculations and observations needed to work out the correct day on which to celebrate the feast of Easter. Without calendars, the monks had to work out the answer for themselves – and it's no easy task.

Bede spent the time between his ordination as a deacon and his ordination as a priest eleven years later producing these books. They no doubt served him well in his own teaching, but he was also writing them so that later monks could carry on his work: one of the key features of the monastic life is that while its eyes are turned towards the next world, it pays greater heed to the long-term practicalities of living in this world than almost any other calling.

That Bede was concentrating particularly on education during this period is made clear by the fact that he only wrote one more textbook afterwards, *The Reckoning of Time*, which is an expansion of his previous work *On Time*. Having laid the educational foundations for his monastery and his own teaching practice, Bede went on to work on his later books, the ones that gave him his lasting reputation as an exegete and a historian. But these all rested upon the foundation of educational textbooks that he had already written.

The students at Wearmouth-Jarrow were divided into elementary and advanced groups. Bede writes of his love for children and their joy in learning, which suggests that he must have been involved in teaching the younger boys as well as more advanced students. The first step for students was learning how to read and write. And as they were training for the monastic life, the psalter was the basis of their practice.

Learning began with the students writing the letters, and then syllables and words on wax-coated tablets (allowing the tablet to be wiped and made ready for the next exercise). The students had to learn the sounds of the Latin they were going to be chanting, committing these to memory. To accompany these basic lessons, the young students were also taught spelling, grammar and word order – all important in understanding a language with a very different structure to Old English. *On Orthography* could be renamed *Latin: Its Traps and Pitfalls*. Listing words in alphabetical order, Bede goes through the words that experience showed his students most often got wrong. For example:

> *Altum* [= high, deep] signifies both up and down
> *Gracilis* [= thin] in the superlative is *gracillimus*, not
> *gracilissimus*
> *Tabes* [= corruption] is only used in the singular

While Bede was probably in charge of teaching the novices Latin, instruction in the chant and its melodies would have been the province of the cantor. With John having come from Rome to teach the monks how they did it in Rome, the monastery at Wearmouth-Jarrow had the tunes from the pope's own choirmaster. These melodies were precious, living things that could only be sustained by repetition. As yet, no forms of musical notation had been devised, so music had to be committed to memory and then taught directly to the next generation of monks to keep it alive.

But while Bede had no influence on the teaching of music, he transformed the teaching of Latin and he did so personally.

To teach Latin at an advanced level, previous educators had always relied on Classical authors for their models and, particularly, Virgil, who supplied the examples of Classically correct Latin verse that were used in first-century Gaul and sixth-century Gaul. Indeed, Virgil was still the source of textbook examples when Theodore and Hadrian set up their school in Canterbury and when Bede first learnt Latin in Jarrow. But when Bede came to write his own textbooks on Latin poetry, *The Art of Poetry* and *The Figures of Rhetoric*, he generally replaced the Virgilian quotations with quotes taken from the Christian poets of Late Antiquity, poets such as Fortunatus, Paulinus, Prudentius and Arator.

The secular poetry of Virgil and his ilk was, for Bede, frivolous and unworthy of the attention of a serious monk, called to contemplate the eternal things of God. However, as a teacher, Bede was committed above all else to teaching his students how to read and understand the Bible, the written source of God's revelation. Coming to the Northumbrians in the Latin of the Vulgate translation by St Jerome, understanding God meant understanding Latin in all its modes – and among these were the metres of Classical Latin poetry: dactylic hexameters and pentameters, which were used for heroic and elegiac verse. Bede also deals with the lyric metres, but his main attention was on the heroic and elegiac modes.

A student proved his mastery of these metres by composing quantitatively correct poetry. *The Art of Poetry* takes the student through these mysterious metres, setting out the rules for the length of syllables (short or long) for the first, middle and last syllables of words. On the face of it, this might not seem such a difficult task, but Bede was asking his students to follow the strict rules of Latin verse and apply them to a language that no longer had native-tongue speakers.

This was not easy, particularly with a master whose ear for poetry was exacting. When discussing poetic style, Bede said that:

> the best and most beautiful arrangement of a dactylic hexameter verse is where the next to the last word agrees with the first word and the final word agrees with a word in the middle . . . However, this should not be done constantly, but only after intervals of several lines. For if you always arrange your feet and your verses in the same way, even if it is the best way, your composition is at once cheapened.

This was a sophisticated understanding of the use and misuse of metre in poetry – and one that few of Bede's successors understood. Medieval poets writing in Latin took Bede's admiration of internal rhyme to almost ridiculous extremes, creating verse that became so artificial as to almost lose its ability to convey meaning. If they had listened to the second part of Bede's comment, they would have known not to do so.

Bede's interest in rhetoric stemmed from his Biblical exegesis. To understand the Bible, it was necessary to interpret it at four levels. The first was the literal, the words and events as written. So, for Bede, God really did part the Red Sea to allow the Jews to escape dry shod. But there were three further levels of interpretation: typological (or allegorical), which referred to Christ or the Church; tropological, which was reflected in the Christian life of individual sinners; and anagogical, which illuminated the heavenly kingdom. To explore the layers of meaning in the Bible required a solid understanding of the various tools of rhetoric in order to better employ these exegetical techniques. While Bede accepted and sometimes used the fourfold scheme of interpretation, when it came to his own commentaries he tended to stick to the literal and the typological, with rarer excursions into the tropological and the anagogical.

As an example, let's look at Bede's commentary on the Apocalypse, and one short sentence from chapter one: 'And his head and his hairs were white, as white wool, and as snow, and his eyes were as a flame of fire.' (Revelation 1:14) In this case, the typological interpretation is that the colour white represents the majesty and purity of God; the tropological interpretation sees the eyes of fire as Christian preachers, bringing light to the faithful; and the anagogical interpretation is that the faithful who are saved are like the individual white hairs clinging to the head. That's quite a lot. While to our eyes these interpretations frequently seem somewhat far-fetched, concluding that is to miss the purpose of these commentaries. No commentator ever claimed to exhaust the meaning of scripture; indeed, that would be impossible. What they were trying to do was illuminate it. It's as if each different commentator offers to the reader a different key to unlock the meaning of that particular passage. For some readers, one key might work; for others a different key. What mattered more was that there were lots of keys so that the meaning of scripture might be opened to as many people as possible.

So an obscure Christian monk at the edges of the world became a skilled and subtle Latinist, as well as a teacher, a scholar and a monk. It was the clarity of mind that Bede brought to all these, and his ability to synthesise a vast array of knowledge into comprehensible wholes, that made his writing so important and so accessible.

It was only after writing his textbooks that Bede turned to writing the works of exegesis and Biblical commentary for which he was most celebrated in the later medieval centuries, and the works of history for which he is best known now. But even when composing his *Ecclesiastical History*, he continued to teach his younger brethren.

In the *Ecclesiastical History*, Bede presents a wide variety of figures as worthy of emulation, from Oswald and Edwin in the political field to Cuthbert and Aidan among the religious. But he also, subtly and not so subtly, signifies his disapproval of others: King Oswiu and his ruthless realpolitik and Wilfrid and his episcopal magnificence. But perhaps Bede's greatest praise was reserved for the religious Marthas, the men and women who worked in the world but were not of it, men such as Benedict, the founder of his own monastery, and Hild, abbess of Whitby.

Before Bede, there was a definite religious hierarchy, with those men who withdrew from the world into solitary contemplation of

God viewed as the spiritual heroes to whose lives and examples all religious should aspire. But by highlighting people such as Benedict and Hild, and by his own example of a lifetime of teaching, learning and writing, Bede provided another example for the fully formed Christian life. The life of the mind was the example Bede gave and followed. It opened up a new path for the men (and some women) who came after him: a life of study. The way of the scholar.

## CHAPTER 7

# The World in Books

This was his favourite place. For Bede, all the monastery was holy ground, with the church its most sacred space, but here, in the library, this was where he was most content. Bede looked around the room, his gaze lingering on the books, each of them as old and dear a friend as his brethren. The light, coming in through the window, was midsummer bright. This was the best time of year to read; when the sun lit the words, and the days lingered long in light. In winter, it was much more difficult: hunched over a book, squinting at the words in the flickering light of a lamp, hands tucked into his armpits to keep them warm and only removed to turn the page of the book. But now was summer, when his fingers were warm and the books, warm too, opened easily. In winter, the books creaked when he opened them, as if they also felt the cold, their spines protesting at its grip. As with men, books welcomed the coming of the warmth, their spines relaxing, their pages softening.

Bede walked around the room, his gaze wandering over the many books gathered safely in its cupboards. He knew them all intimately; many he knew almost by heart. When he wrote one of his own books, he rarely needed to check the wording of a quotation, for the words were engraved in his memory. Without thinking, as he walked he trailed a finger over the covers and spines of the books, relishing the feel of the leather to his skin. Some of the books he knew so well that he could tell them with his eyes shut by their feel.

He did occasionally wonder if he loved books too well. Perhaps that had been true when he was young and first discovering their magic. Then he would spend whatever time he might reading the books of the old pagans: Virgil, Cicero, even Ovid. The adventures of Aeneas had entranced him until, with a start, he realised its allure and he had pulled his reading back to the one thing needful: the knowledge and understanding of God.

To that end, and to protect the young when they were learning to read and write Latin, Bede had gone through the old grammar books and replaced the examples given in them, all taken from the old pagan writers, with extracts taken from suitable Christian poets and writers such as Prudentius. The novice might rest easily among their words, finding them as correct and pure as the words of Virgil but without the temptations to wallow in fantasy that the old pagan authors posed.

'Brother Bede?'

At his name, Bede turned to see who called for him. Standing in the door was a boy, one of the oblates given into the monastery's keeping that he might test his vocation to the monastic life.

'Yes, Wilberht?'

'Brother Cuthbert asks if you would come; he is copying one of your books and would check that he reads it aright before writing the words.'

'Run and tell him that I am coming, Wilberht.'

'Yes, Master.'

Bede held up his hand. 'Not "master" but "brother". Remember that, Wilberht. You have but one master and you know who He is.'

The boy, initially chastened by the rebuke, smiled at this chance to redeem his mistake. 'Yes, I know, Brother Bede, I know who my master is.'

'Very well. Tell Brother Cuthbert to wait until I arrive before he writes; better a minute of waiting than the long business of scraping the skin clean again for fresh words.'

The boy scurried off and Bede followed. He could remember the energy of boyhood, when to run was easier than to walk and each night's sleep was an imposition upon the possibilities of the day. But he was an old man now and he would rather walk than run, and sleep each night came as a friend.

Ah, to be young again, with his sight sharp and his mind as agile as a squirrel and, like a bucket, waiting to be filled with the life water of holy knowledge.

Books were no temptation: they were the keys to life.

*

The library at Wearmouth and Jarrow was the quarry that Bede mined during a lifetime of learning. To understand his thinking, we need to understand the books that he worked from. Unfortunately, the Wearmouth and Jarrow library catalogue has not survived. To work out the books in the library, generations of scholars have trawled through Bede's own books, looking for quotations, allusions, examples and general points taken from the works that he might have had access to, comparing and contrasting what he wrote with the surviving examples of these other works. No easy task, as the texts of Bede's sources as we have them today are not necessarily the same as the texts that Bede himself read. Then it's quite possible that some of the books that Bede used did not survive to the present. In these cases we're trying to decide if Bede read a book through reading Bede's possible allusions to a book that no longer exists. It's a difficult task. Some books might have been missed and others wrongly attributed. But it's the best we can do.

Bearing all these considerations in mind, the most widely accepted figure among scholars is that the library at Wearmouth and Jarrow held about 200 books, although some of these books were collections of more than one work. Adding in multiple works in one volume, we come to around 250 discrete works in the library.

It doesn't seem many. But as a later Anglo-Saxon proponent of learning, King Alfred the Great, remarked, the library did contain a wide selection of the works 'most necessary for men to know'. Most necessary, in Bede's context, meant chiefly for the correct understanding of scripture, the Bible. But, as Bede and his fellow monks knew well, correctly understanding the Bible is not just a matter of sitting down and reading it. For men whose native language was Old English, it meant mastering Latin so that they could understand the language of the Bible in the first place. But not just that. For while they worked, and prayed, with Latin scriptures, Bede and his fellow monks knew well that the Bible had not been written originally in Latin. The New Testament was written in Greek while the Old Testament was written in Hebrew. Not only that, the Hebrew Old Testament had also been authoritatively translated into Greek in the third century BC, this version being known as the Septuagint as it was supposedly translated by seventy-two translators.

So even at its most basic level, proper knowledge of the Bible required understanding Latin and Greek, and preferably Hebrew as well. Not only three languages but three different scripts as well – and all in a country where there were no native speakers of any of these languages. That's a task that would be beyond most of us today, even with access to all the devices and books for language learning that now exist.

Benedict Biscop and Ceolfrith painstakingly assembled the books in the monastery library during their journeys to Europe. The destruction of Viking raiders and the gnawing of time has almost utterly destroyed all the books that were in that library: all that certainly survives is a thin strip of vellum containing lines from the First Book of Maccabees (one of the books of the Bible). The book was written in Italy in the sixth century before being brought to Northumbria. It's a tight and narrow piece of writing, packed onto the vellum; very different from the expansive, illuminated manuscripts that have survived from the time, but by that indicative of the more common run of books. This was a book intended to be read and used, rather than displayed, venerated and read (for make no mistake, even the most splendid of illuminated manuscripts, such as the *Lindisfarne Gospels*, were read from as well as displayed: they were books adorned for the splendour of the words they contained and not the other way round).

As to what versions of the Bible they had in the library at Wearmouth and Jarrow, Bede tells us, in his *Lives of the Abbots*, that Ceolfrith 'doubled the number of books in the libraries of both monasteries with an ardour equal to that which Benedict had shown in founding them. He added three copies of the new translation of the Bible to the one copy of the old translation which he had brought back from Rome.' These three new copies were the complete editions of new translations of the Bible that were undertaken, produced and scribed at Wearmouth and Jarrow, so they made them themselves. However, Ceolfrith had brought back a complete copy of the old translation of the Bible from Rome, which was in itself a significant asset for the monastery library. (The reference to doubling the number of books more probably refers to the work Ceolfrith initiated in copying books rather than that he brought back as many books again as Benedict had collected.) This copy of the old translation of the Bible was significant in itself as it was the *Codex Grandior*, the pandect from the library of Cassiodorus.

Cassiodorus (c.485–c.585) was a remarkable statesman, politician, scholar and abbot of Late Antiquity, a bridge between the dying Classical world and the nascent Christian civilisation. He came from a high-ranking family and himself took on the highest appointments in the Ostrogothic kingdom that ruled Italy in the sixth century, including that of chief magistrate and effective prime minister. During his public career, Cassiodorus spent nearly twenty years in Constantinople, giving him time to thoroughly familiarise himself with the Greek-speaking eastern Mediterranean part of Christendom.

While serving the Ostrogothic kings, Cassiodorus had conceived the idea of founding a library in Rome to serve a school dedicated to educating Christians serving the kingdom. Cassiodorus had the enthusiastic support of Pope Agapetus I for this enterprise. But the pope died after a short reign, the Byzantine Empire reconquered much of Italy from the Ostrogoths, and Cassiodorus's career took him from Italy to Constantinople, so the proposed institution never materialised.

However, when Cassiodorus returned to Italy from Constantinople around 544, he decided to retire from public affairs and founded a monastery on his family's land in the south of Italy, near Squillace in present-day Calabria. The monastery, which was called the Vivarium, became the repository for the books he had collected for the library he had once proposed and, as abbot of the Vivarium, Cassiodorus employed his monks in the task of copying and preserving many of the works of Classical Antiquity, as well as Christian books. As Cassiodorus lived for a long time after his retirement from public affairs, around 40 years, he and his monks had ample time to devote to their task of copying and preserving the important texts of the past. And the wealth that Cassiodorus and his family had amassed during at least three generations of service at the highest reaches of government ensured that he had the funds to finance the copying and making of books.

Among the works he bequeathed to the future were his own letters and judgements in his service to the Ostrogothic kings, as well as at least one pandect of the Bible – the *Codex Grandior* – written in an older translation into Latin rather than Jerome's Vulgate, which was becoming the standard Latin version.

While not himself a great scholar, Cassiodorus's example was hugely important in the preservation of Classical texts. Following his death, after a particularly long life of roughly a century, his carefully assembled library was gradually broken up. However, much of it came to Rome, and it arrived there at around the time when Benedict Biscop and Ceolfrith were visiting in 679. The two men, both inveterate book collectors, took the chance presented and snapped up many of the books from Cassiodorus's library, including the *Codex Grandior*, as well as many of Cassiodorus's own works.

While the remnants of the library of Cassiodorus were a significant source in the library that Bede used, they were not the first and not the largest. Through his travels, Benedict Biscop had made many useful contacts among the religious of Francia, Italy, Spain and Ireland. He used those far-flung friends to collect his library.

Given that Benedict spent two years living at the monastery on Lérins, it's reasonable to suppose that he obtained some books from the monks there. He clearly had people collecting books for him in Francia, as Bede mentions him stopping at Vienne, a town in south-east France, to pick up books that he had left there on his way to Rome. Within Britain, Benedict spent two years as an abbot in Canterbury having escorted Archbishop Theodore from Rome to Britain. Theodore and Hadrian did not rely solely on their memories; they brought books with them, too, and Benedict may either have been given some of these or had some copied while he was in Canterbury. Or, indeed, later: holding the abbacy there helped cement the connection between Kent and Northumbria that Bede tells us endured to his own day. Those books that Theodore and Hadrian could not spare would have been copied at the monastery and sent up to Northumbria or supplied on loan. While we don't have a catalogue for the library in Canterbury, scholars have reconstructed it from later *glossae collectae*. These are collections of glossaries, lists and explanations of difficult terms in the text, which could become little books in their own right. From these, it's possible to work out, with reasonable accuracy, the books from which the glossed terms came. The overlap between the books of the Kent and Northumbrian libraries was almost total.

The final conduit, funnelling books to the library in Northumbria, ran through Ireland. Some of the books probably arrived with Aidan and the other monks from Iona. There is one work, however, that we know was brought to Northumbria and handed over, for Bede tells us that Adomnán, the abbot of Iona, came to Northumbria and presented a copy of his book *Of the Holy Places* to King Aldfrith in 698. It was a happy choice of present. Aldfrith was a notably scholarly king, who had spent much of his early life living in Ireland. Aldfrith had the book copied and Bede used the copy of the book presented to the library at Wearmouth and Jarrow as a key source in his own guide to the sacred sites of the Holy Land.

Ireland was also probably the channel for some of the material Bede used in understanding and writing on the vexed question of the dating of Easter, the field of study known as *computus* which we will look at in more detail later.

It also seems likely that it was via the well-established sea trade routes connecting Spain to Ireland that the books from Spanish and North African writers arrived in Northumbria. It was an easier matter to transport books by boat than land. These were hefty, heavy works, with pages made from the skin of animals and leather bindings – very far from lightweight paperbacks. One scholar, Paul Meyvaert, worked out that just the works of Pope Gregory held by Benedict Biscop's library weighed 45 kilograms; a lot to shove on the back of a mule.

So, we can see that the library of a monastery a long way from anywhere else was connected remarkably well to a network of people and places that could provide it with books.

*

As to what was in the library, its reconstructed catalogue remains a work in progress. However, we can say that it contained books on Latin grammar: basically, language textbooks, and probably quite a few of them, although the exact number is difficult to tell, given that grammar textbooks have a marked tendency to till the same ground.

Standing at the centre of Bede's life as a scholar and a monk was scripture. The monastery had possession of a rare one-volume edition of the whole Bible, the *Codex Grandior* from the library of Cassiodorus, but it also had books containing sections of the Bible in the newer translation by St Jerome, as well as the psalters vital for the work of the monastery.

But reading the Bible was not enough for Bede and his community: belief was the path to understanding. To that end, the largest section of the monastery library was composed of commentaries on the Bible by early Christian saints and scholars, known as Church Fathers, who worked in the centuries of Roman persecution and afterwards to understand the mysteries of the faith and place it in relation to the Greek philosophical tradition. These were books by men such as Augustine, Jerome and John Chrysostom. But deep understanding of scripture required understanding of the context from which it came, and Bede made use of books of history – in particular the Jewish historian, Josephus, and the Church historian, Eusebius – natural history, geography, particularly of the Holy Land, and medicine.

If we can measure the degree of debt Bede owed previous writers by the number of times he cited or alluded to them in his writings, then we can make a list of those authors most important to him outside the Bible itself. This is not necessarily accurate. The work of some writers, such as Augustine, covered such a breadth of topics that it necessarily occurs more often in Bede's writing than the work of someone such as Gildas who is only important to Bede in his *Ecclesiastical History*, but extremely important in that context. With that caveat in mind, these are the writers that did most to form the mind and work of Bede:

St Ambrose (c.339–397). A key figure in the debate about the nature of Christ sparked by the Arian heresy, which held that Jesus was a created being rather than of one substance with God the Father.

St Augustine (354–430). The greatest of the Latin Church Fathers. His writings continue to inspire and repel in almost equal measure. He is famously, although not entirely fairly, credited with creating the doctrine of original sin and linking that with human sexuality.

Eusebius of Caesarea (c.260–339). The first historian of the Church. His *Historia Ecclesia* was a key influence in Bede's own history of the Church.

Gregory the Great (540–604). The pope who dispatched Augustine to Britain. Alfred the Great would later turn to Gregory's writing, too, as an integral part of the knowledge most important for all men to know.

Isidore of Seville (c.560–636). Isidore was the most important encyclopaedist of the early medieval period, writing works that covered history, natural and human, geography and science. Bede came to rather distrust Isidore's work in his later life.

Jerome (c.342–420). The Father responsible for putting the Bible into a Latin translation, the Vulgate, that was to serve as the key version of the text for the next thousand years.

Josephus (37–c.100). The Jewish historian who escaped the blood-soaked Roman revenge on the Jews for their revolt by changing sides rather than becoming another corpse nailed to a cross outside Jerusalem. In Rome, under the patronage of the Flavian emperors, Josephus wrote important histories of the Jewish war and of the Jewish people.

Pliny the Elder (23–79). The encyclopaedist of the Classical world, writing particularly about natural history and geography.

Virgil (70 BC–19 BC). The greatest of the Latin poets, who wrote the epic *Aeneid* about the origins of Rome, and for his sins became the rote master for generations of unhappy pupils attempting to conjugate Latin verbs and decline Latin nouns.

By frequency of citations, these were the most important writers in Bede's own writing. But others played an important role, even if mentioned less frequently. Among these were:

Adomnán of Iona (c.624–704). Now best known for his fascinating life of St Columba, this abbot of Iona brought his guide to the Holy Land with him to Northumbria, and it formed the basis of Bede's own guide to the Holy Land.

Arator (sixth century). Christian poet who wrote a history of the Apostles.

Athanasius (c.296–373). The key voice raised against Arianism. His life of St Anthony was one of the most widely copied books of the era and a staple of monastic libraries.

Basil of Caesarea (330–378). Bishop and theologian, an important proponent of the Nicene creed.

Benedict of Nursia (480–547). The Benedictine Rule was a key foundation for the Rule by which Bede and his community lived.

John Cassian (c.360–c.435). The man who first brought the monasticism of the desert to the fields and hills of Europe.

Cassiodorus (c.485–c.585). The man whose library the founders of Bede's own library raided.

Cicero (106 BC–43 BC). Among Bedan scholars, it's a matter of some controversy as to whether the work of the great Latin prosodist was present at the library in Wearmouth and Jarrow or not. The argument for its presence is that Bede's rhetoric so perfectly conforms to the rules proposed by Cicero that he must have learnt it from the master's own work, despite there being no explicit quotation or reference to Cicero in his writing. The counterargument is that Bede was just really, really good at Latin.

Dionysus Exiguus (c.470–c.544). In writing his works about *computus*, the dating of Easter, Dionysus Exiguus also suggested a new system of dating, based upon the birth of Christ. Bede would take this idea and run with it.

Gildas (sixth century). The irascible Britonnic monk's history of the ruin of his countrymen provided a vital foundation for Bede's understanding of how his own people had supplanted the Britons.

Macrobius (fifth century). His commentary on Cicero's *Dream of Scipio* transmitted significant portions of Classical thinking on the nature of the cosmos to the Christian Middle Ages.

Origen (c.185–c.253). The most important theologian of the early Church. Origen's commentaries on the Bible leaned heavily towards the allegorical and symbolic, greatly influencing Bede's own work. It's obligatory, when writing of Origen, to mention that, according to Eusebius, Origen castrated himself. As Origen nowhere mentions this in any of his writings (and he wrote a lot), some scholars argue that Eusebius was repeating gossip from one of Origen's enemies, of which there were many. Others point out that Eusebius, who admired Origen, would have had no reason to include such a story unless he believed it to be true. At this point, it's unlikely we'll be able to definitively ascertain the origin of the story of Origen's orchiectomy.

Orosius (c.375–c.420). Important Christian historian whose thoughts about historiography, how historians write about history, influenced Bede.

Ovid (43 BC–AD 17/18). The most delightful of Latin poets but one whose sensuality was very far from Bede's sensibilities. Still, it's good to know that Bede read at least some of his *Metamorphoses*.

Paulinus of Nola (c.354–431). A high-ranking official in the empire, Paulinus gave up his position and wealth when he converted to Christianity. He became the bishop of Nola, and many of his letters to other Christian figures survived.

Prosper of Aquitaine (c.390–c.455). The great proponent of Augustine's teachings about grace and free will. His *Sententia* was a collection of short extracts from Augustine's writing that Bede used extensively.

Prudentius (348–c.413). One of the Christian poets of Late Antiquity whose work Bede used in preference to Classical writers. His *Psychomachia* became a model for later medieval allegorical poetry.

Sedulius (fifth century). A relatively minor poet but one whose work Bede used for his teaching of Latin.

Venantius Fortunatus (c.530–c.600). A Latin poet who wrote poetry for the Merovingian inheritors of the Roman province of Gaul, Venantius Fortunatus was one of the key links between Classical Latin and medieval Latin poetry.

These, then, were the writers upon whose books Bede built his own work. They are a mixture of Christian and pagan authors, with an important Jewish strand from the Bible and Josephus. The range of Christian writers is broader, in time and space, than the old Classical writers that Bede read, but the Classical writers carried their mastery of Latin and the pale nimbus of empire to Bede's time.

This was the word soil that Bede ploughed; a fertile soil, and a rich one, fertilised with many minds and traditions. But it was not a field without rocks that had to be cleared before the land could be ploughed, and the most constant of these was the labour involved in writing and copying books. Unlike later medieval writers, Bede had to write out his own books, as well as working as a copyist, and in the next chapter we will examine how words went from the mind and memory to a new page. It was a long process.

# CHAPTER 8

# Bookmakers

Bede sat with the book open and resting on his thighs. He flexed his feet, trying to work some blood back into his toes. Then he shifted his bottom. The stool he was sitting upon was hard and he had been sitting upon it since Sext. His back ached and there was no longer any feeling whatsoever in his bottom. Taking the goose feather pen he was holding, he dipped it into the ink well and bent back to the book, squinting to see the page more clearly. When he was younger, he had been able to sit straight-backed and still see the words clearly. But now that he was old, he had to bend his back to bring his face much closer to the page, otherwise the words were blurred. Sitting hunched like that, it was no surprise that his back ached.

But these pains were small prices to pay for the joy and wonder of what he was doing. It was through and by and in books that men learnt how they should live in accordance with God's law. By these words they might come to his house in the next life while giving praise at the wonders with which he clothed the world.

Just as Bede began to write, the pen's nib gliding smoothly over the parchment, the bell in the church rang, summoning him, and all his brethren, to prayer. It was now Nones, three hours after noon. Bede carefully lay the book he was writing aside, placing it on a table, and covered his inks that they not dry out. He would have to cut a new pen when he returned to his work after the Nones prayers. He put the used goose feather with the others he had discarded.

Standing up, Bede stretched up and out as the blood returned to the parts of his body it had abandoned during the three hours he had been sitting and writing. The time of prayer and song would move the blood that had settled and he would return to his labour refreshed, working on the book until the brethren gathered for their light evening meal. Then, after food, Vespers.

The work of a monk. When he was younger, Bede had done his share of the threshing and the winnowing, the drawing of water and the scraping of skins. But now that he was older, Abbot Hwætberht confined his labours outside the church to teaching, reading, writing and copying. Although Bede did feel occasional pangs of guilt when he saw one or other of his brethren elbow-deep in piles of stinking animal skins, he knew, as did his brethren, that few would miss his work at the tannery but many would miss his work with words.

Bede looked at the cupboards with the books of the library carefully laid out on their shelves. He could not stop himself from smiling. For alongside books by St Augustine and St Jerome, books of Virgil and Ovid, there were books that had come from his own mind and hand lying on the shelves. To think that they should keep such company. Noting the old vice of pride in his work rising in his soul, Bede crushed it beneath his heel: this was the work he was called to and meant for: there was no source for pride in it, simply gratitude to the Lord for giving him the place and means to exercise the talents he had been given.

Outside, Bede heard the slap of sandals on wet path: the brethren were making their way to church for prayer. He went to follow, closing the door of the scriptorium as he left so that no wandering animal might stray inside and damage the precious books. As for himself, he would be back, when the psalms were sung, to sit again upon his stool with pen in his hand and his book on his lap.

It was what God, and Abbots Ceolfrith and Hwætberht, had called him to do.

*

Bede was a scribe as well as a writer. For most of his life, the books he wrote, he wrote himself. This was not the case for later medieval writers, where a senior monk would have a secretary to whom he could dictate his writing. But the monks of Wearmouth and Jarrow wrote out their own books in their own hand.

What's more, we have a picture of how Bede, and the other monks at the monastery, carried out the labour of book writing. The greatest undertaking of the twin monastery was its production of three pandects (complete texts) of the Bible. Two were lost but one survived in, of all places, a monastery in Tuscany. The story of how it came to be written, and how it ended up in Tuscany, is told in chapter twelve. But for this chapter, we just need to know that at the start of the surviving Bible there is a picture of Ezra, writing. According to tradition, Ezra was the scribe who wrote out the scripture following the Jewish captivity in Babylon, thus saving the Bible from oblivion. As such, he makes for a good choice as an opening illustration to the Old Testament.[1]

The illustration lies on the facing page to the altered dedication behind which lies the mystery of the *Codex Amiatinus*'s storage in a Tuscan monastery. Ezra is sitting on a stool with a cushion under his bottom. There's no back to the chair and, given the long hours copyists spent over their work, a cushion was a small comfort for the aching back, eyes and bottom that resulted from such long labour. Ezra's feet are raised from the floor, resting upon a foot stool. This has the effect of raising his knees above his waist, making his thighs into an inclined surface upon which rests the book that he is writing – the Bible itself, since the writer is Ezra. Scattered on the floor around the scribe are the tools of the copyist: dividers, stylus, ink pot, pen and, on a nearby table, a bowl of pigment.

A picture of a scribe from what was the most important scriptorium in Britain is a great treasure. But there is another intriguing possibility to this picture. To understand what that is we need to briefly look at one of Bede's earlier works, *On the Holy Places*, which he wrote before 709. It is essentially a travel guide to the Holy Land and one of quite astonishing vividness and precision given that Bede never went there. The book is a testament to Bede's ability to spin narrative gold from various sources as well as his skill on taking his reader on imaginative journeys to places that neither they nor the writer have ever been. But in his efforts to make the recreation more vivid for his reader, in three parts of the book Bede writes some variation of 'and here it is in a picture I drew'. Unfortunately, none of the surviving manuscripts reproduce Bede's original drawings, so we only have his description of what he drew[2] rather than the drawings themselves. The drawings were probably based on the drawings that Adomnán included in his own guide to the holy places, which Bede used as the basis for his own book. But as we don't have Bede's own pictures, we don't know how closely he stayed to the originals.

However, these throwaway comments about Bedan drawings suddenly suggest that maybe Bede was involved in the illustration of the *Codex* as well. Could he have been the artist who painted Ezra? On the whole, it seems unlikely that a man with so many other duties could spare the time to do the painting, too, but the idea of Bede the artist is intriguing. On such a project, the community clearly wanted to give of their best: if Bede was the best artist there, he might have been the one tasked with painting the picture of Ezra. It's not a question we are likely to be able to answer, but it adds another layer of possibility to what confronts us when we look at the image of the scribe.

In the picture, Ezra sits in the foreground and behind him there is a book cupboard with its doors open. The book cupboard is red and on its five shelves are nine books, each lying flat, that together make up the Bible. Although impossible to see in reproductions of the illustration, the spines of these books have written upon them their titles: the Octateuch (the first eight books of the Bible); Kings, Chronicles and Job; eight history books; the psalms; the books of Solomon; the Prophets; the Gospels; the Epistles; Acts of the Apostles and the Apocalypse. (Although I was fortunate enough to see the *Codex Amiatinus* when it was part of the 'Anglo-Saxon Kingdoms' exhibition at the British Library, I couldn't examine the illustration myself then. However, the few privileged keepers of manuscripts who have been able to examine the *Codex* in detail tell us that by getting the light to reflect off the illustration just right, the titles become visible.) Together, these nine books contain the complete text of the Bible. It's also the form in which almost all monastic libraries throughout Christendom would have had the Bible at this time: not as one single book but split into different volumes.

This was because making books was difficult and expensive. Under the Roman Empire, the main writing medium was paper made from papyrus. Papyrus has a tall stalk rising to an umbrella fan of leaves at the top. It is a thirsty plant that grows best when its roots are in water; it is a plant of riverside margins and marshes. But it is not a hardy plant, and it cannot survive in northern Europe, growing best in the Nile delta. Also, while papyrus made for an excellent paper in the Mediterranean countries, it was never so well suited to the more northern provinces of the empire as it does not last well in damp conditions – and Britain is nothing if not damp. By contrast, when stored in a dry place papyrus can last millennia, as demonstrated by such finds as the Dead Sea Scrolls and the Oxyrhynchus Papyri, which both survived for thousands of years in dry desert conditions.

So when the Western Roman Empire collapsed, the successor kingdoms lost access to Egyptian papyrus and had to find another writing medium, something available, light, flexible, durable and not too affected by the damp and cool environment of north-western Europe. The only candidate was animal skin.

Parchment had already come into use throughout the empire as the writing surface best suited for important books because it was more durable and tougher than papyrus. So the production techniques were already known. With the loss of Egyptian papyrus, parchment became the only viable medium for making books and, for a monastery with substantial herds of sheep, cattle and goats, it became the natural medium for book production. Indeed, one of the main reasons that monasteries sought to increase their land holdings at this time was so that they could run larger herds of animals to support their book production.

As with other books, the *Codex Amiatinus* is made up of bundles of pages stitched together. For the *Codex*, the scriptoria at Wearmouth and Jarrow gathered eight leaves of parchment. These were made of eight rectangles of animal skin. Each rectangle was folded in half and then inserted into the next, forming what was, in effect, a little book. This is still how books are produced today, although it's generally easier to see in hardbacks than paperbacks. Close the book and have a look at it from above. You should be able to see how the pages are gathered together into sections. These sections are called quires or, more simply, gatherings. The quires are then bound together to make the complete book. Palaeographers, the scholars who study ancient manuscripts, compare different manuscripts of the same text, in a process known as collation, to discover the true text. But collation may also refer to checking the text of a particular manuscript to see if any pages are missing.

For instance, suppose a manuscript is made up of quires of eight leaves, that is sections of sixteen pages. If you find that one of the quires only has seven leaves, then there is good reason to suspect that one of the leaves has been removed. Alternatively, a quire might have an additional leaf because a page has been added. Both of these are relatively common in old books. Sometimes the same book has had pages removed and others added. Careful examination of the quires allows palaeographers to discover these changes.

The parchment that went into the *Codex Amiatinus* was the finest available to the monastery. To distinguish this top-quality parchment from the more run-of-the-mill material, it is sometimes called vellum. However, the two terms are often used interchangeably so don't take this as Gospel if you come across the terms elsewhere. The skin of calves was used for the vellum as it was smoother and less lined than that of cattle or goats or sheep – the poor animals had not had the chance to develop any crease marks before they were killed. The vast majority of the calves would have been bull calves; in the lottery of farm birth, being born female meant a far greater chance of a long life.

As with his contemporaries, Bede had a far greater range of practical skills than is usual today. He could plant, sow, reap, wash, sew, darn, knit, cook, clean, herd, tend, fish – and prepare animal skins for writing. Although the twin monastery had its specialists, as a new institution the monks had to cover all the tasks themselves. While most of Bede's work time as an adult was spent in teaching and writing, he still would have helped with the basic monastic tasks, including the dirty and smelly labour of parchment production.

First, the animal was skinned. When making leather, it doesn't matter if there are blemishes or creases in the skin as these can be dyed over. However, the scribe writes directly onto the parchment – the skin of the dead animal. If there are blemishes on the skin, they will be there on the parchment. So the first task was to inspect the skins, selecting those free from marks and blemishes for further processing. Since most animals give birth in the spring, there was usually a glut of skins shortly afterwards, far too many to all be used at once. However, by salting, the skins could be preserved for six months or so until they were needed. The storeroom where the skins were kept, probably one of the riverside workshops excavated by Rosemary Cramp, would have been a noisome place. Putting it by the river, away from the main monastic buildings, kept the air cleaner, and river breezes would have helped to clear the smells that leaked out.

The next step in preparation was to remove the hair. To do this, the skins were soaked in vats of limed water. The lime penetrated into the skins, loosening the hair roots. The skins were soaked for a few days until the hair was all loosened. Then the skin was taken from the lime vat, draped over a stand and the hair scraped off. The liming meant that great swathes of hair would come off with each scrape – although care had to be taken with the scraper to make sure that it was smooth, so that it didn't nick or tear the skin.

However, while the liming meant that it was straightforward to scrape the hair off the outside of the skin, there was still the inside, the flesh side, to prepare. Flesh, muscle, fat, fascia, connective tissue, the sinewy, slippery inside bits that are smoothed over by the skin – all had to be scraped off. To do this, the skin was first stretched out in a frame, held taut by leather thongs tied through the margins of the skin to the frame. The flesh was then scraped off using a semi-circular scraping knife called a lunellum. Rather than scraping, the parchminer (someone who makes parchment) punched the lunellum into the stretched skin, tautening it further while bringing more of the skin in contact with the curved blade surface, and then scraped.

It was a laborious business.

With the skin now clean, it was hung up, still under tension, to dry. Once the parchment was dry, it would be given a final rub down with fine sand to remove any final irregularities on the surface and then it was ready for writing.

According to traditional accounts, the process for making parchment was first discovered in the city of Pergamon, in modern-day Türkiye, in the second-century BC, when the local book makers were suffering from a sudden shortage of papyrus and started searching for something else to write on. According to Pliny, the papyrus shortage was down to a royal literary rivalry: Ptolemy V had ordered the building and stocking of the famous library at Alexandria at the same time as King Eumenes II had decided he wanted a library of his own in Pergamon. When Ptolemy decided to hog Egyptian papyrus for his own library, the book makers of Pergamon, with an impatient king breathing over their shoulders, had to come up with a new writing material in a hurry.

Historians tend to dismiss the story, but they do admit that Pergamon was where the parchment process was perfected.

As a boy and a novice monk, Bede would have been involved in the whole process. However, once his teaching duties became greater, it's likely he was largely spared this labour. There were plenty of men who could prepare parchment, but there weren't many who could teach as well as Bede. But while he no longer made parchment as he got older, he remained a scribe almost to the end of his life. Only in his final months, when ill health was taking its toll, was he given an amanuensis, a young oblate named Wilberht.

We don't know the location of the scriptorium at Jarrow. However, we do, presumably, have a picture of what it looked like in the illustration of Ezra in the *Codex Amiatinus*. The general practice of medieval and later art was to place Biblical scenes in contemporary settings. So Ezra was probably depicted writing in the scriptorium at Jarrow or Wearmouth. There's not much detail about the room in the picture. What stands out is the book cupboard, the *armarium*, with its doors open and its five shelves for books. The cupboard itself is painted red with detailed carvings, both geometrical and figurative, including a cross and a bird. The Anglo-Saxons were late to working with stone – Biscop's monasteries were the first stone buildings constructed in England after the Roman withdrawal – but they were master carpenters and smiths. While metal survives quite well, allowing us to see the craft of these master smiths in the Sutton Hoo and Staffordshire Hoard discoveries, wood decays, leaving little but the holes in the ground that tell the ghost story of lost buildings carved and decorated with infinite care.

So while the Ezra painting does not tell us much about the scriptorium at Jarrow, it does provide one striking, and surprising, detail. Ezra is writing on his lap. This is strange because pretty well all the later portrayals of monks writing have them sitting at desks, with the manuscript raised at a comfortable angle to the scribe. But at Jarrow, we must assume that, for whatever reason, the scribes wrote on their laps. While Ezra is shown writing directly into his book, the scribe would normally have been writing onto the parchment, presumably lain flat over a board resting on his thighs, which was only later bound into a book.

The main task of a scribe was to copy. It's via these medieval scribes, labouring away in monasteries throughout Europe, that we have the ancient Classical texts that have come down to us. The Romans and the Greeks didn't save them. It was anonymous medieval monks who saved Plato and Cicero, Tertullian and Herodotus, Virgil and Homer. Yes, we can lament what was lost but that so much was saved was the work of men like Bede. It's an inestimable debt, and one that few people today realise is owed.

It was difficult and weary work. While in terms of physical hardship it did not rate alongside some of the other labours of the time, the life of a scribe had its own pains. A tenth-century Castilian scribe, Florentius of Valéranica, left this description of what was involved in writing a book:

> Because one who does not know how to write thinks it no labour, I will describe it for you, if you want to know how great is the burden of writing: it mists the eyes, it curves the back, it breaks the belly and the ribs, it fills the kidneys with pain, and the body with all kinds of suffering. Therefore, turn the pages slowly, reader, and keep your fingers well away from the pages, for just as a hailstorm ruins the fecundity of the soil, so the sloppy reader destroys both the book and the writing. For as the last port is sweet to the sailor, so the last line to the scribe.[3]

But in order to write, the scribe had to prepare his tools, his pen and his ink. This was not just a matter of opening a bottle of Quink (younger readers will completely fail to understand this allusion but the writer used a fountain pen at school – he was clearly doomed to the writing life from youth – and that required regular refills with an ink made by Parker called Quink, which was short for 'quick ink'); somebody had to make the ink.

Bede undoubtedly had to make his own ink at least some of the time, and the ink he used was made from oak galls. These are the hard, round knobbly bits that you can see on an oak tree. They're made by the female gall wasp. There are over 70 species of gall wasp in Britain, producing different shapes and sizes of galls. The female pierces the host tree with her ovipositor and lays her eggs within the tree. When the larvae hatch, they secrete chemicals that cause the tree to create a hard growth around them that serves as a protective shell for the developing larvae. It's a process similar to scab formation or how an oyster makes a pearl. Once the larvae pupate into wasps (gall wasps don't look like their stinging counterparts, more like little flies), they chew their way out of the gall to begin the cycle again.

To make ink, medieval monks collected sackloads of oak galls. They are hard, so crushing them required a good hammer. Having reduced the galls to a rough powder, the ink maker put the powder into a container and covered it with rainwater, leaving the mixture to stand for a few days. Oak galls are rich in tannin and during this standing time the tannic acid leached out of the galls and into the water. As the mixture stood, the water slowly turned light brown and then, as more tannic acid dissolved out of the galls, it became a dark brown. That dark brown water was then drained off and the soggy powder discarded.

To make the ink adhere to the parchment, some sort of sticking agent was required. The most common was gum Arabic. That this was used shows the extent of trading routes in early medieval Britain, for gum Arabic is the hard resin produced by the sap leaking from the 24 species of acacia tree that grow in the semi-arid expanses of the Sahel, the transition zone between the Sahara to the north and the savannah to the south, stretching all the way across Africa from the Atlantic to the Red Sea. Gum Arabic was imported via Mediterranean traders, but its name indicates who the main middlemen were.

Gum Arabic works well because it dissolves easily in water, but it then makes a layer around the ink molecules leached from the oak galls, keeping them in suspension within the liquid, thus stopping them settling out into a thick layer of sludge at the bottom of the jar. We still use it today although now, in a typical example of modern demythologisation, it is listed on food ingredients as E414.

The gum Arabic produces a sticky solution to which copperas, the medieval name for iron sulphate, was added (iron sulphate is often called ferrous sulphate when used as a food supplement). The copperas slowly darkened the brown until it became the ink that medieval scribes preferred for their work. When traced over the parchment and exposed to air, the iron sulphate oxidised, rendering the ink the deep dense black that we can still see in medieval manuscripts, while the gum Arabic ensured that it stuck firmly to the page.

That gum Arabic should find its way to a monastery on the North Sea coast, thousands of miles away from where acacia trees grow, might seem surprising, but it's testament to the breadth of trade routes at this time. Some of the ingredients for the pigments used in paints also had to come from long distances. Perhaps the best-known example is lapis lazuli. This is a blue rock, made from lazurite, pyrite and calcite. When crushed into a powder, it can be used to produce an astonishingly intense ultramarine pigment. The only source of lapis lazuli at the time were mines in what is now Afghanistan, where it has been dug for 6,000 years. From there, lapis lazuli was traded east and west. It was a high-value, low-volume export. In fact, even gold was a cheaper pigment than lapis lazuli ultramarine. As such, it's not hard to see why trade in lapis lazuli was so enduring: the returns were huge and the costs low.

The other medieval pigments were not so expensive and were generally easier to obtain. The basic palette of earth colours came from materials such as iron, clay and silica, producing the siennas, umbers and ochres that were the workhorses of medieval illustrators. Early reds were made from madder, a common plant that has been used to dye cloth since at least 3000 BC. Cinnabar had been used widely to make vermilion during the Roman Empire, but its usage dipped during the early medieval period, when it also became very expensive. For yellow, a number of earths could be used but the deepest yellow came from orpiment, an arsenic sulphide that looks in its raw form like yellow quartz. It was mined in the Near East and traded widely although, as its chemical name suggests, its use wasn't without dangers.

Medieval painters had their own recipes for preparing paints. It was normally a task given to the novice as he learnt the skill, working with a list of ingredients set by his master, and it varied according to the location, the ingredients available and the work at hand. A more important book required better and more expensive paints.

In general, medieval people had to master a much wider range of practical skills than we need to know today, from lighting a fire through basic carpentry and horticulture, to animal husbandry and fishing. The monks were the same. If anything, they needed a wider range of skills, for on top of the basic skills for living, they had to learn a new language, sing in it, teach and learn, read and write. Bede was one of these multi-skilled monks, walking through the woods near Jarrow, collecting oak galls, pounding them up and then mixing them just right to make the quality of ink he needed as a scribe.

Having prepared his ink, Bede could get down to doing some writing. No doubt he began as a copyist – and continued as a copyist throughout much of his monastic career, particularly when working on the *Codex Amiatinus* – but, of course, he also wrote his own works.

Before Bede could start, he had to prepare the blank page so that it would take the ink. First, he rubbed the parchment with a fine abrasive, such as crushed pumice, to roughen its surface. Then the page was brushed with a sticky powder to help with ink adhesion. Finally, the irregular sheet of parchment had to be trimmed to a regular rectangle so that it could be bound properly into the final book.

Settling down to write, with his feet raised up on a stool and the writing board on his thighs, Bede had his writing tools set up within easy reach so that he did not have to put the page aside to get things he needed: the ink horn, the quill pen, at least one knife.

The pen Bede used to write was made from a bird feather, most commonly goose. Before use, the feather was left to soak in water. Then it was dried and, finally, hardened by placing it in hot sand. To prepare the quill, Bede cut a diagonal section from the end of the feather. He then cut a channel up the feather which would bring the ink down to the nib, and he then trimmed the end of the quill to the proper shape for the writing he was doing: a narrower tip produced a finer line while a broader tip allowed letter production with broader and narrower lines.

The parchment was obviously unlined, so to ensure that the writing did not wander over the page, scribes like Bede had to mark lines on the page. They did this by pricking out tiny holes down the sides of the page using a regular divider and then joining the dots on each side of the page by drawing a blunt edge across the parchment, producing an indentation that marked the line the scribe would write upon.

To write, Bede dipped his pen into the ink well, loading it with ink. The cut down to the tip drew ink to the nib and, with the quill ready, Bede began to write. If you look carefully at medieval manuscripts, you can see on the page the scribal rhythm as the quill writes, easily and smoothly, and then, as the small amount of ink held in the quill is used up, the writing becomes slightly fainter as less ink is deposited on the page, before the sudden return to thick dark writing as the scribe dips his pen in ink again.

The scribes at Wearmouth and Jarrow wrote in two styles, depending on the book they were producing. For the most important books, such as copies of the scripture, they used a writing style called uncial, which followed very closely the writing in the books brought over from Europe, and particularly Rome, by Benedict and Ceolfrith. Uncial is a stately and formal writing style only using capital letters.

However, the scribes at Wearmouth and Jarrow did change uncial in one crucial respect. In Roman books written in uncial, there were no spaces between words but there were gaps between sentences. This was possible for Italians reading Latin as early Italian was still close enough to Latin for native speakers to be able to tell where words began and ended. But for Anglo-Saxons speaking Old English, Latin was an entirely alien language that had to be learnt from books and teachers. To help readers navigate their way round this strange tongue, the scribes at Wearmouth and Jarrow took to writing uncial with gaps between words, starting the written page on the path down towards modern typesetting. However, the scribes did such a good job of imitating Italian-style uncial that, for years, everyone thought the *Codex Amiatinus* was written in Italy.

For less formal writing, the scribes at Wearmouth and Jarrow used a style called insular minuscule. This derived from uncial but was easier and quicker to write.

While scribes wrote with care, they still made mistakes. To correct mistakes, the scribe used his knife to carefully scrape off the ink. This was another advantage of parchment. Unlike papyrus or paper, parchment is tough. The top layer could endure a cack-handed scribe making lots of mistakes before the parchment frayed.

When the weather was good, the scribes probably worked outside. The light was much better there. However, as this was Northumberland, they would have had to spend many long hours working indoors, away from the wind and the rain. With small windows and cloudy skies, the work must have been difficult on the eyes as well as hard on the back and cramping to the hand. But it was how Bede passed the greater part of his life, learning, teaching and writing.

That was unusual enough for his time. But that we have the physical trace of his work, in the bulky shape of the *Codex Amiatinus*, is extraordinary. Bede's hand is surely among the seven or so that wrote out the pandect. Looking at it, whether in digital facsimile or in its squatting bulk, is to be set at his shoulder as he, with his fellow scribes, worked long and hard to put down on parchment the word of God as clearly and legibly as it was possible for hand to do. The time and care they put to it is evident. Writing – passing on first and foremost the knowledge of God but then also that of men – was their duty and their privilege. They clearly embraced both the duty and the privilege. There's none of the complaints that you find in later medieval manuscripts written into the margins as a tired scribe vented his frustration. These were serious men doing serious and important work and they did not complain at the price they paid for doing it.

Civilisation is a delicate construction, one resting upon many foundations. One of those supports is the unsung work done by generations of anonymous monks in the centuries after the fall of the Western Roman Empire when their monasteries were the only outposts of learning in a world whose horizons had retreated to the fields around the village. Bede gives us a name and a life with which to honour the many other men who did similar work, whose names are lost and whose lives forgotten. It's a shame that St Catherine of Alexandria is the patron saint of scribes; it would have been a role better suited to Bede, who really was a scribe, rather than a semi-mythical figure whose martyrdom became the prototype for a firework.

Nevertheless, we can think of Bede, hunched over his writing board, fingertips stained black from the ink. This was how he copied the works of scripture and the Fathers, and how he wrote his own books. Quill in hand, one dip of ink at a time.

# CHAPTER 9

# A Rational World

Numbers matter. They matter to us today and they mattered to Bede 1,300 years ago. But how we think of numbers, how we work with them and how we manipulate them has changed hugely since his day.

As to why numbers were important to Bede, the first and greatest reason was because God employed them. Indeed, God exemplified them by his very being. For according to Christian belief, God was one being in three persons: the Trinity. This profound paradox lay at the heart of Christianity, bound inextricably together with the other paradox that was fundamental: God becoming man and dying on the cross.

Christianity featured one God in three persons, five books of Moses, seven days of creation, twelve Apostles and tribes of Israel. When reading scripture, Bede was faced at every juncture with significant numbers. And since these were numbers used and hallowed by God, they were not just coincidences: applying the laws of exegesis that Bede had learnt meant that the numbers mattered in and of themselves, for each revealed some new insight into the divine mind that employed them. It is no coincidence that the *Ecclesiastical History* is made up of five books; an open allusion to the five books of Moses that begin the Bible.

But there is a deeper and more profound difference in the way we approach numbers today as compared to pre-modern times. This is not just true of Bede but applies to almost all writers and thinkers before the seventeenth century.

Let's take the Bible as our first example. It's full of numbers. The seven days of creation, the ten commandments, the twelve tribes of Israel and the twelve Apostles, 40 years in the wilderness and 40 days in the desert. These are all clearly significant numbers. But there are other numbers given in the Bible, too. Samson kills 1,000 men with the jawbone of an ass. The Israelites frequently assemble armies of hundreds of thousands of men; Jehoshaphat's army numbered 1,160,000 (2 Chronicles 17:14–18), while David gathered no less than 1,300,000 for his army (2 Samuel 24:9). But it's not just large armies: we also read of extraordinarily long lives. Genesis states that Adam lived for 930 years, Seth for 912, Noah for 950 years and, longest of them all, Methuselah for 969 years.

The most common response to reading such numbers nowadays is to assume that, simply, they just weren't that good at maths. The big numbers were scribal number-waving for something really, really big, from people who didn't really understand how numbers work. We might think the same as being true for Bede. For instance, at the Battle of Chester, Bede records that Æthelfrith killed 1,200 monks who had come to pray for his enemy. The number is too large and too exact, as if someone really went around counting up the corpses before they were trundled back to Bangor monastery. Just another example of number-waving by early writers.

But this doesn't work for Bede because we know he could do the maths. The calculations required to harmonise the various dates he gave in the *Ecclesiastical History* were long, complex and precise. In *30 Questions on the Book of Kings*, Bede carefully worked out the exact dimensions of the Temple of Solomon from the account given in that book. *The Reckoning of Time* begins with a primer on methods of calculation, including fractions, before going on to give the formulas for calculating various cycles. For instance:

> If you want to know what the epacts are for any given year,
> take the number of years of the Lord, for example in the

present eighth indiction, 725. Divide by 19: 19 times 30 is 570 and 19 times 8 is 152, with 3 left over. Multiply these by 3, which makes 33. Subtract 30, and the remainder is 3. The epact, that is, the lunar increment, is 3.[1]

So it's clear that Bede could do the maths. In fact, he was better at it than most people today. However, he had a very different view of what numbers are. For him, as for most thinkers prior to the seventeenth century, numbers weren't just numbers: they had qualities.

This is important. For us, numbers are simply numbers, to be manipulated, calculated and used: there is no intrinsic difference between 40 and 82. This utilitarian view of numbers stems in the first instance from René Descartes, who dismissed qualitative considerations from his consideration of matter, the physical stuff of the universe, an analysis that opened the way to the great successes of modern science at the price of essentially ignoring the qualitative aspects of everyday reality. Thus we have come to understand 'red' as light with a wavelength between 620 and 750 nanometres, consigning its 'redness' to the realm of subjective feelings that have no connection to hard reality.

However, this was not the case for Bede, nor for anyone prior to the early modern age. For them, numbers were qualities as well as quantities. Three was different from four not simply by being one less and a prime but by the very nature of 'threeness', which symbolised generation and growth when compared to the stolid completeness of 'four'.

Therefore, whenever Bede uses a number in his work its significance goes beyond its numerical value. Numbers are values in a universal hierarchy, a way of uniting heaven and earth, so when they occur, they matter. For instance, in his history Bede tells the reader that there were three invading tribes that came to Britain: the Angles, the Saxons and the Jutes. Recent investigations of ancient DNA conserved in the teeth of burials from the time convincingly demonstrate that there were more people coming to Britain than that list indicates; in particular, there were a lot of arrivals from northern France. But Bede ignores this group in his history. Of course, he might not have had any information about them but including them would also have ruined the numerical symbolism of having three incoming tribes, the Trinitarian number, arriving in this promised land.

This means that it is always worth looking at the symbolic significance of the numbers Bede uses as part of the overall message he is trying to convey.

So that was the fundamental theological reason for Bede's interest in numbers. But he had practical reasons, too. First and foremost, the calculation of the date of Easter, *computus*, was a fiendishly difficult problem, involving the solution of theological, historical, astronomical, calendrical and mathematical problems. Not only did Bede have to understand and solve this problem but he had to teach others how to do it, too.

Secondly, there were the huge number of calculations he had to do when working out dates. In 703, Bede wrote *On Times* in which he included a chronicle, the *Chronica Minora*, of Biblical and British events. Twenty-two years later, in 725, Bede wrote a much-expanded work, *The Reckoning of Time*, in which he included a much more detailed chronicle, the *Chronica Maiora*. In both cases, Bede dated events from the birth of Adam. So the first event noted in the *Chronica Maiora*, dated 130, is the birth of Adam's son, Seth, which the Bible says occurred when Adam was 130. Bede lists the assassination of Julius Caesar under the year 3910 and the year 4557 for when Pope Gregory sent Augustine to Britain to convert the Anglo-Saxons. In order to do this, Bede had to take a wide variety of date forms and convert them all into the absolute calendar he had created for the purpose of his chronicles.

However, when Bede came to write the *Ecclesiastical History*, he decided to date everything from the birth of Christ: the BC and AD dating system that we are familiar with today. To do so, he had to convert all the previous dates to this new system.

I am a member of the last generation to grow up before calculators became universally available. At school, I had to do all calculations either in my head or with pen and paper. I had books of log tables, and different booklets for sine, cosine, tangent and cotangent tables. I remember my delight in being given a slide rule when I was thirteen, which made these calculations significantly easier. (For those who have never seen one, a slide rule is a sliding ruler set within a larger base ruler. Moving the slide up and down allows for different calculations, including multiplication and division, but also more complex functions. Rather than sitting down with pen and paper and working out 88 x 24, a slide rule allowed me to simply move the slide and read off the answer.)

Bede, however, not only did not have a slide rule, he did not even have Arabic numerals. These were not introduced into Europe until the twelfth century. He had to do all his calculations with Roman numerals. Which, having run some experiments myself, I can say makes for clunky and long-winded calculations that are liable to error.

This was a problem for Bede because he believed that the world made sense. But there is no obvious reason for the world to make sense, for its workings to be explicable. Yes, there are some regularities: the day and the night, the seasons, the movement of the stars in the sky. But in Bede's seventh-century world, the unexpected and the irregular were far more common and usually devastating, from kings dying in battle to famine and disease through to storms and disasters. It was a world in which most people constantly kept an eye open, looking for the unexpected blow from behind that would rip their lives apart. In such a context, expecting the world to make sense flew in the face of everyday experience.

But Bede did believe this, and he cleaved to that belief because of the Bible and the Church Fathers. Scripture itself warrants this, on the face of it, irrational belief. Firstly, it tells the story of creation in an ordered and sequential fashion, suggesting strongly that the mind that ordered it was just as orderly. Secondly, the Bible is studded with verses which aver that the world reflects the mind that made it. For instance, Psalm 19 begins, 'The heavens declare the glory of God; the skies proclaim the work of his hands.' An even more explicit message of the world's rationality appears in Wisdom 11:21: 'But you have arranged all things by measure and number and weight.'

So despite the evidence to the contrary, Bede and his fellow Christian scholars had faith that the world was indeed intelligible. What was more, by understanding the world better, they would therefore understand God a little better, too, for the world revealed, in its own way, some small part of the workings of his mind. This gave an incentive to investigate and understand the world around them.

In this, there was a key difference between Christian thinkers and their Classical forebears. The Christian had to take seriously the idea that God had made the world in its entirety. 'And God saw everything that he had made, and, behold, it was very good' (Genesis 1:31). For the Greeks, it was clear that the closest approach to perfection was in the realm of philosophical thought: there, things from geometrical objects to living creatures including man were truly themselves, beyond the imperfections of this world. So where the two clashed, philosophical thought and physical evidence, then it was the evidence that was wrong, for it was tainted and distorted by the world.

It was different for Christian thinkers. They had to work from an assumption of God's goodness in making the world, and that he had got it right when he had made it. Therefore, when thought and evidence clashed, there was pressure not to simply dismiss the evidence but to deepen it in order to better understand the world that God had made. And here lies the key to why it was the Christian world that invented science. Because for science to work, two acts of faith are necessary. Neither of these are obvious, a priori: they have to be taken as axioms before any progress can be made. The first is that the world does indeed make sense. The Bible and the Church Fathers were warrants for this. The second is that it's worth investigating the world to understand it better: how the world really is, not how you think it ought to be. For this, the faith that the world revealed some part of the glory of God was vital.[2]

With these two beliefs in place, it was possible to move slowly from the thought of Classical Antiquity to the birth of natural philosophy and then science.

While Classical thought used to be held up as an early stirring towards natural science that was cut short by the descent into the Dark Ages, only to be reborn when Classical learning was rediscovered during the Renaissance, this is now clearly known to be wrong. On its own, Classical thought could never have produced science since it was almost entirely a theoretical discipline. If observation contradicted theory, then the observations were wrong (and since instruments were crude, this was not an unreasonable proposition). For science to develop, it was necessary to put a theory to the test, by observation and experiment, to see if what it told married to the facts on the ground.

Scholars now generally recognise that the intellectual foundations for this approach were laid in the medieval universities. There, professors and students engaged in robust dialogue, putting ideas to the test in lectures and seminars. Indeed, it was the work of men such as Thomas Aquinas and Jean Buridan (from the thirteenth and fourteenth centuries respectively) that put in place the intellectual underpinnings that led to the scientific revolution of the early modern era.

However, it's not so widely recognised that it was Bede who played an early but important part in putting into place the intellectual framework that allowed the development of modern science. This is shown most clearly in *The Reckoning of Time*. This was an expansion of an earlier work, *On the Nature of Things*, that Bede had written in 703.

Bede explained in his preface why he expanded his earlier work:

> Some time ago I wrote two short books in a summary style which were, I judged, necessary for my students; these concerned the nature of things, and the reckoning of time. When I undertook to present and explain them to some of my brethren, they said that they were much more concise

than they would have wished, especially the book on time, which was, it seems, rather more in demand because of the calculation of Easter. So they persuaded me to discuss certain matters concerning the nature, course, and end of time at greater length. I yielded to their enthusiasm, and after surveying the writings of the venerable Fathers, I wrote a longer book on time.

*The Reckoning of Time* is a big book. The English translation published by Liverpool University Press runs to 239 pages of Bede's text (plus another 304 pages for introduction, commentary, appendices, bibliography and index). Bede put a lot of thought and effort into this book because it comprehensively dealt with a question that was vital to him: the proper calculation of Easter.

But to comprehensively treat a question that turned on astronomy, theology, the calendar and mathematics, Bede had to cover a lot of ground. He starts with an introduction to finger counting and other methods of calculating, looks at units of time, examines the calendar in detail, moves on to the astronomy of the moon, deals with the solar year, and only then goes on to the detailed technical consideration of calculating the correct date for Easter. It is, in the most literal sense, a magisterial book; and so thorough and convincing was Bede's examination of the whole problem that he effectively ended the Easter controversy. Its importance at the time and in the centuries following is indicated by the exceptional number of manuscripts that survive: no less than 240, although not all of these are complete texts.

What makes Bede's work in *The Reckoning* so important is how he marries astronomical theory to observable fact. He does this because his work in the book is predicated upon finding the correct date to celebrate Easter, which was, Bede believed, a real event that happened on a particular day. It was his job, and the task of the Church, to celebrate it on the correct day and for that to happen, theory had to mesh with observable astronomical facts.

That viewpoint led Bede to look carefully at the Classical knowledge that he was transmitting to the future. The cliché view of

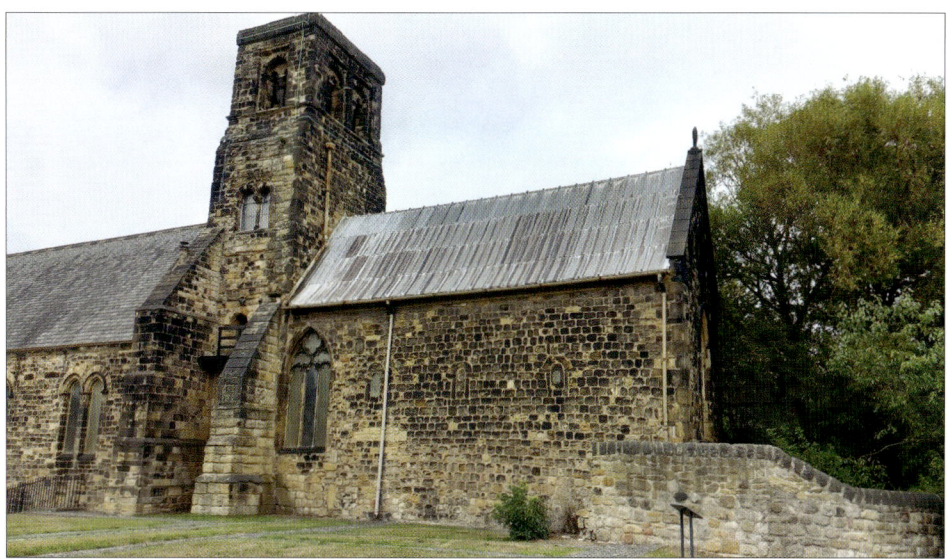

St Paul's Church, Jarrow: Everything to the right of the tower was there when Bede was a monk at St Paul's. The large window is a later addition, but the three small windows (just visible) are all original. The central one is now glazed with glass fragments that Rosemary Cramp discovered during her excavation, making it the oldest stained-glass window in England.

This excellent model of what the monastery at St Paul's looked like in Bede's day is on display at Jarrow Hall, the museum across the park from the church. The building in the top right was a separate chapel, probably reserved for the monks; it is now the chancel of the present-day church of St Paul, making it a direct link to Bede's time.

The original dedication stone of the monastery of St Paul is now set into the arch above the entry to the chancel.

*Left and below*. This close-up of the dedication stone shows how it has weathered and become discoloured over the years, while still remaining in astonishingly good shape for a carving that is so old. There's a convenient, and much easier to read, reproduction at eye level underneath it.

*Left*. The churches at Wearmouth and Jarrow were the first stone buildings built in Britain for a century, objects of marvel for the Angles and the Saxons, who specialised in wood. As well as building the churches, the masons Benedict Biscop brought over from Francia also decorated the stone, carving patterns into stone tiles. These tiles would have been painted too, making the church look as if it was covered in bright stone flowers.

Much less of St Peter's, Wearmouth, is original. In this photo, the wall to the right of the downpipe and the lower section of the tower are part of Benedict Biscop's building in stone, a marvel to the people of the area. (Photo by Andrew Curtis)

While the original *Codex Amiatinus* is locked behind Italian bureaucracy in the Laurentian Library in Florence, Jarrow Hall Museum has an excellent copy. It's as close to physically intimidating as any book I have seen.

CODICIBVS SACRIS HOSTILI CLADE PERVSTIS

ESDRA DŌ FERVENS HOC REPARAVIT OPVS

Ezra the Scribe as depicted in the *Codex Amiatinus*. While Ezra was an Old Testament prophet, the models for the picture were the scribes of Bede's own monastery, providing us with valuable clues as to how they worked.

The monasteries at Wearmouth and Jarrow were closely tied to the kings of Northumbria. Their stronghold lay further up the coast at Bamburgh. The castle was restored by Victorian industrialist William Armstrong, but St Oswald's Gate dates back to Bede's time.

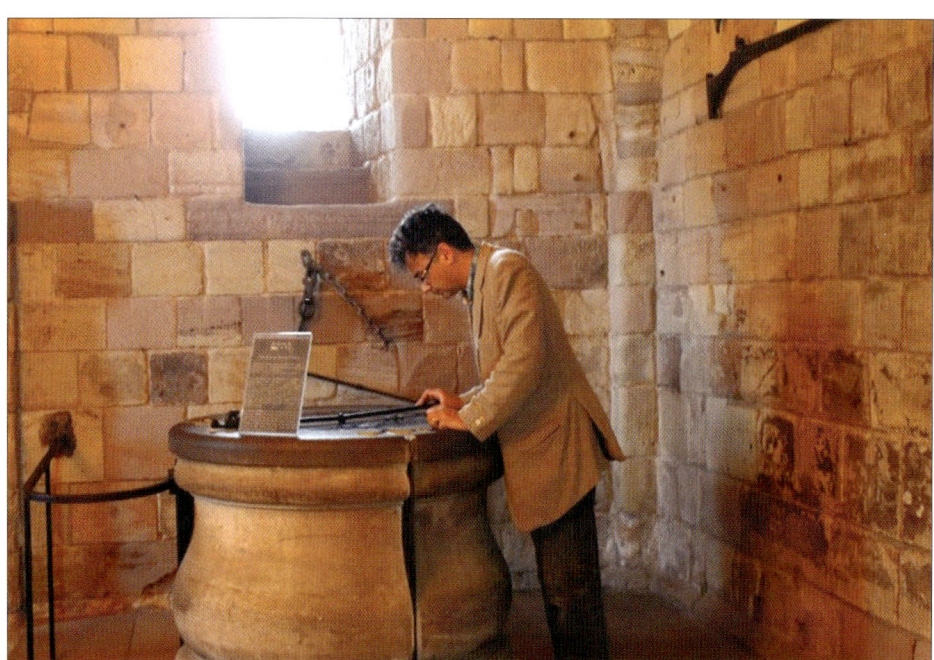

Bamburgh Castle sits atop an outcrop of the Great Whin Sill. It's an impregnable location, save for one thing: no well. A siege would leave defenders dying of thirst. So, sometime in the seventh century, the Anglian kings of Bamburgh had a well dug down through the solid rock. They did this by piling up combustible materials on top of the rock, firing them, then dousing the fire with cold water. The thermal shock shattered the top layer of rock, allowing it to be dug out. They then repeated the process over and over again, digging deeper until they reached water. Bamburgh had its well.

The label in the photograph reads:

**Pattern Welded Sword**

This Anglo-Saxon sword was originally excavated from the west ward of Bamburgh Castle in 1960. Recent research has shown that this is a very rare example of an Anglo-Saxon weapon which was manufactured using six billets of twisted iron to form an open herringbone pattern, tapered and edged in steel. It is probably the most complex sword of its type manufactured in Europe between 650 and 850.

The unprepossessing piece of metal in the centre of the photo was once the top half of possibly the finest sword ever forged. In the seventh century, an anonymous swordsmith took six billets of iron and pattern-welded them together to create a blade of unparalleled flexibility and hardness. It was wielded for 300 years until, finally, it broke, only to be rediscovered by archaeologist Brian Hope-Taylor in the 1960s.

The Farne Islands are further outcrops of the Great Whin Sill, the layer of hard dolerite that underlies much of the geology of the region. St Cuthbert made his hermitage on Inner Farne, isolated from the world but still very visible to that world, in particular the kings of Northumbria, looking out to sea from their stronghold at Bamburgh.

*Right*. The clerics carved into the Dupplin Cross show the delicacy of the accommodation between clergy following Irish and Roman traditions: the carved monks alternate between Roman and Irish tonsures.

*Below*. Jarrow Hall Museum has excellent reconstructions of Anglo-Saxon buildings, including this great hall, given the canine seal of approval by Barnaby.

*Right*. The new Ad Gefrin Museum in Wooler is the best small museum of the Anglo-Saxon world in Britain. I was fortunate to be received in audience by the king, although he appears to be less than impressed.

medieval monks was that they copied without understanding, carrying knowledge into the future with all the understanding of the little man inside John Searle's Chinese box, answering questions without understanding the characters fed into the box. The same idea informs Walter Miller's science-fiction classic *A Canticle for Leibowitz*, where monks in a post-apocalyptic world diligently copy the works of their founder, the Blessed Leibowitz, despite having no understanding of what they were copying.

The reality, at least in the case of Bede, was very different. It's best exemplified in chapter 29 of *The Reckoning of Time*. In this chapter, Bede discusses the effect of the moon on the tides.

The Classical works which Bede knew that dealt with the tides were hampered by their Mediterranean origin. The Mediterranean is an enclosed sea. Its tidal range is very shallow, in most places only about a foot (30 centimetres), although at the top of the Adriatic around Venice and in the Gulf of Gabes in Tunisia, the tidal range can reach three and six feet (one metre and two metres) respectively. But for most of the coastline, the tide putters out a few feet and then putters back in.

It's very different on the North Sea. For Bede, living on the River Don and near the River Tyne with the Tyne estuary just a couple of miles down river, the tides were one of the most important rhythms of his life. The normal tidal range at North Shields, just before the Tyne spreads out into its estuary, is fifteen feet (five metres) but, as Bede mentions in his book, some tides can 'be more or less strong than usual when they are pushed onwards or forced back by the wind'. This was a phenomenon that Bede's sources, knowing only Mediterranean tides, were unaware of.

Bede goes on to quote one of his chief sources, the fifth-century cleric Philip the Presbyter, who wrote about the tides in commentary on the Book of Job:

So let him who is capable, see if what Philip says is true or no: *There are those who claim and affirm that an enormous outpouring of the ocean takes place in all the streams of every region and land at one and the same time*. But we who live at various places along the coastline of the British Sea know that where the tide begins to run in one place, it will start to ebb at another at the same time. Hence it appears to some that the wave, while retreating from one place, is coming back somewhere else; then leaving behind the territory where it was, it swiftly seeks again the region where it first began. Therefore at a given time a greater *malina* [spring tide] deserts these shores in order to be able all the more to flood other [shores] when it arrives there.

Bede read the work of one of the Church Fathers, compared it to what he observed, and challenged the received view, having the confidence to invite his readers to compare what Philip the Presbyter wrote to what they themselves could see. This was important as it showed that the authorities of the past were not necessarily right. Bede was saying that, if faced with the question, who are you going to believe, him or your lying eyes? Then you should believe your lying eyes. This was a crucial stone laid among the foundations of science. For it put theory at the mercy of evidence.[3]

Bede might even have gone further. When looking at how tide times vary up and down the coast, Bede says that 'those who live north of me on the same coastline usually receive and give back each tide sooner than I do, and those to the south much later'. Given that Bede did not travel much, Bede must have found this out by asking other monks up and down the coast to measure and time their tides, then convey the information back to him. The monks of Lindisfarne 50 miles north of Bede had particular reason to measure the tides since they were cut off from the mainland twice each day by the sea covering the causeway between the island and the shore. The monks and nuns of Whitby, 50 miles south of Jarrow, also had good reason to be wary of the tides flowing up and down the River Esk.

The hundred-mile spread between the two monasteries would have allowed Bede and his investigators to see, even with the limited time-keeping apparatus they had available, the difference in tide times between the two locations. For instance, as I write today, low tide on Lindisfarne is at 12.20 p.m. and the following high tide at 6.46 p.m. However, at Whitby, low tide is 1.55 p.m. and high tide at 8.01 p.m.; a substantial difference and one well within the capacity for the monks of this time to measure.

So it seems likely that Bede, after writing *On the Nature of Things*, had begun a programme of research, using his correspondents up and down the coast, to investigate the movement and timing of the tides, and then wrote up his findings in *The Reckoning of Time*. It's almost a programme for science.

Almost, but not quite.

Bede, along with everyone else, was severely hindered by having to use Roman numerals. In fact, he devoted the first chapter of *The Reckoning of Time* to teaching students how to count using their bodies as a calculator, in the vain hope that this might ameliorate the difficulties of using the world's most unwieldy numerical system.

Finger counting meant using the fingers of the left hand to denote numbers up to 100 and the right hand for numbers between 100 and 1,000. For instance, one was shown by bending the 'little finger of the left hand and fix[ing] it on to the middle of the palm'. Two and three joined the ring finger and the middle finger on the middle of the palm. However, to mark four, the counter lifted the little finger back up, rather oddly making something very similar to the 'horns' gesture that heavy metal fans wave at concerts.

By varying the finger positions, finger counters could count all the way to a thousand. This had the advantage, when carrying out calculations, that a particular hand position was unique to each number. While neither Bede nor any other ancient source describes how people actually calculated using finger numbers, modern experiments suggest that it would have been possible to work out problems in almost a mechanical fashion by simply observing the rules of finger movement.

Bede would have needed this facility with calculating for his work on the most vexed question of the day. The date of Easter had split the Church in Britain for decades and the breach had still not completely healed in Bede's day. His work on it formed the basis for *The Reckoning of Time* and its fruit would be the framework upon which he hung his *Ecclesiastical History*. So now it's time to look at the problem with dates.

CHAPTER 10

# The Problem with Dates

Calendars are complicated. Nowadays, we can just look at our phone or the calendar on the wall to tell the date. But the present, settled and largely agreed upon system is the result of thousands of years of trials, errors, disputes and disagreements – and Bede played a disproportionately large part in solving these issues.

There are two separate but interlinked problems here. The first is the calendar itself, the splitting up of time so that we are not lost in a featureless stream of 'now'. The second is the surprisingly complicated question of when to celebrate Easter. Unlike Christmas, Easter moves; it's not on the same day each year but varies, with the earliest possible date being 22 March and the latest 25 April. Working out when that date would be occupied hundreds of years and a lot of very complicated debates, turning on questions of theology, mathematics and tradition.

Let's start with the calendar. Imagine you are a nomad, living 10,000 years ago, moving with your family and your tribe across the low-lying, river-crossed hunting grounds that today lie under the North Sea. Writing has not been invented. You have a rich language (we don't know what that would have been, but all known human languages have been able to express every idea and emotion necessary to its speakers, so there's no reason to suppose ancient languages would have been any different) and a long tradition of stories and tales and myths. But how to tell one day from another?

In some ways, this might have been easier for an ancient nomad than it is for us, as the light lids that press down upon us in modern cities make it so very difficult to use natural cues to tell the passing of time. But let us put ourselves back into the position of the people who invented time. What did they use to distinguish its passing?

The alternation between day and night is the clearest and most obvious sign of time's passing. It's so clear that it is encoded into our physical being: at night we sleep, during the day we wake, and this rhythm is brought about by a range of physical processes, from hormone secretion to behavioural changes. The most important thing to note about the day/night cycle is that it is rhythmical. It repeats, day after day after day. This is important to note because time, as we experience it, is a rhythm, not a story: it doesn't have a beginning, a middle and an end.

The next thing to note is that time comes from the sky. After the alternation of day and night, the next rhythm these old nomads noticed was the waxing and waning of the moon. Every 28 days, the moon grows to fullness and then shrinks again, until the night swallows it into darkness, only to be reborn as a sliver of light a few days later. So after the cycle of the day, we have the next rhythm of life: the month.

The moon pursues the sun through the sky, reaching its full phase when it falls furthest behind the sun and declining as it catches the chariot of the sun. The sun, however, follows its own statelier rhythm, rising higher in the sky as the weather warms, swinging lower when the winter arrives. So the rhythm of the sun is connected to the passage of the seasons, showing the intimate link between what happens in the heavens and what happens on earth. We all know that the sun rises in the east and sets in the west. But the point where it rises above the horizon tracks north and south. In the northern hemisphere the sun rise reaches its most southerly point at midsummer, when the length of the day is greatest, and then it starts slowly tracking back northwards, arriving at its most northerly point on the shortest day of the year. So the rhythm of the sun makes for another cycle: the year.

Our lives today are perhaps most governed by a fourth rhythm, the week, but this rhythm has no astronomical root: it is a religious rhythm applied to the cycle of days but has no basis outside the Hebrew story of God's making. Other cycles have been applied to human affairs, from the ten-day week that the French Revolution attempted to impose upon an unwilling population to the twelve-day weeks of the Chinese five-elements calendar.

The calendar is basically an attempt to fit these different rhythms together. Its difficulty arises from the fact that they don't. The Babylonian calendar, for instance, was based on a 360-day year. This was convenient because 360 is such a divisible number; it can be divided by 22 numbers between two and 180. Taking the great vault of the night sky as half the circle which wheeled over the earth, and the more intimate arch of the daytime sky as the other half of the great circle, then those first systematic sky watchers were able to estimate that there were 360 degrees in the circle of the heavens – and bring that down to earth and inscribe it into a circle drawn on the ground. Which is why, in geometry classes, there are 360 degrees in a full circle. The circle on the page drew down the circle of the heavens and linked them.

To the first calendrists, it all seemed one great harmony. But unfortunately, observation revealed that there weren't actually 360 days in the year. If there were, the sun's rising points at midwinter and midsummer would have stayed with the calendar. But they didn't. Counting from midwinter, after 360 days the sun continued moving further north before stopping and starting its journey south a few days later. For people observing with the naked eye, the difference would not have been very noticeable to start with. But the change grows with each year fixed at 360 days, with the sun lagging behind the calendar until it was calendrically spring when the sun was approaching its furthest point north and winter was only beginning.

Regrettably, from the point of view of mathematical utility and harmony, there aren't 360 days in the year. The number of days need to fit into the true length of the year, otherwise any solar calendar will slowly fall out of synchrony with the seasons. On that point, it's clear why the first calendrists lived far enough north for there to be four distinct seasons. In equatorial regions, where the seasons usually simply divide into wet and dry, the disjunction is far less apparent and the length of the year harder to track.

Closer observation revealed that there were more than 360 days in the year: 365. Mathematically, 365 is an awkward number. Its only factors, apart from itself and one, are five and 73. So you can split the year up into five seasons of 73 days each; not much use when most cultures split the year into four or two seasons. (There are some places where the year is divided into three or five seasons. Malawi has a cold, a hot dry and a hot wet season each year, while Japan has a fifth season, *tsuyu*, the season of rain, and China, in some of its many calendrical systems, had five seasons too, with late summer placed between summer and autumn.)

Unfortunately, the passage of years slowly confirmed that the year consisted of slightly more than 365 days. The seasons started to drift apart from the calendar. Awkward for both religious ceremonies and farmers. The calendar reform introduced by Julius Caesar on 1 January 45 BC attempted to correct for this by introducing an extra day to the calendar ('a leap year') every four years. Mathematically, this made the year 365.25 days long. It was much closer to the exact year length, which is 365 days, five hours, 48 minutes and 46 seconds, or 365.2422 days.

This Julian calendar was the one used by Bede for his calculations. However, over the centuries, the difference between 0.25 and 0.2422 gradually built up until the calendar was running ten days behind the skies. The discrepancy became greater and greater, and the need for calendar reform was widely noted, although various proposals fell through. Mandated by the Council of Trent in 1545, the popes set about engaging scientists and astronomers to work out what was necessary for a sustainable calendar, with Pope Gregory XIII hiring the mathematician Christopher Clavius to work on the new calendar. Clavius introduced a correction to the rule for leap years to bring the calendar year length into closer agreement with the astronomical year, removing a small number of leap years from the cycle. The rule is that every year which is divisible by four is a leap year, except for those which can be divided by 100. However, there is a further modification. If the centurial year can be divided by 400, then it is a leap year, after all. So that made 2000 a leap year, but 1700, 1800 and 1900 were not.

The Gregorian calendar was introduced on 4 October 1582. The next day became Friday 15 October 1582. Ten days were skipped out. The Gregorian calendar was initially used in the Papal States and by the Catholic Church for calculating its feasts, but it was gradually adopted by the rest of the world and is now almost universal for civil reckoning.

In his time, Bede had already noted that the Julian calendar was three days out of synch with the astronomical calendar, but he left that matter for later hands.

Within the whole problem of calendars, there remains the question of how to fit the lunar month into a solar year. The exact lunar month is 29.53059 days. Dividing this into the solar year gives an answer of 12.3682662622. It doesn't fit neatly. In fact, the fit is about as awkward as you can get. We will look at this more closely when we move on to the question of the dating of Easter, which involves the lunar calendar as well as the solar calendar.

*

The calendar is recurring. All the reforms over the years have been directed towards ensuring that it fits one year as well as the next. Therefore, it fits perfectly into a rhythmical idea of time. This notion of time was, through most of history and most cultures, the dominant one. The Greeks and the Romans considered history to run through successive ages, gold, silver, bronze and iron, each worse than the next, before the whole cycle began again. The ancient cultures of India had the same view of time as an eternally recurring cycle.

It was a group of recalcitrant nomads wandering around in the Near East who changed how we view time. They gave it a direction. They turned it into a story, with a beginning, a middle and an end.

They fired time's arrow into the future. They were the Jews, and they remade our view of time. The Christian Church took that view and intensified it, for history was moving towards a final end, when Christ would return and judge the living and the dead. Thus not only would the story have a beginning, a middle and an end, but it would have a climax, too.

This gave history a sense of purpose and a point, rather than it being merely the tale of one damn thing after another, which is an implicit consequence of the view of time as cyclical. But while history now had a narrative, situating events within that history was still done by the old system of telling dates according to the regnal year of particular kings. A good example is the dedication stone in St Paul's, Jarrow: 'The dedication of the basilica of St. Paul on the ninth day before the Kalends of May in the fifteenth year of King Ecgfrith and in the fourth year of Abbot Ceolfrith founder, by God's guidance, of the same church.'

It's all very clear, apart from the Kalends part (which comes from the old Roman calendar and means the first day of the month) but unless you know when King Ecgfrith came to the throne or Ceolfrith founded the church at Jarrow, then it is utterly meaningless. The Roman calendar dated events both from the foundation of the Republic and from the regnal year of emperors, but neither system was relevant to a seventh-century monk living by the North Sea.

However, among the books that we know were kept in the library at Wearmouth and Jarrow were works by a sixth-century Greek monk who moved to Rome in c.500. The monk's name was Dionysius Exiguus, and the books by him held in the library at Wearmouth and Jarrow were key texts that Bede used to formulate his view of the correct way to date Easter. This combination of mathematics, theology, scripture and astronomy was known as *computus* and it underlay the dispute over the correct date of Easter that was finally settled in Britain at the Synod of Whitby.

The dating of Easter was a problem a century earlier in Rome. To resolve the matter, in 525 Pope John I gave the task of compiling new and authoritative Easter tables (a list of years with the correct date for the celebration of Easter) to Dionysius Exiguus. The Easter table he produced ran from 532 to 626. As well as the table, Dionysius Exiguus wrote out the rules by which he calculated Easter (known as *argumenta*) and set out how to calculate the date of Easter (*computus*).

When setting out the dates in his Easter table, Dionysius used the customary dating system of the time, stating that his current year was during the consulship of Probus Junior (a man could only hold the office of consul for a single year). To further anchor the date, previous Easter tables had been dated from the start of the reign of the Emperor Diocletian (in 284, as we would say now). But as emperor, Diocletian had been responsible for the last, serious sustained Imperial assault on the Church, which was why the calendar based on his reign was known as the Era of the Martyrs. However, Dionysius Exiguus did not want to base his table for the dates of Easter, the most important of all Christian festivals, upon the reign of a man who had killed so many of his co-religionists. So he used another starting date for his Easter table, which began, he said, 525 years since the Incarnation of Jesus, that is, since his birth.

Although Dionysius Exiguus did not use this start date for any historical calculations, because of the success of his Easter tables, the idea of using a dating system based on the birth of Jesus gradually spread around Christendom, fetching up in Northumbria when Benedict imported his books to the kingdom.

Bede, and his mentor, Ceolfrith, found the rules (*argumenta*) and method (*computus*) that Dionysius Exiguus advanced for the correct dating of Easter to be convincing. They had formed the background to Wilfrid's arguments at the Synod of Whitby that the Roman method of calculating Easter should be used by the Church in Britain rather than the method used by the Church in Ireland (as you will see in the chapter on the Easter controversy, it's all rather more complicated than this. Some areas of the Church in Ireland had already adopted the Roman method of calculating Easter, although the monasteries that traced their lineage to Iona, and St Columba still held to the older dating method that had been in use in Ireland.) So Dionysius Exiguus's work was held as authoritative by both men. It was therefore natural that, when Bede turned his mind towards the reckoning of time – the title of his expanded book on the nature and reckoning of time – he should think of the new system of dating events from the birth of Christ espoused by Dionysius Exiguus. In the final part of *The Reckoning of Time*, Bede wrote a chronicle of world history, starting from Adam through to his own time, using the Bible and Roman history to calculate when events took place. Starting with Adam, Bede numbered the years from the year zero of Adam's creation, reaching the year 4680 in his own day.

Collating dates from the Bible and Roman history was a massive undertaking but one particularly suited to Bede's systematic mind. He liked these sorts of puzzles. Writing a chronicle of history from its putative start, it made sense to number the years from zero. But Bede also had in mind the principle that calculating dates from the Incarnation of Christ was better theologically. When he came to work on his *Ecclesiastical History*, where most of the events took place in the relatively recent past, Bede decided that it also made historical sense to date everything from the birth of Christ. However, it was one thing accepting the idea in principle, quite another to put it into practice.

The great unseen labour behind the *Ecclesiastical History* was Bede's collation and correction of all the different dates he collected while gathering material for his history. From the date of the arrival of Augustine in Canterbury through to the reign of King Oswiu, stretching back to the arrival of the Anglo-Saxons in Britain and through the decades of the seventh century, Bede had to note down dates given to him in many different formats, attempt to fit them into the framework of the new Anno Domini calendar, and then check them against other dates. What's more, he had to make all these calculations using Roman numerals, which are notably unwieldy for such purposes (Arabic numerals, which should really be called Indian numbers, were only widely adopted in Europe in the fifteenth century).

To do this, Bede had to carefully assemble king lists for the various realms in Britain, work out lengths of reigns, fit these dates into different timelines and then map them all onto the Anno Domini timeline. It was a monumental labour and the fact that Bede did this with so few errors shows the punctiliousness with which he approached the task, as well as suggesting that these little kingdoms did take great care in preserving the details of their kings' reigns.

In fact, it's rather a shame that Bede adopted Dionysius Exiguus's calendar without checking it, as we now know that the Greek monk got his calculations wrong. It's difficult to know where he went wrong, as he does not present his method for working out the date of the Incarnation in his work, but Herod the Great died around 4 BC, which means that, if we assume that Matthew's account of Jesus's birth is correct in putting it during his reign, then Jesus must have been born before 4 BC. Most scholars accept a year somewhere between 6 and 4 BC.

As well as developing the calendar that is used almost universally today, making Dionysius Exiguus one of the most accidentally influential people in history, he also played a crucial role in determining the date of the Incarnation, that is Christmas. As part of his argument for his new Easter table, Dionysius accepted the idea, common among many scholars of the time, that God created the universe on 25 March. However, Dionysius then went on to argue that Jesus, being perfect, would necessarily recapitulate that date in his Incarnation, being conceived in the flesh on the same day that God created the universe, that is 25 March. But if he was conceived on 25 March, then he would be born nine months later: 25 December.

Early Christians celebrated Easter as the key Christian feast. Apart from Easter, the other main celebrations took place at Pentecost, 40 days after Easter and, from the third century, Epiphany, the announcement of Jesus's birth. But a celebration of the birth of Jesus did not feature as a major feast – it's unclear whether it featured at all. But the fixing of Jesus's birth on 25 December raised the feast higher in Christian consciousness, starting its steady march upwards, until it stands today as the second-most important feast in the Chistian calendar.

Because of the success of Bede's *Ecclesiastical History*, the knowledge of this new system of dating events spread widely in Christendom, although its general adoption took some time. However, as Bede's work was disseminated more widely, and his students and followers adopted the same system, the practice slowly spread, its utility becoming steadily more apparent, particularly to the international group of religious scholars who wrote in a common language, Latin. Writing in a common language, it made sense to use a common calendar, and dating events from the Incarnation became the normal practice.

However, the new calendar did have one significant problem for a historian: a lot of things happened before Jesus was born. This was less of an issue with older calendars, such as the Roman one which ran from the foundation of the Republic, as the vast majority of the events a historian might want to write about had happened after the foundation of the Republic. However, Bede solved the problem in the second chapter of his *Ecclesiastical History*. Having discussed the physical and human geography of the British Isles in the first chapter, in the second he went on to write about its history, beginning with the island's entry into written history when Julius Caesar landed in Kent with an expeditionary force. Given that Julius Caesar was born before Jesus's birth, Bede had to find some way to slot him into the new calendar, which he did by using both the old system, stating that Julius Caesar 'in the year of Rome 693, that is, in the year 60 before our Lord, was consul with Lucius Bibulus'. Before the birth of Christ, or BC, took somewhat longer to become established, but it too became the standard way of dating events before the birth of Christ.

However, the new calendar got Bede into a certain amount of trouble. There was a general belief that world history consisted of six ages, one age for each of the six days of creation as related in the Book of Genesis in the Bible and confirmed in the Second Letter of Peter: 'with the Lord one day is as a thousand years, and a thousand years as one day' (2 Peter 3:8). This Christian belief contrasted with the Roman belief in a repeating cycle of four ages. But if each age lasted a thousand years, then the world would endure for 6,000 years and, by calculating the length of the lives of Biblical figures such as Noah and Abraham, it would be possible to work out how long the world had endured and therefore when it would end. This is exactly what the Church historian Eusebius of Caesarea had done, coming to the conclusion that Jesus was born in the year 5199 of the world – which meant that there were only another 801 years to go until the end of the world. As Bede was working on this problem around about 725, that only left 76 years until the Day of Judgement.

Bede was very dubious of the idea that it was possible to precisely date the end of the world. As part of his argument against this idea, he recalculated the age of the earth, using the new Latin translation by St Jerome (the Vulgate). With this more accurate translation at his disposal, Bede recalculated the ages from Adam to Noah, and Noah to Abraham, and found that according to this chronology the world was much younger than Eusebius thought, with Christ's birth dated to the year 3952 rather than 5199. If you accepted the idea of a six-age history of the world (Bede was clearly dubious), it put Jesus's birth in the fourth age rather than the sixth and final age. An end of time some 2,000 years in the future produced a much milder sense of eschatological urgency than an end due in 76 years.

However, not all Bede's readers accepted his argument. Among those who did not were some associates, presumably monks, of Bishop Wilfrid of Ripon. Discussing the matter, these men accused Bede of heresy, and their charge got back to him in his monastery – a charge of heresy was a serious matter and a profound stab at a man who took the utmost care to ground his work in theological orthodoxy.

In response, and in his own defence, Bede wrote a letter to Bishop Plegwin of Hexham in which he characterised his accusers as 'lewd rustics'. He then went on to eviscerate the idea that world history can be divided into thousand-year ages.

That the attack on Bede's integrity came from the camp of Bishop Wilfrid was perhaps not surprising: there was a profound difference of approach between the flamboyant bishop with his huge entourage and even larger diocese, and the scholarly monk who seldom left his monastery. While Bede's adoption of the Anno Domini calendar became universal, his championing of a more austere conception of Church leadership continued to clash with the regal style of Wilfrid, the first of the prince-bishops who would later lord it over Northumberland.

# CHAPTER 11

# The Problem with Easter

Wilfrid was not accustomed to feeling nervous. He had prayed at the graves of the Apostles in Rome. He had spoken with bishops and talked with kings. He had discouraged men whom beer made too bold and encouraged those whose bravery was failing. But now, as he looked about him at the assembly gathered in the church of the monastery of Streanaeshalch, set on the east-coast clifftop overlooking the Bay of the Beacon, he felt his mouth drying and his tongue cleaving to the roof of his mouth. Never had there been such an assembly in these isles and, right now, his bishop was asking permission that he, Wilfrid, might speak on his behalf before them all.

The young priest's gaze swept up and down the men and women assembled in the monastery, gathered now in the church that God might guide them rightly in their deliberations. For the purpose of the assembly, the monastery servants had brought benches and stools into the church so that all present might sit and listen to the proceedings. But seated upon painted and carved wooden thrones at the head of the assembly were the two kings: the high king, Oswiu, lord of Northumbria and *bretwalda*, overruler of all the kingdoms in the land; and, beside him, on a slightly smaller throne, sat his eldest son, Ahlfrith, king of Deira, in whose realm was the monastery of Streanaeshalch. Ahlfrith sat on the high king's right hand. On his left sat his wife, Queen Eanflæd. Wilfrid had noted what little passed between Ahlfrith and the queen, for she was not his mother, and she had a son of her own, now near full grown himself, who had come also to the assembly, although he remained in the shadows and did not speak.

Beside the queen sat the abbess of the monastery, Hild, of the same family as the queen through her father, the nephew of Queen Eanflæd's father, the late King Edwin. Ranged down one side of the long table that had been brought into the church was Colman, bishop of Lindisfarne, with many of the priests and monks from his monastery, as well as monks and nuns from the monastery of Streanaeshalch, which unlike Lindisfarne was a double monastery with male and female religious gathered under the rule of Hild. Seated at the far end of the table was Cedd, bishop of the East Saxons and a man fluent in the speech of the English and the Irish; he interpreted when a speech was made that was not understood by all present, for not all the monks from Lindisfarne knew the tongue of the English, and few of the English could speak the language of the Irish.

On the other side of the table sat Bishop Agilbert, a Frank who was the bishop of the West Saxons, with his priest Agatho. Wilfrid sat on a stool beside the bishop. Ranged down his side of the table was the venerable deacon James, one of the party of religious who had accompanied Bishop Paulinus to Northumbria when he had first come north with Princess Æthelburh when she travelled to the kingdom to marry the king, Edwin. When Edwin fell in battle against the pagan Penda and the apostate Cadwallon, Paulinus had taken the queen and her children south, but James had remained in Northumbria, ministering to the people through all the trials of those years. His was a venerable and holy presence, a man come all the way from Rome to bring life to the people of the north. Beside James sat Romanus, chaplain to Queen Eanflæd.

It was an assembly of the greatest and wisest and most powerful men and women in Northumbria and, in a moment, they would all be staring at him, at Wilfrid. Normally, the prospect would have caused Wilfrid quiet delight but this day he would be speaking on a subject of great moment. He glanced again at Bishop Agilbert. The

Frank was standing and speaking to the assembly in Latin, for he spoke that language more fluently than the tongue of the English, and Bishop Cedd was translating his Latin into English and Irish so that all might understand what the bishop said.

As Bishop Agilbert spoke, and Bishop Cedd translated, Wilfrid remembered how King Oswiu had opened the assembly. Speaking to all the men and women there, religious and lay people alike, the king had reminded them all of why they had gathered at the monastery by his command.

'All present here serve the one God. To do so more fully, it is meet that we should follow the same rule of life that we might all enter the one kingdom, that is in heaven, and be one in celebrating the sacraments of heaven here on earth. To that end, I have commanded you all to gather that we might consider the differences that separate us, differences that have led to the queen, still in Lent, fasting while I was feasting in celebration of the day of His resurrection. Let the chief proponents of each way speak before us, that we might hear and decide which holds closer to the truth that Our Lord wishes us to follow.'

So the king had begun the assembly, before summoning Colman, bishop of Lindisfarne, to speak on behalf of the practices that the king himself followed. Oswin had learned these practices when, as a boy, he had fled to Dal Riada with his family to escape the vengeance of his uncle, father killer and wife father.

While some of the monks who came from Iona to the Holy Island knew only Latin and the tongue of the Irish, Colman was not one of these. Mindful of his duties towards the people of Northumbria, he had learnt their tongue and spoke it now as well as one born to it. Wilfrid had hoped that the bishop would stumble over his words, or require Bishop Cedd to interpret his speech, but he spoke clearly, the words themselves inflected with the lilt of his native language but still completely understandable – if anything, Wilfrid had to admit, the accent with which he spoke added charm to his voice although he thought it lacked the gravitas of the Latin.

When the king called him to speak, Bishop Colman had stood but he did not rush to speak. Rather, he looked slowly from one end of the table to the other, taking in the faces of all the men ranged on the other side, priests and bishops and monks, who would change his world and force him to adopt new and different ways. It was, Wilfrid admitted, a master stroke. When Colman, scanning down the faces, came to him and their gazes momentarily locked, Wilfrid saw no fear or worry in his gaze, but only the calm serenity of a man secure in the truth of God. Colman, Wilfrid realised, as the bishop's gaze moved on from him, fully expected to win the argument.

For a moment, Wilfrid felt a stab of uncertainty. It pierced, like ice, through the surface satisfaction of his surety to the boy who had, after a fearful row with his stepmother, run away from his father's hall and spent the night wandering, lonely and afraid, through the forest and up on to the moor. When his father was told that he was missing, he had set the dogs to find him. Wilfrid had only to hear the bay of hunting hounds to feel again the same stab of fear he had felt when he heard their call, raised against the sky, following his scent. He had run, stumbling up higher onto the moors, trying to throw the dogs off his scent by wading through becks. But his father's dogs were good hunters: nothing he might do could throw them off the scent and, at last, they had brought him to bay, hiding under the roots of a windblown birch. His father had ridden up, called off the dogs with curses and some blows, then hauled Wilfrid out from his hiding place and proceeded to give him the worst whipping of his life in front of his men.

That night, trying to find some position to lie in which did not send stabs of pain through his body, Wilfrid had resolved to leave this life behind and enter the Church. In this plan he found an unexpected ally in his stepmother. Of course, he should have known: with him gone to the Church there was no obstacle to her young son inheriting their father's position and his land. Realising that, Wilfrid had apparently begun to reconsider, musing that mayhap the life of the warrior was the better calling. In answer, his stepmother had pulled him aside and asked him, to his face, what he wanted from her so that he would go – and leave the inheritance for his stepbrother.

'If you wish your son to have no rival for the inheritance, then may my father give me my portion to take with me, as did the prodigal son. But I will not spend my inheritance on riotous living but in giving glory to God and calling men to his service. Ensure my father does that, and I will leave the rest to you and your son.'

His stepmother had nodded her understanding and left him. She was young and beautiful, and his father's eyes followed her around the hall as a dog noses after a bitch in heat. It took but a few weeks before Wilfrid's father called him and said, that if he would leave to serve God, he might take his share of his father's wealth with him when he left. So Wilfrid, although still only sixteen years of age, had ridden from his father's hall with his followers, servants and warriors, all clad in clothes fit for the court of Oswiu. He had gone south, to the kingdom of Kent before setting out on the long road to Rome with another young wanderer, Biscop. But still, eleven years later, the sound of hounds baying would bring the fear sweat pricking through his skin.

There was something about the way that Colman stared at him that recalled that old fear. He felt the fear sweat pricking at his brow and surreptitiously wiped it away as men's eyes turned to Colman. For a mercy, the Irishman's gaze was no longer upon him. He looked now to the kings, seated at the end of the table. King Ahlfrith glanced at his father, then turned back to the bishop.

'We are waiting for you to state your case, Bishop Colman,' said Ahlfrith.

But Oswiu put his hand on his son's arm. 'Bishop Colman will speak when he is ready.' The high king turned to Colman. 'Bishop?'

Bishop Colman made a courtesy to the kings, then turned to face his opponents on the other side of the table. 'I have come here to speak for my fathers, and my father's fathers. It is by their example that we of the Holy Island follow our Easter customs. These are the customs taught to me by my bishop, customs which he learnt from his spiritual fathers, men beloved by God, their holiness attested by signs and wonders. But lest anyone claim that this is not sufficient, then let him know that these same customs found their origin in the blessed Apostle and Evangelist, John, he whom the Lord permitted to lay his head on His breast at His last supper, the disciple that scripture avers was most beloved to Our Lord. It is John who is our teacher and our warrant for our Easter customs. Those who would have us change do dishonour to the most beloved of the Lord's Apostles.' Colman paused and his gaze swept over the men on the other side of the table. 'Let them give answer, if they may, why we should do other than follow the example of St John.'

As he finished speaking, Bishop Colman looked to the head of the table. There, Wilfrid saw King Oswiu nodding in agreement at his bishop's words, while King Ahlfrith's face was stuck into an expression of sullen annoyance. From the other side of the table, whispers of approbation and smiles of agreement spread among the followers of the Ionan way.

'Thank you, Bishop Colman,' said King Oswiu. 'You have spoken well and eloquently. Now, that none may accuse us of not hearing the argument in full, Bishop Agilbert will speak on why we should change our Easter ways to those that he follows.' Oswiu looked at the man sitting beside Wilfrid. 'Bishop Agilbert.'

The Gaul stood up. Wilfrid felt his throat dry. He knew what the bishop was about to ask. He offered a prayer that the king might allow it – for if the bishop were to speak for their side of the argument, then they would surely lose. For seldom would an argument sway the hearts of men if it were given to them in translation, no matter how faithfully Bishop Cedd translated Agilbert's words.

Bishop Agilbert likewise made the courtesy to the kings, but Wilfrid noted that he directed it also towards Queen Eanflæd, whom Colman had ignored. 'I request that my disciple, the priest Wilfrid, may speak on my behalf, for we are both in agreement with the other followers of our church tradition who are here present; and he can explain our views in the English tongue better and more clearly than I can through an interpreter.'

The words, spoken in English, were halting but clear enough to be understood. Wilfrid had coached the bishop in how to say them as they had made their way to the assembly, having him repeat them over and over again. In the kingdom of the West Saxons, where he was bishop, Agilbert had interpreters to make his words clear to the clergy who knew not sufficient Latin to speak in that tongue. But the two men had agreed that, for this great assembly when the truth would be put on trial, they needed one to present that truth who spoke from birth the language of King Oswiu. So they had agreed that Agilbert would ask the king for permission that Wilfrid speak on his behalf.

Now, all the assembly turned their gaze towards the seated kings. King Ahlfrith was nodding his agreement, but he spoke no words, rather turning his gaze to his father. King Oswiu stared at Agilbert, his expression set and blank, a mask that might not be read. The assembly waited upon the king's words.

But before Oswiu made answer, Bishop Colman spoke. 'Your majesty, it is not meet that anyone other than a bishop should put such arguments before this assembly. For these are matters holy and profound; surely only one consecrated to guard and protect his flock, as a shepherd protects his sheep from the wolves, should touch upon these questions?'

Wilfrid looked to the kings, to see their response to the bishop's objection. King Ahlfrith was shaking his head, but it was not he whose word held sway in the assembly but his father, and Oswiu gave no sign of his thoughts as he listened to Colman's words. Rather, when the bishop had finished speaking, Oswiu held up his hand.

'You are right, old friend: these are matters holy and profound.' Wilfrid saw the bishop begin to nod his agreement but before he could finish, Oswiu continued. 'Wherefore, I have called together in this assembly the holiest and wisest men of my kingdom, to learn their minds on this matter. Therefore, I will ask their thoughts on what you raise.' Oswiu looked down the table to where, at the far end, sat the third bishop present. 'Bishop Cedd, what say you? For you have a gift of tongues whereby to interpret all that is said here, no matter what tongue it is spoken in, and you are a bishop, entrusted with the care of your flock. Should only a bishop speak on these matters holy and profound?'

Bishop Cedd rose from his seat and made his courtesy to the king. 'I am not worthy to answer such questions, but if you would press me for answer, then I would say that matters holy and profound should be debated in such whit that all here present can best understand them: therefore, I would council it better to have one who knows our tongue give the case for the queen's Easter rather than another for whom I would have to give words. For always, when moving from one language to another, some things are lost and others misplaced.'

King Oswiu nodded. 'It is as I thought.' He turned back to Bishop Colman. 'I will give leave for the priest, Wilfrid, to speak the case for the custom of the Romans, for the queen gives surety for his good and holy life and I agree with the wise words of Bishop Cedd: these are weighty matters of import for our immortal souls: let us hear the argument in the tongue we know best.'

Bishop Agilbert turned to the young man beside him, nodded his approval for Wilfrid to rise, and sat down.

Now it was time for Wilfrid to stand up, to speak before kings and bishops, abbots and abbesses, the assembly of his people and, most vitally, God Himself. For as he prepared to stand Wilfrid was all too aware that God and His angels were looking down upon him. He slowly straightened.

The men who sat listening to him across the table were not doing God due honour by keeping the greatest of all feasts on the right day but rather were obstinately following their own customs. It was his duty to speak the truth to Bishop Colman and his followers, that they might be brought back to the right path. It was for the sake of their own souls as well as for the good of the Church. Besides, Bishop Colman was insufferably proud about his spiritual forefathers, as if Columba had been an actual Apostle of the Lord. Wilfrid could see the stiff-necked man staring at him from across the table, his forehead shaved but the hair falling like water down the back of his head to his shoulders. This was no way for a man of God to look.

Wilfrid turned to the head of the table and made his courtesy to the kings and queen sitting there. 'Your majesties, I thank you for allowing me to speak on these great matters – matters vital to our souls and to the strength of your kingdom. For as Our Lord says, "If a kingdom be divided against itself, that kingdom cannot stand." We are here to heal the division in this kingdom, that it may stand. In this matter, the greatest sign of division is the celebration of Easter. For some cleave to one custom and others to another. Bishop Colman tells us that the custom he follows was taught him by his bishop and by his spiritual forefathers, men known to have lived true and holy lives. What is more, he claims that his custom for celebrating Easter comes from the Apostle John himself, beloved of the Lord.' Wilfrid paused. He looked up and down the table. 'These are mighty witnesses to call on his behalf. What can I, a young priest, say in reply to such witnesses?' Wilfrid looked back to the head of the table. 'For myself, I can say nothing, for I am a young man and a younger priest.'

At these words, Wilfrid heard a slight gasp from Bishop Agilbert beside him. While Agilbert did not trust his spoken English enough to speak in the debate, he understood it well enough to know what Wilfrid had just said. It seemed as if he was conceding defeat before the council had even begun. From the side of his eye, Wilfrid saw smiles of satisfaction beginning to form on the lips of Colman and his monks.

'But I am not speaking for myself. I am speaking for what I have learnt in Rome and throughout the rest of the world.'

Although he was still looking at the kings, Wilfrid felt the stiffening from the other side of the table. He sensed Colman lean forward, staring at him. Good.

'The Easter we keep is the same as we have seen universally celebrated in Rome, where the Apostles St Peter and St Paul lived, taught, were martyred and were buried. We also found it in use everywhere in Italy and Gaul when we travelled through those countries for the purpose of study and prayer. We learnt that it was observed at one and the same time in Africa, Asia, Egypt, Greece and throughout the whole world, wherever the Church of Christ is scattered, amid various nations and languages. The only exceptions are these men and their accomplices in obstinacy, I mean the Picts and the Britons, who in these, the two remotest islands of the Ocean, and only in some parts of them, foolishly attempt to fight against the whole world.'

\*

This comes at the halfway point of Bede's *Ecclesiastical History*. The assembly is now known as the Synod of Whitby but at the time, the location of Hilda's monastery was called Streanaeshalch. The Viking invasions and settlements of the tenth and eleventh centuries saw Streanaeshalch renamed as Whitby (the -by ending is characteristic of a place name derived from Old Norse). In one sense, everything before Bede's account of the synod is leading up to it, and everything after it describes its playing out. The debate, and the decision, over when to celebrate Easter was so important to Bede that he structured his entire history of the Church in Britain around it.

Before we go on to look at why it was so vital to Bede, let's look at how the rest of the debate at Whitby proceeded. Bede gives lengthy accounts of the speeches of the two main protagonists, Bishop Colman, speaking for the Ionan method of calculating Easter, and the young Wilfrid, arguing for the custom of Rome. While these would not have been the exact words the men used in the debate – which likely lasted over some days rather than being concluded in an afternoon – there's no reason to think that Bede has not accurately summarised the key arguments given by both sides.

As we have seen, Colman averred that the Ionan practice was sanctioned by it having been used by his spiritual forefathers, men of undisputed spiritual merit, before going on to claim that the Ionan practice had its origin with the Apostle John himself.

In answer, Wilfrid basically trumped Colman's one Apostle with two, these two being no less than Peter and Paul, before pointing out that the 'Roman' method of dating Easter had become almost universal, with all the Church adopting it, apart from the Britons, the Irish who looked to St Columba, and the Picts. (The dispute is often painted as one between 'Roman' and 'Celtic' Christianity, but by this time most of southern Ireland had already changed. Those Irish, mainly in the north of the island, who traced their spiritual lineage back to St Columba kept to the practice because of the great prestige and honour attached to his name. The Picts, evangelised by the Columban Irish, followed their practice. In the end, the Britons kept to the practice longer than anyone else, a function of their continuing dispute with the Canterbury-based Church hierarchy.)

Wilfrid's pointed mention that only these 'two remotest islands in the Ocean' hold out against the otherwise universal practice was meant to contrast the parochialism of the hold-outs against the cosmopolitanism that he espoused and, indeed, embodied through his travels. It was a conscious framing of the argument both in terms of the universal against the local (although Colman certainly did not see his position as parochial), and the sophisticated versus the rustic. It proved a potent framing device. And, showing how similar debates recur through history, it bears more than a passing resemblance to the rhetoric and the substance of the arguments for and against Brexit – although it should be noted that, in Bede's time, those arguing most fervently for the integration of British practices with those of Europe were the ancestors of the English, while those opposing were the ancestors of the Scots and Irish.

Following the opening statements by Colman and Wilfrid, Bede reports the debate continuing. Apparently somewhat nonplussed by the ferocity of Wilfrid's attack, Colman responded, rather weakly, by returning to his point about the authority of the Apostle John.

Indeed, to start with, the argument as given by both men revolved largely on the question of authority, and whose testimony was stronger: Ss John and Columba and Colman's spiritual forebears, or Ss Peter and Paul. Colman continued to rely on this for his argument but, in answer, Wilfrid went into a long and formidably technical explanation of why his method of calculating Easter was superior to Colman's. It's unlikely that more than a handful of people at the debate would have understood the depth of Wilfrid's argument, for the simple fact is that calculating the date of Easter is formidably technical, involving problems of astronomy, the calendar, theology and liturgical practice, both Jewish and Christian, all of which Wilfrid included in his answer to Colman. But there's no doubt that Wilfrid had mastered the technicalities of the argument, and his presentation of them must have been impressive to all the people listening.

Faced with Wilfrid's masterful display of technical knowledge, Bishop Colman once again resorted to an appeal to authority, this time calling on St Anatolius, a third-century Syro-Egyptian who was the first man to develop the nineteen-year lunar cycle that became the basis for the system espoused by Colman. But assuming that Bede reports Colman's arguments correctly, he again did nothing more than advance Anatolius as an authority. To this, Colman added the witness of St Columba, arguing that his witness was confirmed by the signs and wonders ascribed to him. Essentially, his argument amounted to an appeal to the authority of John and Anatolius, developing that by implying that St Columba would not have been able to perform his miracles if he was not keeping to the true Catholic faith, so therefore his method of calculating Easter had to be true – otherwise he could not have worked his miracles.

Wilfrid's reply first admitted Anatolius as worthy of the respect accorded to him but then, with a dizzying lash of disdain, he claimed that Colman and his peers did not understand what Anatolius taught because they did not keep to his precepts. Then, in a move calculated to enrage Colman and his followers, Wilfrid went on to cast doubt on the holiness of their beloved founder, Columba, say-ing, 'So far as your father Columba and his followers are concerned, whose holiness you claim to imitate and whose rule and precepts (confirmed by heavenly signs) you claim to follow, I might perhaps point out that at the judgement, many will say to the Lord that they prophesied in His name and cast out devils and did many wonderful works, but the Lord will answer that He never knew them.'

In his account, Bede then presents Wilfrid rowing back a little on his grave insult to St Columba and his followers. One suspects that, at the assembly, there was general uproar when Wilfrid laid this charge against Columba, and only when some order was restored did he go on to say, 'Far be it from me to say this about your fathers, for it is much fairer to believe good rather than evil about unknown people. So I will not deny that those who in their rude simplicity loved God with pious intent, were indeed servants of God and beloved by Him.'

Wilfrid really was a masterly debater, who in a later age would have made a fine lawyer, insinuating ideas into the mind of the jury before apparently retracting them following objections from the opposing counsel. But he had done what he aimed to do: call into question the whole idea that Columba's miracles necessarily supported the Ionan method of calculating Easter.

Concluding his argument, Wilfrid returned to his opening theme: that the Easter system he was proposing was testified to by the practice of the universal Church against whom stood 'a few men in a corner of a remote island'. Then, even granting Columba's miracles, Wilfrid played his trump card, the one he had been withholding until the debate reached its climax: 'And even if that Columba of yours . . . was a holy man of mighty works, is he to be preferred to the most blessed chief of the apostles, to whom the Lord said, "Thou art Peter and upon this rock I will build my Church and the gates of hell shall not prevail against it, and I will give unto thee the keys of the kingdom of heaven"?'

Wilfrid addressed this final claim directly to King Oswiu, a man whose authority to rule had been questioned in the past, too. It evidently struck a chord in the listening king, for he asked Colman to confirm the truth of Wilfrid's claim as to Peter's authority, a truth Colman could not but agree to, for it is in the Gospel of Matthew. King Oswiu then asked Colman if St Columba had been granted similar authority, to which Colman could only, helplessly, answer, 'No.'

Faced with the debate boiling down to a question of authority, what could Oswiu do? His own authority to rule had been hard won through years of struggle: he had murdered Oswine, the rival king of Deira; he had fought against and run from and bought off King Penda; he had even married his children to Penda's children – until, finally, all questions of authority came down to the contest of blood by the banks of the River Winwaed. It had taken Oswiu years of struggle to establish authority over his own kingdom and over the other kingdoms of Britain. Not surprisingly, he was sensitive about the issue.

When Colman admitted that Peter, and by implication his successors, both the popes in Rome but also the general testimony of the Church as advanced in the great Church councils, had authority, the choice became clear to Oswiu: 'Then, I tell you, since he is the doorkeeper I will not contradict him; but I intend to obey his commands in everything to the best of my knowledge and ability, otherwise when I come to the gates of the kingdom of heaven, there may be no one to open them because the one who on your own showing holds the keys has turned his back on me.'

Having come to this decision, the Synod of Streanaeshalch became binding upon the whole Church in Northumbria, with the decision expanded to take in all the Church in the Anglo-Saxon parts of Britain following the Synod of Hertford in 673 that was convened by Archbishop Theodore.

In the aftermath of the synod, Bishop Colman, his arguments rejected, had either to accept the decision or leave. He left, returning to Iona with many of his brethren and any other clergy who could not accept the decision. Iona clung to its method of dating Easter until 716, when it finally abandoned its old practice. The last hold-outs against the new practice were the Britonnic Christians. Hemmed in by the expanding Anglo-Saxon kingdoms, they maintained their old ways until 768, the final part of the Church to accept the new method of dating Easter – nearly 40 years after Bede wrote his history of the great dispute.

It's clear that the dispute roused passionate feelings and engaged the deepest beliefs of the participants. Bede, usually so calm and balanced, regards the hold-outs against the Roman Easter with barely concealed loathing, referring to them as *perfidi*, a term he only employs elsewhere about the Pelagians. For Bede, the men holding to their customary practices at Easter were not merely mistaken, they were *heretics*, which meant a wilful disregard of the saving truth. This was not just a matter of being wrong: this was a sin of pride. And pride, the greatest of the vices, when joined to the practices of the Church, lead to heresy and the breaking of the body of the Church into schism.

But the problem from our distance in time is to try to understand why it was such a big deal. It seems an awful amount of sound and fury about a date.[1]

There was also the related question of the tonsure, with the Irish sporting their shaven foreheads and flowing locks while the Romans had their hair in a torus. The tonsure, like different-coloured football shirts or the blue and green chariot factions of Constantinople, visibly proclaimed the allegiance of its wearer. The different tonsures ensured that the factions remained opposed even when their Easter dates were in agreement – as they were most of the time.

So why was the date of Easter so important to Bede and his contemporaries? After all, it's clear it was not just his own hobby horse but a question that affected everyone.

Firstly, there are practical reasons. Muslims use a lunar calendar to determine their year and the start and end of Ramadan, the month of fasting. While these dates are now officially proclaimed from Saudi Arabia, in principle any Muslim can decide when Ramadan starts and ends by observing the first rising of the crescent moon.

Easter, based upon the Jewish festival of Passover, is also linked to the moon, so why can't it be decided by observation? One reason is that Easter is preceded by Lent, the 40 days of fasting and preparation that lead up to Easter. If you can't predict the date of Easter, then you can't tell when to begin Lent. The season of Lent commemorates the 40 days Jesus spent fasting in the wilderness before he began his public ministry. (The more observant might notice that the period from Ash Wednesday to Easter Sunday is actually 46 days. The forty days of Lent is counted by excluding the Sundays during Lent.) Because of this long lead-up to Easter, it is vital to be able to give accurate dates for the festival. Otherwise, you might get to Easter and find that you've cut Lent short or, alternatively, that you've got another week to go. Given the austerities of medieval fasting, this would have been a fairly dreadful discovery.

It was also necessary for local churches to be able to calculate the dates of Easter for themselves. Communication was slow and often interrupted. This was not something that could be worked out in Rome and the news sent out to the churches elsewhere: the message might never arrive, or come too late. No, each church – or each diocese, at least – had to be able to work out the date of Easter itself. While the technicalities of the calculation were beyond most churchmen (or indeed most other people even today), the production of Easter tables enabled the dissemination of an accurate method of dating Easter – so long as the Easter table was itself reliable.

But aside from these practical matters, there were important theological reasons for the intensity of the dispute over Easter, reasons that were summarised in a surviving letter written by Bede's abbot, Ceolfrith, but which Bede may well have contributed to and which he certainly agreed with. The letter derives from an analogical view of the world and scripture, where the physical reality of the world and the literal meaning of scripture are granted their surface appearance but are then mined and scrutinised for a deeper meaning that reveals and throws refracted light on divine truth.

Contra modern ignorance, Bede and the early medieval world were well aware that the earth was round and that the moon revolved around the earth, shining by the reflected light of the sun. As the calendar is derived from astronomical observations, the timing of Easter, which depends upon the position of the moon and sun, reveals theological truths. So as Ceolfrith says in his letter, Easter falls just after the vernal equinox (the day in spring, usually around 20 March, on which day and night are of equal length at every latitude) because Christ's resurrection is the physical and spiritual triumph over darkness and after the vernal equinox, the power of darkness wanes as the sun rises higher in the sky and the grip of winter is loosened. The solar year (365 or 366 days) and the lunar year (354 or 355 days) do not match. To bring them into alignment, the lunar year was matched to the solar year on 22 March, which was therefore regarded as the first month of the lunar year. The first month of the lunar year was also believed to be when God created the world, so Easter necessarily had to fall in the first month of the lunar year, as that was the month when the world was first created and it was therefore also when Christ, through his resurrection, re-created it. Finally, Easter had to fall on the Sunday nearest to when, in this time frame, the moon begins to wane in the sky. This might seem counterintuitive but in fact it shows how detailed early medieval knowledge of astronomy was. For when the moon starts to wane in the sky, it is because it is rotating away from the earth and towards the sun. Read analogically, this was seen as the astronomical embodiment of turning away from the earth and towards heaven, as symbolised by the sun.

These were the detailed theological reasons for the importance attached to getting the date for Easter right. But there were other reasons, too, intimately bound up with the fragility of life. In the early medieval period, unity was a hard-won and highly prized aspect of any household, kingdom or church. That the Church could not agree on the date to celebrate its chief feast was a scandal in and of itself. The scandal, in the early medieval imagination, grew the greater when there was a strand of thought that had the prayers and masses of the faithful as a necessary part of Christ's breaking down the gates of hell and opening the underworld to eternal life. By dividing their prayers on to different Sundays, the Christians of the time risked undermining Christ's saving mission – at the least, they were failing to play their proper part in it.

This might help us today, for whom the dispute seems abstruse and the passions it aroused unnecessary, understand it a little better. People being people, and clerics sometimes reckoning in that assembly, there were of course issues about episcopal power, as well as a bunch of impatient young churchmen pushing against their elders, but unity as an expression of the theological significance of the date of Easter was the overriding matter.

The synod decided for the method of calculation used by Rome. Some of the monks of Lindisfarne, unable to accept the decision and the implied repudiation of their father in faith, Columba, withdrew to Iona where the old ways still held. Others were thrust out by that most thrusting of young churchmen, Wilfrid, who never saw an Irish tonsure without wanting to shave it off. By the time Bede came to write his history, some 70 years later, the wounds were still sore in the Northumbrian Church. One aim of Bede's writing was to chart a path through to healing these wounds, a path that acknowledged that Aidan and the Ionan monks had been wrong about Easter, but that nevertheless accepted the crucial role they had played in the conversion of the Northumbrians. In this, Bede was helped hugely by the remembered virtues of Aidan and how they mapped precisely on to the virtues taught by Pope Gregory the Great, the man who had sent Augustine's mission to the Anglo-Saxons, as the most important for a bishop to practice (and which, by implied contrast, were largely not virtues displayed by Wilfrid, the arch Romaniser, who in his magnificence and display anticipated the prince-bishops of later times).

The central place of the Synod of Whitby in Bede's account of the history of the Church signifies how important this dispute and its resolution was to Bede. Settling the dispute reunited the Church in Britain with the Church in the wider world. For Bede, this was a vital sign of the orthodoxy of his local church and its rightful place as part of the universal, or Catholic, Church.

## CHAPTER 12

# Bede and the Bible

The *Codex Amiatinus* is as close to physically intimidating as a book can get. I saw it in the vellum and leather at the British Library exhibition of Anglo-Saxon manuscripts, 'Anglo-Saxon Kingdoms', in 2018. It squatted, unbelievably huge, on its display stand. It's 20 inches high, 13 inches wide and 9 inches thick (51.5 centimetres by 34 centimetres by 23 centimetres). If I could have picked it up, it would have been even heavier than I expected: 77 pounds or five and a half stone (35 kilograms). That's the weight of my ten-year-old son, or as archaeologist Rupert Bruce-Mitford put it when measuring the book fifty ago, the equivalent of an adult female Great Dane.

But it's not just its size – although that's certainly part of it! – that lends the book the sense of immense gravitas that it conveys. It's the impression of worlds contained within its covers, as if one might see the book spontaneously open and pull all its surroundings within. It is a book not to trifle with. And it was the book that Bede's life as a Biblical scholar made possible.

The *Codex Amiatinus* was an edition of the complete text of the Bible that was produced in the twin monastery. Because of the length of the complete Bible – the *Codex Amiatinus* contains 2,060 pages – it was very unusual at the time for a scriptorium to produce a complete volume of the holy book. What was much more common was the production of parts of the Bible, with the Gospels and the psalms being the most frequently copied sections. A monastery would probably have a complete Bible, but not in one volume: it would be split between different books. But the twin monastery at Wearmouth and Jarrow decided to produce not one, not two, but three complete editions of the Bible – or pandects, as they're known in scholarly jargon (a word of sufficient obscurity as to offend the spellchecker on my computer as I write).

But producing a Bible was not just a matter of printing out a Word file, nor of printing from a press. It meant a scribe transcribing, word by word, from a proof text onto the vellum in front of him, using a goose feather quill. The techniques were all familiar to the monks at Wearmouth and Jarrow, and Bede himself takes the title of 'scribe of Scripture', indicating that he took his turn at the laborious work of copying. A minimum of seven, and possibly nine, different hands have been identified as contributing to the writing out of the *Codex Amiatinus*, and it's highly likely that one of those hands belonged to Bede.[1] It's rare to have a direct physical link to someone who lived so long ago. This connection with Bede makes the *Codex Amiatinus* a doubly precious link to the past.

Copying books was serious, holy work but copying the Bible raised the seriousness of the enterprise to a new level. The book itself required the skin of 515 calves to furnish its 1,030 folios. But of more import were the words written upon all those pages of skin. Abbot Ceolfrith intended these Bibles to not just look good but to carry the incorrupt words of God – and that meant producing editions that combined all the Biblical scholarship that he and his monks could bring to bear on the project.

The problem in producing an authoritative edition of the Bible in Britain was one of translation and editing. In his commentaries, Bede calls the Old Testament the Law and the New Testament the Gospels – in many ways, it's a better way of distinguishing between the different sections of the Bible, particularly as it avoids the implied Christian triumphalism of New against Old. The Law was originally written in Hebrew. However, by the second century BC knowledge of Hebrew had declined among Jews, particularly those who lived outside the traditional boundaries of Israel. Greek and Aramaic were their main languages. As such, many Jews were unable to understand their own scriptures. This was obviously an untenable situation.

However, the story that came to be attached to the translation into Greek that was produced in the third century BC was curious: the request for the translation supposedly came from the chief librarian of the library in Alexandria. The account, as related in a letter written by Aristeas to Philocrates, has the chief librarian urging the Egyptian Pharaoh to have the Hebrew Law translated into Greek so that its wisdom might be added to the works collected in the great library in Alexandria.

It's worth adding that, while the pharaoh in question, Ptolemy II Philadelphus, was certainly the ruler of Egypt, he was in no way Egyptian. In fact, he was the second member of the Ptolemaic dynasty that would rule Egypt for 275 years until Cleopatra picked the wrong side in the struggle between Octavian and Anthony, and Egypt became part of the Roman Empire. Ptolemy II was, as the name suggests, the son of Ptolemy I, who was not Egyptian at all but Greek, one of Alexander's generals. Following Alexander's death, Ptolemy brokered the attempted settlement between the various contenders for Alexander's vast empire. The terms of the treaty gave Egypt to Ptolemy, and it was to Egypt he clung during the wars that followed. Unlike the other pretenders to Alexander's empire, Ptolemy made no effort to bring all Alexander's possessions under his rule: he was content with Egypt. With the Nile as a defensible border and the other generals expending their men in internecine wars, Ptolemy survived and founded a dynasty.

According to the letter, the pharaoh, Ptolemy II Philadelphus, enthusiastically assented to the idea, freed Jews captured by his predecessors, and sent messengers to the Temple authorities in Jerusalem, asking them to provide translators. The Temple authorities selected six men from each of the traditional twelve tribes of Israel, 72 in total, who travelled to Alexandria where they met the pharaoh and engaged in philosophical debate before settling down to translate the Hebrew text into Greek.

According to Aristeas's account, when the 72 translators had finished their work, all 72 versions were taken to the pharaoh and compared – and found to be identical. As evidence of their inspiration, all the translators had produced the same translation.

As the work of 72 translators, the translation became known as the Septuagint, and it accrued further credibility when the story of the translators' work was recounted in works by Philo of Alexandria, Josephus, the Babylonian Talmud and Augustine. For the early Christian Church, the Septuagint became the authoritative version of the Old Testament.

Naturally, scholars regard this story as a pious fiction. However, the period of Ptolemy II's reign as being the correct timeframe for the translation of the Hebrew scriptures into Greek is supported by the Greek of the Septuagint being typical of the Greek spoken in the third century BC. It's likely that the Torah, the first five books of the Bible, was translated first, with the other books translated later. Further evidence for this being the time when the translation was made is provided by quotes from the Greek text appearing in other books from the second century BC. We have also found fragments of the Septuagint text in papyri that can be dated to the same time.

The Septuagint is written in Koine Greek. This was the form of the language that was used as a lingua franca among the soldiers of Alexander the Great and, following his conquests, it became the de facto language of international communication through the area controlled by the generals who survived him and parcelled out his conquests among themselves. Koine Greek was the language of the Hellenised world, taking in the eastern Mediterranean, the Levant, the coast of the Black Sea, Egypt and Libya. With there being a large and culturally significant Jewish population living in Alexandria, the very definition of a Hellenistic city, it was natural that Koine Greek became their main language and the Septuagint the common version of Jewish scripture for Koine-speaking Jews.

When the first Christians began writing about their religion, they also wrote in Koine Greek. Some scholars maintain that there was an original collection of the sayings of Jesus written in Aramaic, but the letters of Paul, the oldest parts of the New Testament, were all written in Koine Greek, as were the Gospels, the other Apostolic letters and the Apocalypse.

This was all very well in the Greek-speaking half of the Roman Empire but as the new faith spread, it moved into parts of the empire where Latin remained the main language. This was the western Mediterranean, northern Italy (not Rome itself, which was largely Greek-speaking), Hispania, Gaul and Britannia. Perhaps the greatest and most influential of the Church Fathers, Augustine of Hippo, famously did not know Greek. So Augustine, with other Latin-speaking Christians, used translations of the Bible from the Koine Greek of the Septuagint and the New Testament into Latin. These Greek-to-Latin translations were produced by Christians for their own communities and then were copied and passed on. Many of the second- and third-century Church fathers made their own, off-the-cuff translations. That there were a lot of different translations floating about is confirmed by Augustine, who wrote in *De Doctrina Christiana*, 'Translators from Hebrew into Greek can be numbered, but Latin translators by no means. For whenever, in the first ages of the faith, a Greek manuscript came into the hands of anyone who had also a little skill in both languages, he made bold to translate it forthwith.' These various Latin translations came to be called the Old Latin (*Vetus Latina*) versions of the Bible when a newer translation appeared in the late fourth century.

The different translations of the Old Latin Bible did become somewhat more standardised over time. However, there remained many different readings. In response to this situation of confusion, in 382 Pope Damasus I decided to commission an authoritative translation of the four Gospels. The man he chose for the task was brilliant, impatient and irascible: Eusebius Sophronius Hieronymus, better known as Jerome. While originally commissioned to translate the four Gospels from their Koine Greek originals into Latin, Jerome's work of translation expanded to take in most of the Bible, the Old as well as the New Testaments. In order to translate the Old Testament more accurately, Jerome, who had moved to Bethlehem and learnt Hebrew, went back to the original Hebrew text rather than using the Greek Septuagint.

It was a monumental task, and Jerome wrote in one of his many letters of the reaction he feared his new translation would provoke:

> You urge me to revise the old Latin version, and, as it were, to sit in judgment on the copies of the Scriptures which are now scattered throughout the whole world; and, inasmuch as they differ from one another, you would have me decide which of them agree with the Greek original. The labour is one of love, but at the same time both perilous and presumptuous; for in judging others I must be content to be judged by all; and how can I dare to change the language of the world in its hoary old age, and carry it back to the early days of its infancy? Is there a man, learned or unlearned, who will not, when he takes the volume into his hands, and perceives that what he reads does not suit his settled tastes, break out immediately into violent language, and call me a forger and a profane person for having the audacity to add anything to the ancient books, or to make any changes or corrections therein? Now there are two consoling reflections which enable me to bear the odium – in the first place, the command is given by you who are the supreme bishop; and secondly, even on the showing of those who revile us, readings at variance with the early copies cannot be right. For if we are to pin our faith to the Latin texts, it is for our opponents to tell us which; for there are almost as many forms of texts as there are copies. If, on the other hand, we are to glean the truth from a comparison of many, why not go back to the original Greek and correct the mistakes introduced by inaccurate translators, and the blundering alterations of confident but ignorant critics, and, further, all that has been inserted or changed by copyists more asleep than awake?

Jerome went ahead with his work and his translation, which became known as the Vulgate. This slowly became the authoritative version of the Bible in the Catholic Church. But it was a slow process. Books were not the throwaway items they have become but were treasured and read and re-read until they had to be copied for the text to survive. Also, it's important to remember that complete texts of the Bible were very, very rare. What were copied and read were particular books of the Bible, in both *Vetus Latina* and Vulgate translations.

\*

When Ceolfrith and his monks decided to produce three volumes of the complete text of the Bible, the question arose: which Bible? The library of the twin monastery did have its own pandect already, the *Codex Grandior*, which had been written for Cassiodorus during his long retirement at Vivarium, his monastery near Squillace in Italy, and brought to Northumbria by Benedict Biscop. But that was an Old Latin translation and thus clearly not an ideal template for their aim: to produce an authoritative, reliable copy of the Bible that, in Latin, came as close as possible to the meaning of the original Hebrew and Greek text.

To do that required giving minute attention to every single word of the text. Bede had already gained much valuable experience through writing commentaries on various books of the Bible. As commentaries are no longer much read, a quick word of explanation. A commentary takes a text, originally a text from the Bible, and attempts to understand it more completely. For example, in his commentary on the Book of Tobit, which was the first major commentary on this book (while canonical for Catholics and Orthodox, Protestants place the Book of Tobit among the Apocrypha), Bede writes, on chapter three, verse seventeen, that 'there was sent the Lord's holy angel, Raphael, (whose name is translated as medicine of God) to free Tobias from blindness and Sarah from the demon. [In like fashion] was the Lord sent into the world; he said of himself, *A doctor is not needed for the healthy, but for the sick.*'

Bede's interest in the etymology of words is shown by his giving the meaning of the angel's name, while he links the simple events of the passage – the angel Raphael healing Tobias from blindness and freeing Sarah from the demon who had afflicted her by killing seven bridegrooms, one after the other, before they could consummate their marriage to her – to the overarching theme of Christian commentary, which sees the Bible as essentially a commentary upon the life and teaching of Christ (Jewish commentary, not surprisingly, has a different point of view).

This is an example of allegory, one of the four different ways of interpreting the text of the Bible. In this case, an event in the Old Testament, namely the angel Raphael healing Tobias and delivering Sarah from evil, is taken as a foreshadowing of the New Testament, where Christ fulfils the implied promise of the Old Testament and makes it universal: where the angel saved Tobias and Sarah, Christ comes to heal everyone of their ills (allegorical interpretations are sometimes also called typological). As we saw in chapter six, the other three ways of interpreting scripture were the literal, historic sense, the tropological and the anagogical.

On the surface of it, interpreting the Bible literally would seem the most straightforward way to understand it. But it's not as simple as it appears – a fact of which Bede was well aware. Firstly, there's the difficulty of accurately translating from one language to another, and whether the translator is aiming for a literal or an interpretive translation. Add to that the fact that the Bible was written in a time and a place very different from seventh-century Britain. To take an obvious example, the vast majority of Bede's countrymen had never seen a desert. Neither had Bede himself. So readers needed some explanation as to the sort of territory the Jews wandered through after leaving Egypt, the same sort of land that Jesus withdrew to in order to pray and fast before beginning his public ministry. Bede at least had heard Abbot Adomnán relay the tales of Arculf, who had visited the Holy Land himself, and had at his disposal the book Adomnán wrote about the holy places, so he could form a picture of a desert landscape.

But the key challenge in the literal reading of the Bible is understanding the very different style and aims of its different books. Some are meant as history, such as the books of Joshua and the two books of Kings; others are essentially poetry, including the psalms and the Song of Songs; and then there are the prophetic books, including Isaiah and Jeremiah. Standing outside this division is the Pentateuch, the first five books of the Bible.

One of the key reasons that Bede spent so much time and effort analysing the different forms of Classical poetry was so that he could apply this knowledge to his understanding of the Bible, for he believed that similar literary tropes were found in scripture. The Bible is chock full of wild imagery, metaphors, hyperbole, paradox and synecdoche (where a part of something is written for the whole, or vice versa), and many others. It's vital for understanding. For example, when Jesus said, 'If thy right eye offend thee, pluck it out,' did he really mean for most of the male population to go around one eyed as a result of looking with too much interest at beautiful women? No, this is an example of hyperbole. Jesus's teaching is full of hyperbole, paradox and metaphor: he must have been a remarkable storyteller.

So even discerning the literal meaning of the text was no easy task. While Bede was a masterful Latinist, there's been considerable discussion among scholars as to how much Greek he knew. But by the time the twin monastery took up the production of its Bibles, Bede's knowledge of Greek must have become at least sufficient to refer to Septuagint versions of the texts and compare them to Old Latin versions and Jerome's Vulgate, for in places the *Codex Amiatinus* improves upon Jerome's translation.

As to Hebrew, it is likely that Bede knew enough Hebrew to be able to understand and critically evaluate Jerome's own notes about his translation from the original Hebrew. Quite a feat for someone who probably never met a native Greek or Hebrew-speaker in his life.

Once Bede had nailed down to his satisfaction the literal sense of the text, he could move on to the other modes of interpretation.

The allegorical or typological sense sought to understand the Old Testament in terms of the New Testament, applying the same tool of understanding the scriptures that Jesus often applied to himself.

This is shown most clearly in Luke's Gospel when two of Jesus's disciples are walking to Emmaus, despondent and distraught after the crucifixion of their friend and teacher. As they are walking, a man joins them on the road and asks where they're going, and why. The two disciples, not recognising who they are talking to, explain what has happened. Then the mysterious stranger explained why all this had to happen by interpreting 'to them the things about himself in all the scriptures'. So this approach had warrant from Jesus himself. Augustine, in *Seven Questions Concerning the Heptateuch*, which he wrote in 419 and 420, makes the connection explicit: 'In the Old Testament the New is concealed, in the New the Old is revealed.'

One example occurs in John's Gospel, where Jesus says, 'Just as Moses lifted up the snake in the wilderness, so the Son of Man must be lifted up, that everyone who believes in him may have eternal life.' This refers to an incident during the long wandering of Israel after the Exodus, when the Israelites were afflicted by poisonous snakes. Then, in a rather mysterious command given the previous commandment against the making of graven images, God tells Moses, 'Make a snake and put it up on a pole; anyone who is bitten can look at it and live.' So Moses made a bronze snake and put it up on a pole. Then when anyone was bitten by a snake and looked at the bronze snake, they lived (Numbers 21: 8–9). For Christians, this passage, otherwise refractory to understanding, was explicable as a prefiguration of Christ's crucifixion.

The third of the fourfold ways of understanding scripture that Bede employed was the tropological, which is more easily understood as the moral of the story. It's a way of applying scripture to the personal moral life of the reader or listener. The final method of interpretation was the anagogical or eschatological. This is to do with the last things, death, judgement and what might happen in future in a Christian context. It's the prophetic interpretation.

However, Bede's breadth and depth of knowledge was not seen by everyone as a good thing. Just as his work on the ages of the earth had drawn criticism and accusations of heresy, so did his commentary on the meaning of the symbols traditionally associated with the four evangelists (an angel for Matthew, Mark a lion, the ox for Luke and an eagle for John). The bishop of Hexham, Acca, wrote to Bede warning him that he was again being accused of heresy. In a scathing reply, Bede pointed out that his accusers were basically too ignorant (he called them illiterate, which meant that they were ignorant of Latin) to know that his writing was based on that of the Church Fathers and thus perfectly orthodox. To protect himself against any such future accusations, Bede invented the footnote, inserting marginal marks to indicate when and which Church Father he was referencing.

Many religious of the time saw their duty as to pass on to the future their inheritance from the past, specifically the Christian past, although some people, such as Cassiodorus, expanded the role to include the most worthwhile elements of pagan Antiquity. In the chaos and violence following the end of the Western Roman Empire, this was a difficult and sometimes dangerous task, but the Church did achieve it. However, a drawback of this attitude was to foster a deep suspicion among some clergy of anything that smacked of innovation and independent thought. The job was to pass on the message of Jesus, the teaching of his Apostles and the wisdom of the Church Fathers, not to expand on it. Indeed, any attempt at expansion ran the risk of being perverted and leading the faithful astray, as had happened during the great heresies of the early centuries.

So far as Bede was concerned, he was doing exactly this: passing on the inheritance of the past by explaining it more fully to his contemporaries. He was painfully aware of the low level of education of most of the clergy; few knew enough Latin to do more than recite the mass, mangling the Latin and, in the worst cases, rendering it invalid. Bede noted that the English are particularly bad at learning new languages – something which has not changed over the centuries – but rather than merely bewail that fact, towards the end of his life, Bede set about translating some key texts into Old English. He wrote out a translation of the Pater Noster into Old English so that rustic priests had a prayer that they and their people could understand; and, right at the end of his life, he was working on a translation of St John's Gospel into Old English. Sadly, this has not survived. Presumably, while Bede saw its necessity, not enough of his successors did to ensure sufficient copies were made to assure its survival. If it had survived, it would have been the earliest long text in Old English.

Steeped, as he was, in the Bible and the Church Fathers, Bede's commentaries were full of allusions and references to them. Indeed, it was precisely such allusions that had gone completely over the heads of the men who had accused him of heresy. So, to ensure that he did not have to face such charges again, Bede started putting markers into his books to let readers know when he was quoting from the Bible and when he was alluding to the Church Fathers. The mark for a Biblical quotation was a squiggle shaped like an 's' in the margin beside the quote, while where he was alluding to or quoting from a Church Father, he put the first letter of his name in the margin (so 'A' for Augustine, 'O' for Origen). The device was noted and copied by later authors, since it protected them against similar accusations, until it evolved into fully fledged footnotes.

*

While the other two Wearmouth/Jarrow pandects did not survive the ravages of time, Viking raids and the dissolution of the monasteries, the *Codex Amiatinus* set off for Rome with Ceolfrith and . . . disappeared. Bede writes, in his *History of the Abbots*, that following Ceolfrith's death in Langres some of his company continued on to Rome with their great gift for the pope. It does seem that the monks entrusted with getting the codex to Rome and giving it to the pope succeeded in their task, for the anonymous life of Ceolfrith, written by another monk at the twin monastery, asserts that some did so, reaching Rome and then returning with a letter of appreciation for the gift from the pope. In what turned out to be a particularly useful note, the anonymous life also recorded the dedication at the front of the codex. It read: 'To the body of sublime Peter, justly venerated, whom ancient faith declares to be the head of the Church, I, Ceolfrith, abbot from the furthest ends of the earth send pledges of my devoted affection, desiring that I and mine may ever have a place amidst the joys of so great a father, a memorial in heaven.'

And that's where the story went cold for hundreds of years. The great Bible, scribed by Bede and the monks of Wearmouth and Jarrow, disappeared. The assumption was that it had been lost to the ravages of time: water, fire, neglect, worms. Time is hard on books if they are not well cared for. Besides, the two Bibles that were kept at St Peter's and St Paul's had been lost too. If the two Bibles in Britain were gone, what was the chance of the one that had been sent thousands of miles away surviving?

However, in 1854, the German Biblical scholar Constantin von Tischendorf was working on the text of the Bible in Latin. Tischendorf had already become famous for his discovery of the *Codex Sinaiticus*, the oldest complete text of the Bible, in the remote monastery of St Catherine at the foot of Mount Sinai in Egypt (according to Tischendorf, he found the first 43 pages in a rubbish bucket). For his work on the Latin text, Tischendorf consulted what was reputed to be the oldest version of the Vulgate translation, a Bible that was kept by the monastery of San Salvatore (Holy Saviour) on the shoulder of Mount Amiata in the province of Siena in Tuscany. Tischendorf confirmed the faithfulness of the Latin to the original Vulgate translation, but he noticed that the dedication inscription had been altered. The dedication said that the Bible had been presented to the abbey of the Saviour by Peter, abbot of the Lombards, 'from the furthest ends of the earth'. Since the Lombards, a Germanic people who conquered most of Italy between 568 and 774, lived in Italy and even had a province named after them, Lombardy, placing them at the 'furthest ends of the earth' seemed a trifle excessive. However, it was not entirely beyond the bounds of possibility. Italians, to this day, have intensely local identities. A Lombard might conceivably, with tongue firmly in cheek, present a book to a Tuscan monastery as a present from the 'furthest ends of the earth'.

While Tischendorf noted that the original inscription had been altered, he could not work out what was written originally. That was left to the Italian archaeologist, Giovanni Battista de Rossi. De Rossi was already famous for his rediscovery of the Catacombs of Callixtus, and in 1888 he turned his formidable epigraphic skills – he was the official scriptor of the Vatican Library – to what turned out to be the *Codex Amiatinus*. It was Rossi who discovered that the name of the donor had been changed to 'Peter Langobardorum' ('Peter of the Lombards') and that the original words were 'Ceolfridus Anglorum' (Ceolfrith of the English').

So at some point in the past, the codex had come to the monastery on Mount Amiata (hence *Codex Amiatinus*), for reasons that we can only guess at. With the great codex in his keeping, an otherwise unrecorded abbot of the monastery decided that he could ensure it remained at his monastery permanently by making it seem like his own gift to the monastery.

While de Rossi had deciphered the original dedication, he did not realise its significance. It was only when the news reached Cambridge, and the ears of F.J.A. Hort, professor of divinity, that anyone realised that the dedication in the *Codex Amiatinus* now exactly matched the dedication recorded in the anonymous *Life of Ceolfrith*: the Bible hidden away in the Abbey of San Salvatore was the very book that had gone abroad in 716, never to be heard of again.

This was big news. The late nineteenth century saw many remarkable discoveries, including the Oxyrhynchus Papyri, and this discovery, the lost Bible of Bede, was as important as any. For patriotic Victorians, it brought their own proto-Englishman into the centre of the Christian world, his bluff goodness hidden by Catholic Italian perfidy. It was a perfect summation of Protestant English Victorian ideas of how they related to Catholic Europe.

The *Codex Amiatinus* was a statement book. For Ceolfrith, the man who conceived the idea of taking the book to Rome as a gift to the pope, it was a statement, 'from the furthest ends of the earth' of how the people who lived there, the English, were now worthy members of the universal Church, returning with a great gift to the successor of the man who had first sent missionaries to bring them into that Church. The *Codex Amiatinus* was expressly written to express Romanitas and it did that so well that, once the dedication was forged, no one thought it could have had any other source than Italy. The scribes at Wearmouth and Jarrow who wrote the book did so in a self-consciously Roman way, using a writing style that was closely identified with the Church in Italy. Indeed, they did it so well that no one realised it came originally from the farthest ends of the earth rather than the heart of the empire. So when knowledge of the book first resurfaced in the sixteenth century, its production was, in an ironic reversal, ascribed to Pope Gregory the Great, the man who had dispatched Augustine's mission to Britain, setting in motion the train of events that had led to the creation of the codex. So while the attribution to Gregory was wrong, in fact it was correct in spirit.

But while the creation and dispatch of the codex was Ceolfrith's statement of the place of his people at the heart of the Church, despite their position on its periphery, for Bede there was another lesson to be learnt from the book. For by stating that the book was a gift from Ceolfrith of the English, the abbot was making himself a member of a tribe that existed only in the dedication he had written in the Bible.

To Bede was left the task of making the English a people.

## CHAPTER 13

# The Invention of Northumbria

The kingdom of Northumbria was a sword marriage. Two separate, rival kingdoms were forced into union by the most formidable warlord of his day: Æthelfrith. The two kingdoms were Bernicia, centred on the royal stronghold at Bamburgh and including the coastal strip running up to the Cheviot Hills, and Deira, which covered the Vale of York and the old Roman legionary city of York.

The early history of both kingdoms is sketchy. Scholars suspect that the Anglian kingdom of Deira was first established in the latter part of the fifth century, which would make it significantly older than its neighbour and rival, Bernicia, which was founded in 547. However, while we have king lists for Bernicia from its founder, Ida, onwards, the first recorded king of Deira was Ælla, who reigned from about 560 to 589. The king lists of Bernicia feature a swiftly rotating cast of kings after Ida, with no less than six men reigning in the 34 years between Ida's death and the accession to the throne of Æthelfrith in 593 (so that's an average reign of 5.67 years; short even for those violent times). For our purpose, we don't need to know whether the king list is accurate. What's interesting is that it exists and that it was transmitted.

On the other hand, in Deira, the king lists starts with Ælla and has only one other entry, Æthelric, before Æthelfrith, the king of Bernicia, took over the kingdom. This suggests that Æthelfrith, to bolster his own legitimacy as king of Deira, suppressed the memory of the older kings so that it would appear his own lineage was longer and nobler.

While Æthelfrith united the two kingdoms by conquest, it appears that they continued as separate realms. In that respect, it was an earlier example of the personal union of Scotland and England during the reign of James VI (Scotland) and I (England): the two countries remained separate entities with their own laws and customs but shared the same king. However, it's clear that the union of Bernicia and Deira was a rather more forced affair than that between England and Scotland. While the sources aren't entirely clear, it seems likely that Æthelfrith did not negotiate his way to being ruler of Deira. We can say that because Edwin, Ælla's son, went into exile for many years when Æthelfrith became king, moving around various kingdoms further south, both Anglo-Saxon and Britonnic, before Æthelfrith finally tracked him down in East Anglia.

What makes the whole matter even more tangled is that, having taken Deira, Æthelfrith married Ælla's daughter, Acha, who was Edwin's sister. Since Æthelfrith and Acha had eight children together, it seems to have been a relatively successful marriage. It could of course be the case that Acha took the pragmatic view that having been forced into marriage at swordpoint she might as well enjoy the benefits of being queen. But it might also be the case that there were problems between her and her brother, Edwin. Certainly, when Edwin finally returned to Deira, having killed Æthelfrith at the Battle of the River Idle in 616, Acha did not wait around to make peace with her returning brother. Instead, she gathered her children and fled.

Edwin, as the scion of the house of Deira, had little difficulty in persuading the locals of the kingdom to accept him as their returning king while his sister and his nephews and nieces remained in careful exile throughout Edwin's reign. There is, at least, no record of Edwin trying to track down and kill his sister and her family, which in the ruthless calculus of seventh-century kingship would have made sense, as his nephews had a blood obligation to avenge their father by killing their uncle. However, if Edwin ever did try to have them assassinated, the attempt failed; it would not have been something he wanted recorded and nor would it have been an act that Bede, our main source, would have wanted to record.

What Bede did want to record was Edwin's conversion to Christianity. This came via his marriage to a Christian Kentish princess who brought with her to Northumbria a priest, Paulinus, who was part of the follow-up group of missionaries dispatched by Pope Gregory to help Augustine in 601. So Edwin and his court adopted Christianity in its most thoroughgoing Roman form.

There was also a junior third partner to Bernicia and Deira: Lindsey. This covered an area that roughly maps onto modern-day Lincolnshire. Then, though, Lindsey was almost a separate island, cut off to the north by the Humber estuary and to the south by tidal marshes that ran inland all the way up to Lincoln. There was only a narrow overland way into the kingdom, between Torksey and Lincoln over the Foss Dyke. It's not entirely clear when Lindsey was conquered by the kings of Northumbria, although Æthelfrith, from whom Edwin fled for the first part of his adult life, is a possible candidate.

When Edwin did finally decide to convert to Christianity, he seems to have conducted a ritual process of conversion in each of the three kingdoms he ruled: in Catterick for the Deirans, at Ad Gefrin with the Bernicians and in Lincoln for the people of Lindsey. So Edwin seemed to regard himself as the king of three separate kingdoms.

When Edwin was killed and his returning nephew, Oswald, took the throne of Bernicia and Deira, he had the great advantage of being a member of the royal families of both kingdoms: Æthelfrith of Bernicia was his father and Acha of Deira was his mother. So in his person he united the two kingdoms. Oswald also brought into his realm monks from Iona, introducing the Irish flavour of Christianity to his kingdom.

However, the two kingdoms retained their separate identities. When Oswald was killed and his brother became king, Oswiu was initially only able to claim the rulership of Bernicia. Oswine, a member of the Deiran ruling family, took control of the southern kingdom. Even when Oswiu killed Oswine and took over Deira, the kingdom remained restive. Oswiu initially installed his son, Ahlfrith, as sub-ruler of Deira but a conflict appears to have broken out between father and son, with Ahlfrith disappearing from the historical record after 664.

So throughout this time, the inhabitants of Northumbria did not see themselves as Northumbrians but as Bernicians, or Deirans or people from Lindsey. Indeed, it's likely that not even the kings saw themselves as kings of a single realm but rather as kings of three separate kingdoms, as James was king of England and Scotland. Indeed, so disconnected from any idea of a general kingdom of Northumbria were some monks in Lindsey that they initially refused to accept relics of Oswald into their monastery, leaving them locked outside overnight. But then a vision of a shaft of light rising from the relics up into heaven convinced the monks of Bardney monastery that, just maybe, they ought to accept Oswald's relics after all. Curiously, the reason the monks gave for initially refusing the relics was that Oswald had conquered Lindsey. This is odd as Lindsey had certainly been under Northumbrian domination before Oswald's rule. It's possible that Lindsey might have briefly regained its independence after Edwin's death, only for Oswald to reclaim it, but we have no other source to confirm that. Alternatively, the monks might have seen their loyalty as lying with Edwin and his family, rather than with Oswald and the Idings.

In fact, so far as we can see, the first person to refer to a unified kingdom of Northumbria was Bede.

Did Bede invent the whole idea of a single kingdom of Northumbria? While on the face of it unlikely, it would have served some of his purposes in writing the *Ecclesiastical History* very well. For one of the key themes of his history was how the twin streams of Christianity, the Roman and Irish, that met in Northumbria had been, by his time, fused into a single unified Church that took the best of both and made them into one.

As Christianity was initially Roman in Deira and Irish in Bernicia, having both kingdoms become one served as a political metaphor for what Bede was attempting to show had happened with the Church. However, Bede tended to ignore Lindsey. King Ecgfrith permanently lost that part of his kingdom to the Mercians at the Battle of the River Trent in 679. Indeed, it seems that the loss of Lindsey catalysed the emergence of the unified kingdom of Northumbria. Following that defeat, Northumbria remained a unified kingdom until the arrival of the Vikings and the establishment of the Norse kingdom in York.

From a simple authorial viewpoint, it also made the writing of Bede's history considerably easier, and smoother to read, if he could refer to Northumbria rather than having to trot out the kingdoms of Bernicia, Deira and Lindsey under the rulership of King Whoever each time he wrote about the whole. Of course, Bede might also have been putting down on parchment the wishes of his royal patron when writing the *History*. It would have made political sense for the king that his realm be seen as a single kingdom. Or there may have been an interplay between Bede and his royal sponsor, with each of them contributing to the framework into which he lay his history. This latter seems the most likely scenario.

Whatever the truth of the matter – and at this juncture we will never be able to know for certain – it remains the case that it was Bede's pen that first named in an enduring record the kingdom as Northumbria, subsuming Bernicia and Deira into a political and religious unity that they might never have known without Bede's literary midwifery.

But it was not just his local kingdom that Bede baptised into being. As he turned his mind and his writing towards compiling the chronicle of history that concluded *The Reckoning of Time*, it became clear to him that he was gathering the material necessary to tell the story of his people's conversion to the faith he espoused. He realised that he was writing the story of a people and, by doing that, turning them into a nation.

To understand this fully, we need to look into the long and complex history of how, when and why Bede wrote his history of the English people.

## CHAPTER 14

# Writing History as It's Happening

The *Ecclesiastical History of the English People* was one of the last books that Bede completed. We know that because, at the end of the book, he helpfully provides the reader with a bibliography of his previous works. This list includes almost everything else he had written. The only work we can definitely say that was written after the completion of the *Ecclesiastical History* was a letter to Bishop Ecgberht, dated 5 November 734. There was one other book that did not make it into the bibliography, for Bede was working on a translation of the Gospel of John into Old English in the months leading up to this death. The account of Bede's death, written by his pupil and friend Cuthbert, suggests that he did finish the translation shortly before he died but sadly the translation has not survived.

The usual date given for completion of the *Ecclesiastical History* is 731. By then Bede was 58 or 59. This was a good age for the time. Benedict Biscop died when he was about 61. Bede must have suspected that he did not have too many more years to live. In fact, he died four years later, in 735.

So the book was in many ways the completion of his life's work as a scholar. Bede intended it to be a work that would last (although its continuing importance so many years later would surely have surprised and delighted him). To understand how the book was the summation of Bede's life work, we will begin by looking at how he wrote the *Ecclesiastical History*. Yes, it was with a pen and parchment, but what made the work on this history stand out was the labour that went into assembling the material that went into the book.[1]

The monastery at Wearmouth and Jarrow was, of course, famous for its library. Benedict Biscop and Ceolfrith spent much labour, travels and effort in establishing and expanding the library, and Bede made full use of it in his work, particularly his Biblical commentaries and scholarship. One of the great advantages of having such a library available was that within it Bede had pretty much all the works necessary to him when he wrote his commentaries. These are chock full of allusions, extracts, extrapolations and arguments from the Church Fathers whose books were in the monastic library, as well as Bede's own extensions and interpretations of their work. When Bede wanted to check on one of the wilder flights of anagogical interpretation in Origen's commentaries, he could look up the relevant passage in the book.

Bede could also do that when writing the *Ecclesiastical History*, for the first few chapters at least. Up to the end of chapter 22 of the first book of the *History*, Bede told the story of Britain from the first incursion by Julius Caesar up to just before the piquing of Pope Gregory's interest in these people at the edge of the world. Beginning with Julius Caesar's invasion, Bede also unveils his system of dating right from the beginning of the *History*, dating Caesar's consulship to 693 years after Rome's founding and 60 years before the birth of Christ.

Bede had the material to write these initial chapters in the library at Jarrow. His sources included Jerome's *Chronicle*, Constantius's *Life of Germanus*, *The History against the Pagans* by Orosius and *The Ruin of the Britons* by Gildas. But what we don't read in the completed text are the many other books that Bede must have read and digested in order to compile his early history of Britain. To put it simply, Bede trawled through all the Classical and Christian sources he had, looking for material about, and references to, Britain. Given that Britannia was an outpost of empire which rarely figured in any narratives, he had to cast his net widely. Even in those books which did mention Britain, Britannia generally played a minor part. So Bede had to find and extract the relevant information from all the sources available to him – without the help of indices, research assistants or search engines. It was all done by reading, recall and note-taking.

Sometimes, Bede found and included just the tiniest detail from these sources. He quoted a few lines from a poem by Prosper of Aquitaine because it included a short description of the origin of the heresiarch Pelagius: 'sea-girt Britain's porridge bred this twaddle'. A lot of reading for a short quotation.

However, in terms of material, these first chapters giving the history of Britain were relatively straightforward for Bede to write. He had a lot of it to hand in the monastery library; it was simply a matter of reading books and collating the history from them. (Although trying to fit Gildas's completely date-free narrative into his history must have caused Bede no end of head scratching. This might come as some mild consolation to generations of later scholars who have struggled just as much to wring the history out of Gildas's jeremiad.) But it was one thing collating the history, quite another assembling it into some sort of coherent narrative. Looking at the sources that Bede used to write his history of Britain up until the start of Augustinian mission, one is left amazed. Bede took disparate bits of material, ranging from hagiographies to histories of elsewhere, and turned them into a history of Britain, spinning a haphazard string of anecdotes into historical gold.

This was all very well when it came to writing about the events prior to the conversion of his own people. But when his narrative moved onto the conversion, Bede faced a problem. He had no written sources for the ecclesiastical history of his people because, before him, no one had written about that history. So for the vast majority of his book, he had to find, gather and collate the information that went into it. Bede did that by asking people.

For the Church history of Northumbria, he had people to hand who could tell him much of the information: the monks of his own monastery and even more so the monks of Lindisfarne. They had an oral tradition of passing on the lives of their founders as well as their institutional history. Being monasteries, they also had the first sets of written records: lists of the abbots, grants of land to the monastery, books of benefactors (the *Liber Vitae* recording the names of those who had helped the monastery that the monks might pay them back in perpetual prayer), records of local bishops and, possibly, king lists, giving the names of the ruling dynasty back to a legendary founder of the line. In most Anglo-Saxon kingdoms this founder was Woden, although a couple of the ruling dynasties traced their lineage back to Tiw. Tiw and Woden were both gods of battle, although Tiw seems to have been a more straightforward warrior god than Woden, whose favour could never be taken for granted.

But outside of Northumbria, Bede had to look to other sources for his material. Rather helpfully, Bede himself tells us who many of these informers were, right at the beginning of his book, in his preface. First and foremost, he lists Albinus, the abbot of the monastery of Ss Peter and Paul in Canterbury, connecting him directly to Theodore and Hadrian who, Bede says, educated Albinus. As the channel of information to him from Albinus, who, being abbot, could not leave his monastery to go jaunting off round the countryside, Bede expresses particular gratitude to Nothhelm, who would later become archbishop of Canterbury. Nothhelm was the messenger who brought Bede the information stored in Canterbury about the early history of the mission there, as well as later visiting Rome in person and copying from the papal archives many of the letters that Bede quoted in his book.

For events in other parts of the country, Bede lists as his sources Daniel, bishop of the West Saxons; the monastery at Lastingham provided information about the history of the Church in Mercia and among the East Saxons; Abbot Esi told Bede about the history of the Church in East Anglia; and Bishop Cynibert was his source for the history of the Church in the kingdom of Lindsey.

This is probably not an exhaustive list of Bede's sources but it surely represents his key informants, those whom he really had to name-check at the start of his book. But let's think of what communicating with these people actually entailed. Today, we can phone, email, WhatsApp, etc.: instant communication is taken as a given in everyday life. It was different for Bede. While it's clear that there was correspondence between monasteries and bishops in Britain, there was no postal service. If you wrote a letter to someone, you had to find a courier to take the letter. He then either had to wait until a reply was written and bring it back to you or another messenger had to be employed to bring back the answer.

Ships were the main channel of communication. Jarrow was on the coast, and there were merchant vessels that plied up and down the North Sea, supplying monasteries and, in particular, the kings whose strongholds lay on the coast, with exotic imported goods. Just up the coast from Jarrow at Bamburgh, the Bamburgh Research Project has excavated the remains of luxury imported items, including garnets that were mined in Sri Lanka and lentils, found preserved in coprolites, that were harvested in the south of France.

Jarrow itself was home to a thriving port and Rosemary Cramp's excavations reveal the monastery had wide-ranging contacts up and down the seaboard. Indeed, when the incidents that Bede relates in the *Ecclesiastical History* are mapped, they show a marked tendency to occur within a few miles of the coast, suggesting that most of his contacts lived north and south along the east coast of Britain. Looking at the list of informants that Bede provides, Abbot Albinus in Kent, Abbot Esi in East Anglia and Bishop Cynibert in Lindsey would have been most easily contacted via naval mail.

But one drawback of waterborne messages was that they were seasonal. The ships that plied the east coast did so from the middle of spring to early in the autumn, when the weather was gentlest. Outside these times, only fishing boats would generally go out, save in dire need – and replying to an inquisitive monk asking who was bishop before you in your diocese did not qualify as dire need.

We don't know if Bede sent letters via the masters of the ships that plied the coast or whether someone from his monastery was sent as courier and messenger. A messenger could carry a personal message from Bede, amplifying the request and sweetening the labour involved, as well as being on hand to carry a reply back to Bede as soon as it was written. A letter was easier to transport but carried less urgency, and a reply would have depended more on finding a suitable ship to carry it. A courier could take the reply on the first ship heading in the right direction and then switch ships as necessary. A message would have had to wait until a ship could be found that was definitely travelling to Jarrow.

Some of Bede's correspondents were inland. Road travel was slower than sea travel and often more dangerous. When Ceolfrith left for Rome with the *Codex Amiatinus* he travelled as part of a group of 80 people. On longer journeys, people banded together for mutual protection against thieves and bandits. So Bede's messengers had to wait until they found a sufficiently large group of people travelling to Wessex before taking his letter to Bishop Daniel asking for information about the conversion of the West Saxons.

Despite these difficulties, the travelling itself did not take that long: a couple of days to a week or so down the coast, the length chiefly determined by how many ports the ship docked into along the way; a week or two by road to Wessex.

No, what dragged this correspondence out was the reply. Upon receiving Bede's request, and supposing the recipient was favourable, he still had to identify the material he had that he thought was relevant, assemble it and then arrange for it to be copied – it's unlikely that original documents were sent to Bede. This all took a considerable amount of time. For seaborne communication, it probably meant that a reply would not be forthcoming until the next sailing season in the following year. If, upon receiving the reply, Bede had further questions or wanted more information, that would take another communication cycle before the answer could reach him.

So gathering the information for the *Ecclesiastical History* took a long time. Most sources list the book as having been written in 731 (some scholars think, however, that Bede continued to work on it until a few months before his death). But this was the date of the book's completion – it was a book that took years of baking before it was ready.

Among the chief labours involved in writing the *Ecclesiastical History* was sorting out the dates. The material that his informants sent to Bede included dates but they were written according to a large number of different systems. Take, for instance, the dedication stone that Bede would have read every time he stepped into the church of St Paul in Jarrow. That gave the date of the foundation of the church as the ninth day before the kalends of May, in the fifteenth year of the reign of King Ecgfrith and the fourth year of Ceolfrith's abbacy.

All the other dates supplied to Bede came in forms as unhelpful as this. Even the papal letters that Nothhelm copied and brought back from Rome were difficult, as they gave the year in indiction. The indiction was the Roman fifteen-year tax cycle that was adopted by Constantine as the dating system for the empire and which continued to be used in the early medieval period until it was eventually supplanted (due, in no small part, to Bede's work) by the Anno Domini system. By Bede's day, the terminology had changed so a date given as the third indiction represented the third year of the fifteen-year cycle. The indiction itself was usually anchored to the reign of an emperor or a pope but without that, and with no further information, it would be impossible for Bede to derive an absolute date from an indiction date. The list of bishops of East Anglia, for instance, included lengths of each bishop's respective reign but no anchor date, meaning that Bede was never able to give definite dates for any of these bishops or, indeed, their kings.

To put this cacophony of dates into order, Bede needed some system of sorting them. And through his work on calculating Easter, he had that system to hand: the Easter tables that he had produced. The paschal tables produced to give the dates of Easter were split into columns on the page with wide margins. Monks were already beginning to add the year's events into the margins, starting down the road to the chronicles that became a key part of monastic record-keeping in the later history of the country.

As Bede received the wealth of disparate material that was to go into his book, the obvious way to sort through it and establish some sort of order was to expand the paschal tables that he had already produced to accommodate the new material he was receiving. To set everything into order, he probably put a column for the AD year first, followed by a column for the indiction, and then added other columns to cope with the other dating systems he was receiving. According to Richard Shaw, who has attempted to reconstruct the dating table that Bede produced, the next two columns probably consisted of the regnal year of the Northumbrian king and his age in that year (both of which Bede could work out from the Northumbrian king list); then the regnal year of the Deiran king if there was one; the regnal year of the king of Kent; the regnal year of the Mercian king; the regnal year of the West Saxon king; the regnal year of the Northumbrian bishop; the regnal year of the archbishop of Canterbury; the regnal year of the pope; and the year of the abbot of Wearmouth and Jarrow. To these, Bede may have added other columns as material became available.

The great advantage of this table was that, as it grew and developed, Bede could add new events and information, fitting them into the scaffold of dates that he had already constructed, and then use this information as he wrote his *History*. There were still difficulties. In particular, his table did not cope well when one king died and another took over: the table tended to show the king who died as reigning for the whole of the year he had died and the first year of his successor's reign beginning the year after.

But despite its limitations, Bede's table was a brilliantly successful method for arranging and sorting the information he received, enabling him to create a coherent historical framework for the events of the previous century and a half. He made mistakes. Of course he made mistakes, but their paucity shows the order and care that Bede put into his research. Even now, we remain in his debt.

*

Having looked at how Bede wrote his *Ecclesiastical History*, we now need to consider when he wrote it. As shown above, the *History* required a huge effort of time and thought. To expend so much work on a single book suggests a motivation beyond that which Bede ascribes to himself in his preface. There, he states that the writing and reading of history has a moral purpose: 'Should history tell of good men and their good estate, the thoughtful listener is spurred on to imitate the good; should it record the evil ends of wicked men, no less effectually the devout and earnest listener or reader is kindled to eschew what is harmful and perverse.'

Some scholars take Bede at his word and accept that this was why he wrote the *History*. But others suggest that while there's no reason to doubt what he says here, it's not exhaustive. There were other reasons for writing the book, too. Most of these explanations locate his motivation in the religious and secular politics of the day. But unless we can establish when he worked on the book, we won't know what the religious and secular context was when he was writing it. So let's first try to establish some sort of time frame for when he wrote the book.

For that we have a clue in the second person named in Bede's preface, Albinus, the abbot of the monastery of Ss Peter and Paul in Canterbury. Bede states that 'it was chiefly through the encouragement of Albinus that I ventured to undertake this work'. Bede also mentions that Albinus was taught by both Theodore and Hadrian, who died in 690 and 710 respectively. Albinus died in 732, not long after Bede finished his *History*. We don't know when Albinus became abbot of the monastery but to have been taught by Theodore he must have been in his teens at least during the 680s, giving a latest possible date of birth of 675, and probably a bit earlier. Bede was born in either 672 or 673, so the two men were likely close contemporaries.

Richard Shaw argues convincingly that Albinus suggested Bede write an ecclesiastical history of their people as early as 713. If that's the case – and I think it is – then the book took even longer to go from conception to publication than *The Lord of the Rings*. This is important because the ecclesiastical and political context in which Bede was writing changed a lot between 713 and 731 – and even more so if the book wasn't really finished until 734. It was a period of instability in Northumbria, with four kings ruling and the first three apparently ending their rule in blood (Ceolwulf, to whom Bede dedicated the *History*, dodged the sword, abdicating and retiring to Lindisfarne to live out his life as a monk).

A sponsor was a vital part of a book's inception. It wasn't like today, where the imagined idea is that a writer sits in his leaky garret feverishly trying to catch the passing trail of inspiration, and only then giving out into the world, for its appreciation, the fruits of his genius. Then, with much shorter parchment runs, a book was written at the request of a specific reader or audience. The monks of Lindisfarne commissioned Bede to write a biography of Cuthbert. Other works were direct answers to questions posed. His teaching books were written to help with the education of the monks of his own monastery.

In the case of the *Ecclesiastical History*, it was Albinus who suggested the project to Bede, thus ensuring an audience for the work. And not only did he suggest the subject, he provided a lot of the material. In his list of sources, Bede lists Albinus first and one can see why: not only did the abbot commission the work but he also provided material about the Augustinian mission and, when that proved insufficient to Bede's requirements, he dispatched one of his priests, Nothhelm, to Rome, to ferret about in the papal archives for the texts of the letters that Pope Gregory sent to Augustine. Nothhelm had already been once to see Bede in Jarrow with the first tranche of material from Canterbury. Having come back from Rome with a historical hoard, Albinus sent Nothhelm up to Jarrow again to convey the papal letters to Bede personally.

Bede tells us that Canterbury also contributed information about Kent, the East Saxons and the West Saxons, East Anglia and even Northumbria, particularly with respect to the list of bishops of each diocese and the events of the Christian conversion of these kings and their peoples. As such, it appears that not only was Albinus the original sponsor of the book but that he, and the Canterbury diocese, provided a lot of the information that went into the *History*.

The question therefore arises as to why Albinus, and the wider community in Canterbury, wanted a book written about the history of the Church in Britain. The monks of Lindisfarne wanted a biography of Cuthbert to praise and glorify their founder, that his fame might spread and his cult grow. This is not meant pejoratively. We tend to view medieval attempts to bolster the cult of a particular saint as purely the efforts of venal monks to increase their monastic income through a swelling of the pilgrim stream. But pilgrims were not yet a feature of early medieval Britain. Rather, spreading the news of Cuthbert, was like me, when I was a teenager, taking a new record that I'd been listening to again and again round to a friend and saying, 'Listen to this!' I had found something I loved and I wanted to share it. Cuthbert's monks wanted to share the news of their saint, for his glory and for the benefit he could bring to the people who prayed to him. So, yes, spreading a saint's cult did bring material benefits to a monastery or a church holding his relics, but these were secondary benefits compared to the good that he might do for those who prayed to him.

Working from that, the first part of the answer would seem to be that Albinus, and the Church in Canterbury, wanted to commission a book that would give their founder, Augustine, his due as the Apostle to the Anglo-Saxons. What's more, they had a good tranche of material about Augustine to present to Bede (although some of the anecdotes appear to have been modified over the years). Highlighting Augustine's role in the conversion of the Anglo-Saxons would increase his profile and allow more people to benefit from his intercession.

This was undoubtedly a factor in Albinus commissioning Bede to write a history. But it was not the only one. Around the time we think that Albinus asked Bede to write the book, there were two issues that were particularly important to the Church in Canterbury: who was in charge of the Church in Britain and harmonising the celebration of Easter to the Roman/Canterbury dates. While the Synod of Whitby had regularised Easter for the Anglo-Saxons, Iona and its daughter monasteries only accepted the new dating in 715. This was an important event for the Church in Canterbury as it brought all but the Britonnic churches back into harmony. The Easter controversy plays a central role in Bede's narrative and having its almost final resolution as a backdrop provided further reason to write an account telling how the matter was resolved.

But the other key issue was episcopal oversight. When Theodore became bishop of Canterbury, he brought with him the title of archbishop; he alone in these islands held that title. Throughout his tenure as archbishop, Theodore sought to divide the other dioceses in the country so that they covered smaller areas. On the face of it, this might look like episcopal arrogance, an attempt by an overmighty bishop to ensure that no other diocese could compare to his own. But to be fair to Theodore, this was actually clerical best practice, and the practice elsewhere in the Church; many of the dioceses in Britain were huge in comparison to those elsewhere in Europe. Such large dioceses meant that the bishop was necessarily disconnected from much of his people and his clergy. As only a bishop could consecrate new priests, having only one bishop to cover such huge areas tended to lead to a drastic shortage of priests to minister to the people.

There was also a tendency for dioceses to map onto kingdoms, leading to a conflation of spiritual and political aims, as well as the relative importance of the various dioceses rising and falling according to the political fortunes of their accompanying kingdoms. This was particularly so for Kent. When Augustine arrived, it had been the richest kingdom in Britain as a result of its close contacts and trade with the Merovingian kingdom in Francia. However, Kent's political importance and strength steadily declined through the seventh century, leaving the archbishop of Canterbury somewhat exposed: he had to rely on clerical authority to buttress his claims for spiritual supremacy, as the king of Kent could no longer support him politically.

Thus, while splitting over-large dioceses was clerical best practice, it also meant that smaller dioceses were easier for Canterbury to handle. There was considerable opposition to Theodore's efforts but, by the beginning of the eighth century, all the old one-kingdom dioceses had been split into smaller areas, although much of the actual credit for this went to Theodore's successor as archbishop, Berhtwald, who managed to divide the last single-kingdom dioceses. We can see just how important an issue this was for Canterbury because, in a surviving letter from c.705, the bishop of London wrote to the archbishop of Canterbury to tell him that a synod had threatened to excommunicate the West Saxons unless they agreed to divide the diocese in two. The threat worked, and bishops were consecrated in Sherborne and Winchester.

By the early decades of the seventh century, Canterbury had upped its claims. Not only did Archbishop Berhtwald claim authority over the other bishops among the Anglo-Saxon kingdoms but over all the Christians in the island. The ancient Britonnic churches resisted this claim mightily, but the progress that Canterbury had made over the previous half-century suggested that it might reasonably think that it could extend its authority to take in all the Christians of Britain.

Apart from the area a bishop controlled, the celebration of Easter was the other key question under authority. The monastery at Wearmouth and Jarrow appears to have played a key role in the adoption by the Picts and Iona of the Roman Easter. As such, it's likely that Bede came to the attention of Albinus as a result of the monastery's work in convincing the Picts and Iona to change their long-cherished Easter celebrations. Here was a man who could write a book that would cement Augustine's position as the Apostle of the English, affirm the primacy of the see of Canterbury over the whole country and present the case for the Roman dating of Easter as being the correct one.

While this was Albinus's idea in asking Bede to write a history of the Church, it was not necessarily Bede's. Bede certainly believed just as strongly that the Roman method for dating Easter was the correct one, so he had no problem in presenting that as a key theme of his *History*. Augustine's importance was also undeniable. However, living in Northumbria, Bede had first-hand evidence for how the Augustinian mission had, after initial success, failed in his own country, only to be rescued by missionaries from Ireland – monks who professed the wrong system for dating Easter and who certainly did not accept the authority of Canterbury. What's more, Bede's brethren at Jarrow and their near neighbours at Lindisfarne had played key roles in the adoption of the correct Easter tables, first by Lindisfarne itself and then, in the end, by Lindisfarne's mother house at Iona. It had been a hard-won peace, but it was a settlement nonetheless. To cement the settlement, Bede needed to write an account that gave due place to the monks of Iona for their role in the conversion of the Northumbrians while allowing for their earlier errors. It was a difficult balancing act, but it was one that Bede accomplished.

It's clear that it was a thorny and delicate settlement. The question involved profound matters of faith and thought, and the origin of these. Although Easter was the crux of the problem, there were other differences between the Roman and Irish practices, of which the most visible was the tonsure. This was the mark of a monk, showing that he had been consecrated to God. The Roman practice was to shave the crown and the back and sides of the head, leaving a torus of hair. Irish monks, and these included those whose traced their lineage back to Iona, shaved the front and side of the head, to the crown, but left the hair at the back to grow long. They would have looked something like the young Brian Eno in his glam Roxy Music days.

In his *History*, Bede carefully balanced the achievements of the Roman and Irish missions, noting the failure of the Irish to observe the correct dates for Easter but just as carefully noting their commitment to preaching and simplicity of life, clerical practices that Bede wanted to hold up as important for his own and later generations. Maintaining this balance between the two streams of Christianity was important for the settlement that had been achieved, and it remained important for at least three generations after Bede's death. This is illustrated by a discovery made by the publishers of this book – a discovery that has not been published before now.

In the church of St Serf, which is in Dunning, a village eight miles south-west of Perth in Scotland, is an eight-foot-high free standing cross carved from sandstone. The cross originally stood in the open air, on a hillside between Dunning and Forteviot, part of the tradition of freestanding crosses in the north. The cross, known now as the Dupplin Cross, was moved into St Serf's Church in 2002 to ensure its preservation. The Dupplin Cross was carved in c.800, so some 65 years after Bede's death. It was raised during the reign of Causantin, who reigned as king of the Picts between 789 and 820. As with other free-standing crosses, it is intricately carved, knotwork weaving around stylised figures, as well as having an inscription in which only the name of Causantin remains legible.

Which is where my publisher comes in. They decided to use a picture of part of the Dupplin Cross on a book jacket cover. The part they photographed showed a line of clerics, and the photo was duly dispatched to the designer. Having spent 1,200 years enduring all that Scotland's weather can throw at them, the carving of the clerics had become pretty worn, so to make them stand out more clearly on the book cover the designer set about colouring the image. And this was where something extraordinary was revealed. For in doing that he had to go into the grain of the stone, and it became clear that the line of clerics had different hairstyles: some had the Roman tonsure, others the bald foreheads and flowing locks of the Irish tonsure. In fact, the line of clerics depicted men with alternating tonsures, one Roman, one Irish, one Roman, one Irish. So even at this stage, three or four generations after Bede's death, it was still necessary to maintain balance between the two parties when carving a royal cross.

So despite his original sponsor's probable wish, Bede maintained a balance between the Roman and Irish streams of Christianity, seeking to foster the rapprochement that was developing between them rather than subsuming one beneath the other. Bede was further encouraged in this approach by an unexpected consequence of his request for further information from Albinus.

As mentioned above, Albinus put a great deal of effort into providing the material necessary for Bede to write his *History*. When

Bede requested further information after sifting through the original tranche of material, Albinus went so far as to send his aide, Nothhelm, to Rome to conduct research in the papal archives. Among the material that Nothhelm unearthed and brought back to Canterbury were copies of the original letters that Pope Gregory had sent to Augustine, giving advice and setting out Gregory's aims for the mission.

It must have been a shock for Nothhelm, as he read the letter, to see that far from Pope Gregory giving the whole of Britain to the guidance of Canterbury, his original plan was for there to be two archbishoprics, one based in Londinium, the capital of Britannia Superior, and the other in Eboracum (York), the capital of Britannia Inferior. It is to the credit of Nothhelm, when he first read the letter, and to Albinus, when he read the copy Nothhelm brought back to Canterbury, that neither attempted to suppress its contents. For in a sentence Gregory's letter undercut their justification for the supremacy of Canterbury. An archbishop in York would be of equal rank to the archbishop in Canterbury; he would necessarily command the Church in the north of the country, leaving Canterbury with the south.

Canterbury's policy, which it had followed unswervingly since Theodore's arrival in 668, was undone. In 735, the year of Bede's death, Ecgbert, the bishop of York, was made into an archbishop – in the very same year that Nothhelm himself became archbishop of Canterbury.

It's a testament to Albinus and Nothhelm that, despite what must have been their shock and disappointment in reading Gregory's plans for the Church, they did not try to hide what the letter said. Instead, Nothhelm travelled up to Jarrow with the copies he had made and gave them to Bede, who incorporated their text into the evolving framework of his *History*. With Gregory's letters now copied into his *History*, Bede had proof that Canterbury's claims were overstated. The Church in Britain would have two centres of power, in the north as well as the south. York was, of course, one of the key centres of Bede's own Northumbria. Ever the advocate for his own people, Bede must have been delighted to have their status receive such a boost from the pope.

Canterbury's downgrade led to other changes. While Albinus had been the first sponsor of Bede's *History*, by the time the book was nearing completion his place had been taken by the king of Northumbria, Ceolwulf. What's more, Ceolwulf was no hands-off sponsor but an active partner in the book's final editing prior to its completion. In his preface, which begins by dedicating the book to King Ceolwulf, Bede says that he had sent an earlier draft of the work to the king for him to read and comment upon, and that he was now sending him the final version having incorporated into the book the king's suggestions. This indicates that Ceolwulf was alive to the implications of writing history and wanted to ensure that it addressed some of the matters that were of concern to him.

Unfortunately, Bede does not extend his book as far as Ceolwulf's reign, which began in 729, and our other sources for him are very thin. What we do know can be boiled down to a short paragraph.

Having come to the throne in 729, Ceolwulf was deposed in 731, tonsured and forced into a monastery by parties unknown. However, he was restored to the throne later the same year and reigned until 737, when he abdicated the throne to his cousin, Eadberht, and entered the monastery at Lindisfarne, remaining there until his death in 765.

Given this chronology, it's noteworthy that Bede gives the turbulent year of 731 as the year he finished writing the *Ecclesiastical History*. Placing its completion then suggests his support for the king.

The chronicle from which we hear about Ceolwulf's deposition and return goes on to laconically record that Bishop Acca of Hexham was expelled from his see. It's hard not to see the two events as related, and that Bishop Acca had played a part or supported the failed coup against the king.

Bishop Acca had been an important figure in Bede's life and work. As bishop of Hexham, he was the diocesan bishop of Bede's monastery, and Bede wrote several works in response to queries from Acca.

They evidently had enjoyed a long and close relationship, with Bede likely making use of the extensive library at Hexham. But despite these years of collaboration, Bede omitted all mention of Acca from the preface to the *History*.

Hexham was founded by Wilfrid. Its monastery was a key centre of his cult, and Acca himself had been a pupil of Wilfrid. Acca's expulsion meant the removal of the chief remaining proponent for an exclusively 'Roman' and Wilfridian view of the history of the Church. In contrast, Ceolwulf clearly had close links with Lindisfarne, since it was to there that he withdrew for the final 30 years of his life. With Acca gone and a king keen to support a history of the Church that gave greater credit to Irish influence, Bede had a sponsor who favoured the blended view of history that he himself preferred.

That's not to say that Bede wrote to order. But his books were aimed at their sponsors rather than their readers. The changing ecclesiastical and political circumstances through the long writing process of the *Ecclesiastical History* meant that Bede's aims in writing it shifted throughout its gestation. These changes mean that no single purpose is discernible in the book because the book's purpose changed during its writing. While this meant that Bede had to rewrite and revise it many times, it produced a book of many aims and purposes that has proved impossible to pigeonhole. Indeed, its long writing history served to ensure that the book became in itself a mosaic of the shifting tensions within the Church in Britain, held together in almost perfect literary symmetry by Bede's supreme talent as a writer and historian.

Bede did not start writing the *Ecclesiastical History of the English People* with the aim of it becoming his masterpiece, but its long writing, the input it received from so many different people and places, and the time and effort Bede expended writing it served to turn it into his testament. Indeed, the way that Bede writes about himself and lists his other works at the book's end indicates that he himself saw it as the culmination of his life's work. By including his own bibliography in the *History*, he was also preserving the rest of his work while laying modest claim to the book which the reader had just finished reading.

The preface, coming at the start of the book, was probably the last part of it that Bede wrote. At the end of the preface, Bede reached out to his contemporaries and to posterity, asking for their prayers and intercession. Few men have so deserved them, from his own time and from a future he could have never imagined.

## CHAPTER 15

# The Invention of England

We know more, and in more detail, about Bede's death than any part of his life. We know when he died and where he died and how he died. We know what he was doing in the weeks before he died and much of what he said to his brethren in his final days and hours. We know all this because a fellow monk and pupil of Bede's, Cuthbert by name, undertook to write an account of his death in a letter to another monk, named Cuthwin. It turned out that not just Cuthwin wanted to learn about the manner of Bede's passing from this life: there are 65 surviving manuscripts describing it.

The death scene was an important part of medieval hagiography. Indeed, sometimes, as in this case, the saint's death was written up independently of his life. Cuthbert says at the end of his letter that he intended to write an account of Bede's life later but if he ever did, it has not survived. As Cuthbert later became the abbot of Wearmouth and Jarrow, he may simply not have had the time necessary to devote to the task.

As Cuthbert notes many times in his letter, he was one of Bede's pupils and, at the time of Bede's death, he was still being taught by Bede. No doubt his master would have been gratified to read Cuthbert's work because it evinces the same mastery of Latin, and the various literary techniques employed in the Bible, as Bede's own work. By the pupil's work we can see that Bede really was an excellent teacher.

When establishing the cult of a saint, the manner of his or her passing was important. For Bede, the lifelong monk and scholar, there could be no bloody martyrdom – although if he had lived a century later, he would have had that opportunity. But the manner of the death was still important. No true saint could die in fear and doubt: even when in pain, he must die in joy and anticipation, or no true saint he. Since relatively few people sit with someone dying today, I should add that dying with joy is by no means impossible. A member of our church choir was diagnosed with liver cancer. She was a spinster, living alone, but her fellow choristers and parish priest visited her regularly through her final weeks – her decline was swift, from singing in the choir to too weak to move within six weeks. On the morning of her death, the priest visited her to administer the last rites, for her end was near.

While the priest was anointing her with oil, Maureen whispered to the priest, 'It's not long now, is it?'

Father David, realising she wanted to hear the truth, confirmed that it wasn't. The nurse looking after her, an experienced palliative care nurse, had confirmed that Maureen had at most a day or two to live.

Maureen looked at Father David. 'I can't wait.'

So the accounts in medieval hagiographies of saints accepting their approaching death with joy are not, in principle, far-fetched.

Cuthbert tells us that Bede had been ill for a while, in particular suffering from breathlessness. However, the worst symptoms of his illness improved two weeks before Easter 735 and Bede continued, weak but able to work, until the feast of the Ascension on 26 May. He carried on teaching his pupils, Cuthbert among them, and singing the Office as well as he could manage. He generally prayed through most of the night, too, frequently quoting a line from the Letter to the Hebrews – 'It is a fearful thing to fall into the hands of the living God' – and taking only short sleeps. Bede knew his time was near. The urgency of repentance was clear to him in a way that it is difficult for the hale to share, but he sought to remind his brethren that the day of their own deaths would surely come, soon or late. To drive this point home, Cuthbert writes that Bede composed a poem in English, saying:

> Before that enforced journey no one becomes
> Wiser in thought than he may need be,
> For considering his going hence
> What for his spirit of good and evil
> After his death day might be judged.

In another valuable insight into Bede's attitude towards his native language, Cuthbert notes in an aside that he gave them this poem 'in our own language (as he knew our poems well)'.

As a final summation of Bede's life and work, he would also sing this antiphon, often lingering over and repeating the third line:

> O king of Glory, lord of Might,
> Who rose today in victory above all the heavens,
> Do not leave us orphans,
> But send us the Father's promised Spirit of Truth.
> Alleluia!

During these final sufferings, Bede's attitude encompassed both poles of Christian thoughts on coping with pain and death. He accepted the pain as a share of Christ's suffering and a promise of future vindication, for as he told his brethren, 'God chastises every son whom he receives.' But he also affirmed that he was at peace with his conscience, quoting the words of St Ambrose: 'I have not lived in such a way that I am ashamed to continue life among you, but I do not fear to die, because we have a uniquely good God.'

Apart from teaching, Bede continued writing through to the end of his life. In his final months he was engaged on a unique task: the translation of the Gospel of St John into English. Bede had become increasingly concerned about the paucity of priests sufficiently versed in Latin to be able to understand the Bible and explain it to the people. He had already made a translation of the Our Father into Old English so that those priests who knew only enough Latin to muddle through a mass could at least recite the prayer that Jesus had taught his disciples, in a language that they and their people understood. But evidently he had come to the conclusion that more needed to be rendered into English, so even as he was struggling towards death he dictated his translation of the Gospel to his scribe, a young boy, presumably an oblate as he had been himself, named Wihtberht. Sadly, this is one work of Bede that did not survive, for it would have been the oldest substantial Old English text we have.

Underlining Bede's commitment as a teacher and scholar, the other task he continued until the end was his revision of a work by Isidore of Seville. Isidore (c.560–636) wrote a summa of knowledge, his *De natura rerum*, which Bede used a great deal but of which he became increasingly critical. So rather than have his own students labour through the *De natura* trying to work out which bits were right, Bede compiled a digest of the best bits, leaving out everything he had decided was wrong. As he said, 'I do not wish my students to read lies, or to work at this task in vain after my death.'

Bede continued teaching and working, even though his breathing became markedly more laboured, and on Tuesday 24 May he told his pupils, 'Learn quickly now, for I do not know how long I shall live.' On the next day, when a pupil pointed out that there was a chapter missing from the book he was dictating, Bede had him scribe while he dictated the missing chapter. This was presumably his edition of Isidore, for we learn later that he was still working on the translation of John's Gospel.

At the ninth hour of the Wednesday, which is about 3 p.m., Bede said to Cuthbert, 'I have a few treasures in my little box: pepper, handkerchiefs and incense. Run quickly and fetch the priests of our monastery to me, so that I can distribute to them these little gifts which God has given me.' Pepper was a valuable gift at a time when few other spices were available, although the monastery gardens made much use of herbs.

After Bede distributed these gifts to his priestly brethren, amid promises of prayers for the repose of his soul, Cuthbert records him as making his final speech. As given, it is full of allusions and quotations from the Bible. It might be doubted that a man labouring to breathe could say anything so elaborate, and Cuthbert might have tidied up the speech for his account, but Bede was so steeped in the language of the Bible there's little reason to doubt that, as he approached his end, its words would have supplanted his own.

'It is time, if it should so please my Maker, that I should be released from the body and come now to Him who formed me from nothing when I did not exist. I have lived a long time and the Holy Judge has provided well for me my whole life. The time of my release is near; indeed my soul longs to see Christ my king in all his beauty.'

But, as it turned out, it was not yet quite time for Bede to depart. For the boy, Wihtberht, Bede's scribe for his translation of John's Gospel into English, spoke, saying, 'Beloved master, there is still one sentence left, not yet written down.' So Bede told him to write it and, when he had, Bede said, 'Good. It is finished.'

His life very nearly was. Bede asked for his head to be raised so that he could see the place where he used to pray. From Rosemary Cramp's excavations at Jarrow, we have a good idea of where he was and what it was like. Bede's room was small, roughly ten feet square, with a low screen made from wood separating the sleeping area, where Bede was lying, from the prayer space. Presumably Bede had one or two religious items in the prayer space, perhaps a picture or a psalter or a Gospel book. With his head lifted he could see into that place where he had spent many hours praying and thinking.

According to Cuthbert, these were Bede's last words on this earth: 'Take my head in your hands, for it pleases me very much to sit opposite my holy place where I used to pray, so that as I sit I may call upon my Father.' This was followed by a doxology, a short phrase of praise to God: 'Glory be to the Father, and to the Son, and to the Holy Spirit.' Then Bede died.

It was Thursday 26 May 735, Ascension Day, the feast in the Church's calendar that commemorates Jesus's return to heaven. A fitting day for Bede to die. He was 64 or 65 years old – a good age certainly but not that old for a man who is invariably thought of as hoary with age at death.

Unlike other accounts of saints' ends, Cuthbert does not follow Bede's dying with spectacular healings or other miracles; instead merely saying that the people present at his end agreed that they had never seen anyone else die at such peace and with such devotion.

Cuthbert finishes his account with the promise to write more about Bede's life but either he never wrote his proposed life or it did not survive – much was lost from the library at Wearmouth and Jarrow when the Vikings attacked the monastery in 794, the year after the attack on Lindisfarne. We don't have anything more than an outline of the attack, but given their normal modus operandi, the Northmen stole anything that was valuable, which would have included books bound with precious metal hasps and inlaid with jewels, as well as taking prisoners to be sold as slaves. Indeed, it's now clear that the taking and selling of slaves was the single largest economic driver to Viking raiding. Those monks at Wearmouth and Jarrow who were not dead or fled were driven onto the drakkar, there to have the iron rings of slavery bound around neck and ankle. Archaeologists have uncovered such iron shackles in Sweden, Germany and Denmark. It took only a few boatloads of armed men to leave the civilisation that had been so painstakingly built up over the previous century tottering. Civilisations require many supporting elements, any one of which can be destroyed with relative ease. Degrade enough of them and the civilisation will disintegrate.

\*

Bede did not live to see his brethren lying dead in the choir and church. Between his death and the first Viking raid in 793 there was a period of relative peace in Northumbria, when missionaries set out from Britain to cross the North Sea to take the new religion their parents and grandparents had embraced so enthusiastically to their still pagan cousins in the Low Countries, Frisia and Germany. It was through this missionary activity that we have some of the letters Cuthbert wrote after becoming abbot of Wearmouth and Jarrow. Writing to Lul, archbishop of Mainz, in 764, Cuthbert thanked him for the gifts he had received from Lul to clothe the relics of Bede that they had at the monastery: 'And indeed it seems right to me, that the whole race of the English in all provinces wherever they are found, should give thanks to God, that he has granted to them so wonderful a man in their nation, endowed with diverse gifts, and so assiduous in the exercise of those gifts, and likewise living a good life; for I, reared at his feet, have learned by experience this which I relate.'

Such was Bede's renown by the time of this exchange of letters that Cuthbert had to excuse his monastery for not sending more of Bede's works to Archbishop Lul:

> Now truly, since you have asked for some of the works of the blessed father, for your love I have prepared what I could, with my pupils, according to our capacity. I have sent in accordance with your wishes the books about the man of God, Cuthbert, [the archbishop had asked for a copy of Bede's *Life of St Cuthbert*] composed in verse and prose. And if I could have done more, I would have gladly done so. For the conditions of the past winter oppressed the island of our race very horribly with cold and ice and long and widespread storms of wind and rain, so that the hand of the scribe was hindered from producing a great number of books.

Writing to Archbishop Lul 29 years after Bede's death, we see that Cuthbert refers to the 'whole race of the English in all provinces wherever they are found' and the 'island of our race'. These are expansive terms, apparently taking in all the English. Scholars have argued long about what is meant by 'race', and it is certainly true that it carries different connotations today than it would have done in the eighth century, when Cuthbert wrote his letter. But it's also clear that Cuthbert ties the 'whole race of the English' to Bede, 'so wonderful a man in their nation'. For it was Bede who invented the idea of the English as a people and set the framework for England as their home.

To comprehend how and why he did this, we have to look at the world he wrote about. Bede sets his understanding of it out clearly in the first chapter of the *Ecclesiastical History*. After reviewing the physical geography of Britain, he goes on to its human geography: 'At the present time, there are five languages in Britain, just as the divine law is written in five books, all devoted to seeking out and setting forth one and the same kind of wisdom, namely the knowledge of sublime truth and of true sublimity. These are the English, British, Irish, Pictish, as well as the Latin languages; through the study of the scriptures, Latin is in general use among them all.'

It's important to note how Bede reads the historical situation of Britain in the same way that he understands scripture, applying the four tools of understanding the Bible – the literal, allegorical, moral and eschatological – to his understanding of the 'why' of the history he was setting out to relate in his book. For Bede understood history as fundamentally teleological: it had a point and a destination; it told a coherent story of salvation, with people and nations and events – and God – as the actors in the story. In this, the Jewish and Christian idea of history was very different from the cyclical view that dominated the ancient world.

By viewing the five languages and four nations of Britain through a prism of Biblical metaphor, Bede put them implicitly into the same story that runs through the Bible. While Bede was all too aware how late his people had come to knowledge of Christ, and how far away they were from the land in which Jesus had walked and taught, by fitting them into the story of the Bible he was bringing them out of the dark and into the story.

The other point to note is that Bede calls his own people, the ones who share his language, the English. This seems obvious. What else was he going to call them? But the people to whom the 'English' had first become known had called them by a different name.

Stretching from Norfolk, round Essex, around Kent and then on along the Sussex and Hampshire coasts there are a string of Roman forts which were built in the late third century. They include the forts at Reculver and Richborough in Kent that guarded the two entrances to the Wantsum Channel between the Isle of Thanet and the mainland, as well as Burgh Castle in Norfolk and Pevensey Castle in Sussex.

Across the Channel there was a matching line of forts stretching from near Calais in the east all the way along northern Gaul to the tip of Brittany. According to the *Notitia Dignitatum*, a document describing the official positions of the Roman Empire, the line of forts was under the command of the *Comes Litoris Saxonici per Britanniam* (Count of the Saxon Shore in Britain). There is some disagreement among scholars as to whether the count in command of the Saxon Shore was defending it from Saxon invaders or using Saxon mercenaries to man the forts under his command, but for our purposes the key point is that these Germanic peoples were known as Saxons.

We now come to that obscure period in British history, the 200 years between the Romans leaving in around 410 and Augustine arriving in Kent in 597. But Bede was writing a century and more after these events, so what is important is what he *thought* happened then, rather than what actually did happen during the *adventus Saxonum*.

Bede relates that the Angles and the Saxons were invited to Britain as mercenaries by a Britonnic king whom he calls Vortigern. He names the leaders of the mercenaries as Hengist and Horsa and tells how, as unreliable mercenaries, they turned on the people who had hired them and began carving out kingdoms of their own in this new land:

> They came from three very powerful Germanic tribes, the Saxons, Angles, and Jutes. The people of Kent and the inhabitants of the Isle of Wight are of Jutish origin and also those opposite the Isle of Wight, that part of the kingdom of Wessex which is still today called the nation of the Jutes. From the Saxon country, that is, the district now known as Old Saxony, came the East Saxons, the South Saxons, and the West Saxons. Besides this, from the country of the Angles, that is, the land between the kingdoms of the Jutes and the

Saxons, which is called Angulus, came the East Angles, the Middle Angles, the Mercians, and all the Northumbrian race (that is those people who dwell north of the river Humber) as well as the other Anglian tribes. Angulus is said to have remained deserted from that day to this.

Bede told the story of his people as one of migration, of their ancestors taking ship across the North Sea, leaving their native land unpopulated to his own day, and coming to Britain.

Now the question arises as to where Bede got this information from. One source was undoubtedly the Britonnic monk, Gildas. In the library at Jarrow was a copy of his book, *De Excidio et Conquestu Britanniae* (*On the Ruin and Conquest of Britain*). In the most frustrating book ever written, Gildas launches an unbridled jeremiad against the Britonnic kings and clerics of his time, proclaiming that the tribulations visited upon the Britons in the hairy shape of the Saxons was down to the sins of their own kings and the mendacity of their priests. Part III of *De Excidio*, which concerns the clergy, memorably says, 'Britain has priests, but they are fools; numerous ministers, but they are shameless; clerics, but they are wily plunderers.'[1]

However, all peoples throughout history have been concerned with understanding and remembering their origins. We want to know, and to pass on to our children, the tale of our beginnings. So there's every reason to think that the Anglo-Saxons had stories of their own origin that Bede would have heard and known well. As Cuthbert said, concerning Bede's knowledge of the oral culture of his people, 'he knew our poems well'.

While Gildas wrote *De Excidio* in excellent Latin, his everyday language was probably one of the rapidly dividing forms of Britonnic that was evolving into Welsh. Elsewhere, Britonnic was becoming Old Cornish and Old Breton. When he talked about the invaders in the vernacular, he used a name for them that has come into modern Welsh as *Saesneg*. *Saesneg* now means English, but it derives from Saxon. Scottish Gaelic, which also evolved from Britonnic, calls the

English *Sasannach*, another word derived from Saxon. In Breton the English are *Saoz*, in Cornish *Sowsnek*.

To the other peoples of Britain, the incomers were Saxons not Angles. So why do the English call themselves 'English' and not 'Saxons'? (If they had named themselves after the Saxons, then one must presume, working from place names derived from Saxon settlers such as Essex and Sussex, that their kingdom would have been called the land of the Saxons, or Sexland.)

We will put that question to the side for the moment and return to it later. When reading Gildas's *De Excidio*, Bede could hardly have failed to appreciate the point that Gildas set out to make when writing the book: that the disasters that had befallen the Britons were due to their moral and spiritual failures. The Saxons coming over the sea and taking their land was, according to Gildas, God's punishment for their sins. In this, Gildas was reading the Bible, and particularly the Old Testament, onto the history of his own people. For much of the Old Testament can be read as the story of God's covenant with his chosen people, their failure to live up to the terms of the covenant, and the consequences following from that failure. Those consequences usually involved invasions, defeats in battle and, finally, deportation to Babylon and slavery, before the slow return to the Holy Land and the rebuilding of the Temple.

Bede also had copies of the books of the Jewish historian Josephus in the library at the twin monastery, so he knew what had happened to the Jewish people in the century after Christ. In particular, he knew the history of the first Jewish-Roman war, that had ended with the destruction of the Temple in Jerusalem in AD 70. From Eusebius's *History of the Church*, Bede further learnt the devastating consequences of the Bar Kokhba revolt between 132 and 136. The Romans, under Emperor Hadrian, responded with their customary military brutality to rebellion. The Jewish rebels were crushed, although it took six legions to break the revolt. The rebels taken prisoner were crucified. The rural population of Judaea either fled or died. Determined to finally crush this stiff-necked people and to wipe them from their own memory, Hadrian ordered the name of the province changed from Judaea to Syria Palestina, while Jews were forbidden to even set foot in Jerusalem. The Jews who survived dispersed, creating scattered communities throughout the Roman Empire and beyond, communities based upon worship in the synagogue rather than the now destroyed Temple in a city they could not visit.

Furthermore, from his reading of many of the commentaries written by the Church Fathers on the Bible, Bede also knew that there was a strand of thinking among Christians that explained the disasters that had befallen the Jewish people in the century following Christ as God's punishment for their refusal to accept Jesus as the promised Messiah. This strand of Christian/Jewish polemic, deriving from a time when both sects were subject to Imperial persecution, would go on to have disastrous consequences when Christianity became the major religion of the new European countries. The internal quarrel of what was, at the start, two Jewish sects led finally to the growth of Christian anti-Semitism, culminating in the Holocaust.

The bitter rows between Jews and Christians during the first centuries were made more bitter by the fact that many of the early Christians were Jews. While this is obviously so in the era of the Acts of the Apostles, recent statistical work on the spread of Christianity through the Roman Empire in the first four centuries show that a relatively high percentage of the Jewish population among the diaspora did become Christian in the century following the life of Jesus. Suffering the trauma of the Roman response to the Bar Kokhba revolt, with Jews banned from Jerusalem, the conversion of many Jews to Christianity must have seemed like the greatest of betrayals. No wonder that the polemic, on both sides, became so bitter.

Some Christian apologists began to argue that the disasters that had befallen the Jews were directly caused by their refusal to accept Jesus as the Messiah and, working on from that, these commentators proposed that the disasters showed that God had abrogated his covenant with the Jewish people, transferring it to the Christian Church. Thus the Church was the new chosen people while the Jews were forsaken by God and thus, by implication, could be persecuted by the secular authorities. Of course, this had little application in the first few centuries when Christians were themselves persecuted by the state, but when Christianity became the religion of the empire and then of the successor states of Europe, it would produce bitter fruit.

Of course, there were no Jews in the Britain of the eighth century when Bede started writing his *Ecclesiastical History of the English People*. But there were Britons, Picts, Irish and English. Bede appears to define a nation or people by its language. Thus, while Bede writes of the Angles, Saxons and Jutes as having distinct origins, he labels each of them as one people because of their different languages.

This probably goes some way to explaining why the English are called 'English' and not Saxon. If the common language spoken by Angle, Saxon and Jute was known from their arrival in Britain as English, then it would become a synonym for the people speaking the language, even if they had different origins. Unfortunately, we don't have any examples of Old English from the fifth and sixth centuries to know whether English was indeed the common name for the language spoken by the various tribes of newcomers.

Once we do start seeing written examples of Old English, it is clear that there were strong regional dialects. It is not clear whether all these dialects went under the general name of 'English'. However, language was also the clearest marker between the different tribes inhabiting Britain, although there were other signs in terms of dress, weapons, jewellery and adornment. But language was the clearest marker of all. So Bede classifies the peoples of Britain by language, naming them for their tongues.

*

When trying to understand the history of his people in Britain, there was another strand of the story of the Jewish people for Bede to consider: the Exodus and their arrival and conquest of the promised land.

According to the Pentateuch, God promised to Abraham and his descendants the land of Israel, which they took. But they were still a wandering, pastoral people and when drought and famine struck the land in the time of Joseph they sought refuge in Egypt, where through Joseph's influence with the Pharaoh they found shelter and a new home. However, they became an overly powerful minority within Egypt, leading to their enslavement. Then a leader arose, Moses, a Jew although one raised in the pharaoh's court. Moses led the Jews from Egypt amid signs and wonders and into the desert. The deliverance from bondage in Egypt remains one of the key festivals of the Jewish year, celebrated each year at Passover. Moses led the Jewish people through the wilderness for 40 years before arriving at the promised land. While Moses died before he could set foot in the promised land, Joshua, his successor, was commanded to destroy and drive out the peoples who had settled there during the Jews' exile in Egypt: 'When the LORD your God brings you into the land you are entering to possess and drives out before you many nations – the Hittites, Girgashites, Amorites, Canaanites, Perizzites, Hivites and Jebusites, seven nations larger and stronger than you – and when the Lord your God has delivered them over to you and you have defeated them, then you must destroy them totally. Make no treaty with them, and show them no mercy' (Deuteronomy 7:1–3).

A few verses later, the text goes on to say: 'For you are a people holy to the LORD your God. The Lord your God has chosen you out of all the peoples on the face of the earth to be his people, his treasured possession. The Lord did not set his affection on you and choose you because you were more numerous than other peoples, for you were the fewest of all peoples. But it was because the Lord loved you . . .' (Deuteronomy 7:6–7).

The Jews had gone to the promised land, driven out or killed its inhabitants, and settled it as God's chosen people. Bede's own people had arrived in Britain, driven out or killed the original inhabitants, and established their own kingdoms there. The parallels were obvious but so were the differences: Bede's ancestors had been thoroughgoing pagans who had driven out the Christian Britons. On the surface, the story of Britain read more like the Jews being driven out of the promised land by pagan invaders. But then . . .

The Jews had been defeated and taken into captivity in Babylon by King Nebuchadnezzar when their failure to keep their part of the covenant finally drew forth retribution. God had used pagans as a punishment to the Jews to fulfil his purposes. In *De Excidio*, Gildas wrote that the disaster that had befallen the Britons was due to their sins – and this disaster was the arrival of the ancestors of Bede's own people. The Angles and the Saxons had left their land and made a perilous journey across the desert of the sea to a new land, a land of promise, and there defeated its inhabitants and secured kingdoms of their own.

The pieces were beginning to slot into place. Bede's people, his own folk, were a new chosen people come into a new land at the edge of the world.

But an implication of this idea was that Bede's people had to be one people, not two (Angles and Saxons) or three (and Jutes) or, as was actually the case on the ground, even more (Mercians, Bernicians, Deirans, West Saxons, East Saxons, East Angles and so on). In fact, the great majority of people probably had distinctly local and tribal identities. We can see traces of these in hints towards the smaller tribal groups that first established themselves in different parts of the country, such as the Magonsæte around Hereford and the Gewisse in the Thames valley around Dorchester on Thames. There are many more of these, with no doubt even more completely lost to history. So if you were to ask someone of the time who they were, the answer would have been their name, their immediate kin, and then their local clan/tribe. If they should also answer that they were an Angle or a Saxon, it would come a long way down the list.

By writing an *Ecclesiastical History of the English People*, Bede was asserting that all these varied tribes and clans, speaking dialects that in some cases verged on mutually unintelligible, and who fought each other as incessantly as they fought the Britonnic kingdoms, were in fact one people rather than a mess of warring groups whose only common characteristic was a language that they roughly shared. It was an assertion that, at the time, would have surprised most of the English people Bede was writing about. After all, even in Bede's own *History* we have examples of Britonnic and Anglo-Saxon king-doms allying together, such as Cadwallon's Gwynedd and Penda's Mercia, to attack a common enemy, and there were likely many more such temporary alliances that did not make their way into his *History* because they did not affect the ecclesiastical history of the country. Nevertheless, by setting out his book as a history of a people, Bede stated in writing an idea that was implied by language and history, even while it was obscured by different local realities. And ideas, once formulated, can take on a vivacity of their own, growing and spreading as they meet and answer questions of identity that were increasingly posed as the different kingdoms of seventh- and eighth-century Britain strove to grow and organise themselves.

However, to fit the English people into the narrative of a chosen people claiming a new land as their own, there was one further problem that Bede had to solve. And it was a major difficulty. For when the Anglo-Saxons expanded their control at the expense of the Britons, they were pagans and the Britons were Christians. On the face of it, the result should have been the other way round, if God was acting to help his people. By rights, the Christian Britons should have defeated the pagans and chased them back into the sea to drown.

Bede found the answer to that in Gildas. It's one of history's ironies that as fierce a defender of his own people as Gildas should find his work pressed into service as a justification for their conquest by the Anglo-Saxons. For if Gildas was right, and the Britons had been subjected to the disaster of the *adventus Saxonum* as a result of their sins, then the pagan Anglo-Saxons were doing God's work, as his scourge and his rod.

But what if the sins of the Britons were such that their own covenant with God as holders of the land by virtue of their faith was rendered forfeit? Then there would be justification, divine justification, for the Anglo-Saxons taking the land from the Britons. It would chime with the covenant, once with the Jews, now resting upon the Church.

However, when it came to justifying such a conclusion, Gildas proved as frustrating to Bede as to later historians: he launches jeremiads against contemporary rulers, likening five kings to the ravening beasts mentioned in the books of Daniel and Revelation, the most apocalyptic in the Bible, but he does not actually say what these kings did that was so bad. Similarly, the final part of Gildas's book excoriates the clergy but does not name any of them, again leaving the accusations vague. Not enough to base an idea of covenantal substitution upon.

But when moving closer to his own time, Bede had other sources. In particular, he knew and corresponded with Nothhelm, the monk in Canterbury who became archbishop in 735. As we've already seen, Nothhelm had access to the records kept in Canterbury of the mission of Augustine, as well as the traditions that had been handed on in story, tale and anecdote down the generations. Nothhelm also visited Rome and, from the papal archive, copied down the texts of the letters sent by Pope Gregory to Augustine.

From these archives, Bede read a history of conflict between the Augustinian mission, dispatched from Rome itself, and the local Britonnic clergy. This chimed all too well with his own experience: while the southern Irish and the monks of Lindisfarne had accepted unity in their celebrations of Easter, and Iona itself came over to Rome in 716, the Britonnic clergy refused to change their ways until 768, long after Bede's death. Coupled with this, there was the language barrier between the Church that ministered to the Britons and the Church that ministered to the Anglo-Saxons: while they shared the same liturgical language, their everyday languages were mutually unintelligible. And while there were sometimes alliances between Britonnic and Anglo-Saxon kingdoms, the more usual relationship between them was warfare or suspicious truce.

The Church in Britain had been established during Roman rule. While we cannot say what proportion of the population had become Christian by the end of Roman rule, or whether this was a largely urban class of believers or if the new religion had penetrated deeply into the countryside, during the obscure fifth and sixth centuries the religious difference seems to have become accentuated by the conflict between the Britons and the Anglo-Saxons. The Anglo-Saxons were pagans. Those Britonnic families who were not Christian beforehand slowly became Christian during the following centuries so that by Bede's time the vast majority – perhaps even all – of the Britons were Christian. What's more, the tradition of Classical education continued among the Britons for more than a century after the end of Roman rule, for Gildas wrote elegant Latin. Indeed, the conflict was not just Christian Britons versus pagan Anglo-Saxons but also Britons who considered themselves still Romans against the barbarians.

Here I must put in a caveat: this is an oversimplification. Conflict was local, one warlord against another, with war resulting from personal rivalries and territorial clashes as much as anything else, and in these small-scale wars the enemy of my enemy was my friend, even if he spoke a different language. These were the gold-and-garnet everyday battles of the time, the vast majority of them forgotten by the time the slain had mouldered in their graves. Nevertheless, with the evidence provided by ancient DNA, we do have grounds for thinking that the old idea of an overarching conflict between Britons and Anglo-Saxons had some reality on the ground during these centuries.

In his *History*, Bede also goes back to Britain under Roman rule, long before there was any significant Anglo-Saxon population on the island. From his reading of the Church Fathers, he knew well the most infamous of Britonnic clerics, Pelagius (c.354–418). Pelagius gave personal testimony to the excellence of the education still available in Britain in the later fourth century, despite the general chaos of the time, for aside from his wide knowledge of theology he was also fluent in Greek as well as Latin. Pelagius travelled to Rome about 380, where he started teaching. As his views became better known, he and his followers came into conflict with men such as Augustine and Jerome. They denounced him for teaching that, since everything God made was good, then men could choose to follow God's commandments of their own free will, without need of divine grace. Augustine denounced his views and they were condemned – although modern scholarship suggests quite plausibly that Pelagius was misrepresented by his enemies – and Pelagius himself disappeared from history. However, his teachings continued to be followed in Britain for a while, and Bede records the visit of a bishop from Gaul, Germanus, to Britain in 429 to combat the teachings of the Pelagians. By recording these events, Bede was pointing out that the Church in Britain had something of a history of accepting heretical teachings, requiring visits from abroad to bring it into line with the wider Church.

Even after Pelagianism was defeated in Britain, Bede states that the Church there remained guilty of one great omission: 'To other unspeakable crimes, which Gildas, their own historian, describes in doleful words, was added this crime, that they never preached the faith to the Saxons or Angles who inhabited Britain with them.'

When Augustine arrived in Britain, he brought with him Pope Gregory's plan for the Church there. Gregory envisaged a Church hierarchy based on the old Roman dioceses, with one archbishop in London, the civilian centre of Britannia, and the other in York, the city of the legions in the north. However, when Augustine arrived in Britain, the situation on the ground did not match Gregory's plan: London was an abandoned ruin rather than the capital and he himself found a hearing and protection from the king of Kent, who had no intention of seeing his priest relocate to a part of the country outside his control. So Augustine set up as bishop of Canterbury, which is why Canterbury remains the chief episcopal see in England to this day.

While Augustine had considerable success in converting the pagans of Kent to Christianity, he and his men also started making contacts with the Christian Britonnic clergy. While it's wrong to think that the Britonnic Church was entirely isolated from the rest of the Church, its normal lines of communication followed the old sea lanes that ran from south-western Britain to Brittany to Galicia in north-western Spain, allowing for little contact with the Church in Rome or the East. Under attack from the pagan Anglo-Saxons, the Church in Britain became fiercely resistant to outside pressure, whether it came from the new kingdoms or from a new bishop claiming to have arrived in Britain with the authority of the pope behind him.

Augustine, however, had received the pallium, the mark of his episcopal authority, from Gregory and was all too aware of the dignity due to his office. Bede records that he summoned the bishops of the Britonnic Church to a meeting at a place later called Augustine's Oak, on the boundary of the territories of the West Saxons and the Hwicce, in what is modern-day Gloucestershire. The location is interesting as the Hwicce appear to have been converted by Irish or Britonnic Christians, rather than the Augustinian mission. It's unclear whether Bede was aware of this – he notably fails to mention any missionary activity of the Britonnic Church towards the Anglo-Saxons – or whether he suppressed the information as contrary to his narrative. If the Hwicce had become Christian through the missionary activity of Britonnic Christians, it makes the site of the proposed meeting between Augustine and the representatives of the Britonnic Church a place where both sides could meet in relative safety.

According to Bede, this first meeting was long, argumentative and without fruit of agreement, with the main sticking point being the dating of Easter. A frustrated Augustine then brought the meeting to a halt by saying that, if they could not come to agreement themselves, then they should let God decide: whichever side could show, by divine sign, that they were right, then the other should follow. It was basically a miracle contest. A blind Angle was brought into the assembly and the Britonnic priests prayed over him to no effect. However, when Augustine knelt and prayed for his healing, the man's sight was restored to him. Despite this sign, the Britonnic clergy cavilled, saying that they needed to consult further about such changes to their ancient practices and asked for a second meeting, to which Augustine agreed.

This is all very laudatory of Augustine and his clergy: exactly the sort of story that would be preserved and passed into the future for Nothhelm to relay to Bede. But what is particularly interesting is the next part of the story, for it casts Augustine in a far less favourable light.

The story goes that, before the next meeting with Augustine, the Britonnic bishops who were to attend it went to consult a holy and venerable hermit, to ask what they should do. The hermit told them that if Augustine was a man of God, then they should follow him. The Britonnic bishops then asked how they could tell whether he was truly a man of God, whereupon the hermit told them that they would know Augustine was a man of God if he was meek and humble. When questioned how they could tell if Augustine was truly humble, the hermit replied, 'Contrive that he and his followers arrive first at the meeting place and, if he rises on your approach, you will know that he is a servant of Christ and will listen to him obediently; but if he despises you and is not willing to rise in your presence, even though your numbers are greater, you should despise him in return.'

The Britonnic bishops did as the hermit suggested and, sure enough, when they approached Augustine, he remained firmly seated. This got the conference off to a bad start and matters did not improve until finally Augustine issued an ultimatum, saying that he would accept their other divergent practices so long as they changed their calculation of Easter to the Roman method, baptised according to Church tradition (which should not have been a problem given the universality of the baptismal formula) and finally joined with Augustine in preaching to the Anglo-Saxons.

However, the Britonnic bishops refused the ultimatum, and likewise refused to accept Augustine's primacy over them as archbishop. Then Augustine prophesied to them: 'If they refused to accept peace from their brethren, they would have to accept war from their enemies; and if they would not preach the way of life to the English nation, they would one day suffer the vengeance of death at their hands.'

This is the story as Bede understood it and wanted to convey it to his readers. However, Richard Shaw has recently argued that there was only a single summit between Augustine and the Britonnic bishops but that Bede had two sources for this meeting. The first source was Canterbury, and Bede related it in his account of the first meeting. But the second source appears to have been Britonnic, for it carries the sort of details about the views and reactions of the Britonnic clergy that are found nowhere else in the *Ecclesiastical History*. Unable to reconcile the accounts, neither of which would have been dated, Bede decided that they described separate meetings. Presumably this Britonnic account was passed on to Bede by one of his normal sources, most likely Nothhelm, but we have no idea where Nothhelm got it from.[2]

And this was not the only Britonnic record to make its way into the *History*.

Immediately following this passage, Bede skips forward about twelve years to another battle of the Northumbrian king Æthelfrith. He was the most formidable warlord of his time and Bede had already introduced him a few chapters earlier in his history, writing of him:

> He ravaged the Britons more cruelly than all other English leaders, so that he might well be compared to Saul, the King of Israel, except of course that he was ignorant of true religion. He overran a greater area than any other king or ealdorman, exterminating or enslaving the inhabitants, making their lands either tributary to the English or ready for English settlement. One might fairly apply to him the words of the patriarch Jacob's blessing of his son: Benjamin shall ravin as a wolf; in the morning he shall devour the prey, and at night he shall divide the spoil.

Now, straight after stating Augustine's prophecy of the dire consequences that will follow from the Britons refusing to adopt the Roman method of calculating Easter and preaching to the Anglo-Saxons, Bede tells the story of the Battle of Chester, which probably took place around 615. Again, the details of this story suggest a Britonnic source, although we have no more idea of where Bede obtained this material than we have of where he learnt of the other account of the meeting between Augustine and the Britonnic clergy.

Æthelfrith, advancing from his northern heartlands, was driving down towards the territory of the Britonnic kingdoms of Powys and Gwynedd. To stop him, warriors of Powys, possibly with reinforcements from Gwynedd and Mercia, took up position near Chester. To support their warriors, a large contingent of monks from the monastery at Bangor had come to pray for victory. They had fasted for three days and, on the morn of the battle, they climbed up on a hill overlooking the battle plain to pray for victory. However, when Æthelfrith saw the monks on the hill he ordered his men to attack them first, since they were praying for his defeat. Exactly 1,200, a symbolic number of the monks, were killed before Æthelfrith turned his men on the enemy army, winning a decisive victory. 'Thus the prophecy of the holy Bishop Augustine was fulfilled, although he had long been translated to the heavenly kingdom, namely that those heretics would also suffer the vengeance of temporal death because they had despised the offer of everlasting salvation.'

So Bede had established, but without flat-out stating it, that the Britons, like ancient Israel, had forfeited their covenant with God and, as a result, had suffered justified divine punishment at the hands of his pagan ancestors who, like Babylon, had broken the Britons, driving them from their land or enslaving them. Similarly, he had set the framework for seeing the Anglo-Saxons as a new chosen people who had travelled to a strange land. There, they had been singled out by Pope Gregory as the object of the mission he dispatched to achieve their salvation.

After the trials and setbacks recorded in his history, the Anglo-Saxons had become Christian and, what's more, they were completely orthodox in their practice, unlike the Britons who clung to their heretical ideas. Furthermore, the Anglo-Saxons were in communication with Rome and the wider Church, while the Britons, Bede implied, refused to listen to what the rest of the Church said: the Anglo-Saxons were international and Catholic, the Britons were parochial and sectarian (if he was alive today, Bede would probably have voted Remain).

By writing of the various kingdoms as united by language and belief, Bede had also set about constructing the idea of an identity that went beyond the familial and the tribal: he was inventing the idea of a unified people long before they were anything like unified. By tying the idea of the English people to the idea of Israel, Bede introduced by implication into the idea the land in which they lived. The promised land of Israel became the actual green fields of England. England, partaking of that identification, became sacred and holy. There is a long but distinct thread running from Bede to William Blake asking, 'And did those feet in ancient time walk upon England's mountains green?' For only to a land made sacred by covenant between earth and people would the young Jesus come. The legends appear to have been first written down in the thirteenth century but could well recount earlier stories. There is, of course, no evidence for an actual visit, but that it was possible to propose such an idea shows the deep, mostly unspoken, underlying mysticism that the English have for their land.

By telling the story of their conversion, Bede had made of them one people, the English, living in a land consecrated to them, England. Although it is not stated, Bede also implied something else: that of a country, Britain, made up of different peoples but with the English as the head of the family of peoples. This was not relevant in Bede's time, when the different realms were still relatively small, but it was something that would be noticed and acted upon a century and a half later, when Alfred and his children and his grandchildren set about reconquering the Danelaw.

But at the time, hardly anyone noticed. After his death, Bede was venerated more for his Biblical commentaries than for his *History*, becoming the last Doctor of the ancient Church as well as the first Doctor of the medieval Church. The sheer fact that almost all of his work survives in multiple manuscripts shows how widely it was valued. But it was the commentaries and the textbooks that were most valuable for the monks and missionaries who first requested copies of Bede's work, although the *History* was widely copied, too.

*

However, everything began to change in 793. That was when Alcuin, the heir to Bede who was driving the Carolingian Renaissance, wrote of his shock at the despoliation of Lindisfarne. A year later, the Vikings attacked Bede's own monastery. The Viking Age had begun.

The highly mobile, sea-based raiders attacking Britain and north-western Europe bore more than a passing resemblance to the ancestors of the Anglo-Saxons. In a decentralised, thinly settled world, landing two or three boatloads of warriors on a quiet beach was almost always enough to ensure local superiority: attack, plunder and retreat before the bewildered locals could react. It was a winning formula, and one that the Vikings were content with for the first half-century or so. But in 865, what the *Anglo-Saxon Chronicle* called a Great Heathen Army landed in East Anglia. This was a force that had come to conquer rather than plunder and, over the next nine years they did exactly that, overthrowing the kingdoms of East Anglia, Northumbria and Mercia. Only Wessex, under the leadership of a youthful king who, as the youngest of five brothers, had never expected to come to the throne, managed to fight off their assault.

King Alfred won a second, decisive victory at the Battle of Edington in 878, following which he signed a treaty with the Viking king, Guthrum, dividing the country between the two of them, with the boundary running along the River Thames, then up the River Lea to Bedford, then along the River Ouse to Watling Street.

Although Alfred had won a victory and a respite, he knew to expect further attacks, if not from Guthrum then from other Viking leaders. So in the systematic way that was characteristic of Alfred, he set out to understand why what had happened, had happened. God had allowed a pagan people to scourge the Christian kingdoms of Britain. That this had taken place could only be a result of some deep moral and spiritual failure of his own people. Alfred identified this as the loss of the deep learning that had characterised the Anglo-Saxons in the time of Bede. Indeed, in his time, learning had declined so greatly that even in Canterbury, the seat of the archbishop, there were no priests sufficiently educated to write intelligible Latin.

So Alfred set to rectifying the situation. He instituted a programme of education throughout his realm. He himself set about learning Latin, and did so well enough to take part in the other strand of his programme: the translation of the 'works most necessary for all men to know' into English. While the overall aim was to reinstitute proper Latin learning, the use of the vernacular would serve so long as men read the right books. Among the books translated was an edited version of Bede's *Ecclesiastical History*. And when Alfred signed his treaty with Guthrum, Alfred, the king of the West Saxons, signed as the king of the English.

Alfred was a subtle ruler. The treaty he signed with Guthrum effectively annexed half the ancient Anglian kingdom of Mercia to his rule. Alfred delegated rule to a local ealdorman, Æthelred, to whom he married his daughter, Æthelflæd, but Æthelred remained subordinate to Alfred and was never listed as a king in the charters he signed. There had been a long and bitter rivalry between Wessex and Mercia. For the Mercians under Æthelred's rule (the eastern half of the kingdom was controlled by Guthrum), having to submit to a king from Wessex must have been bitter. Signing the treaty with Guthrum as the king of the English rather than the king of the Saxons was one way of making the herbs of bitterness a little sweeter.

At some point after 899, Æthelred appears to have become incapacitated, for Alfred's remarkable daughter, Æthelflæd, effectively took over as the ruler of Mercia. With Edward, her brother, succeeding Alfred as king of Wessex at the same time, the siblings ruled the part of the country not under Norse control. The children of Alfred continued with the family project of winning back the country. Working in tandem, Æthelflæd from Mercia and Edward from Wessex, the brother and sister launched the reconquest of the Danelaw, one by one bringing the cities of the Five Boroughs – Leicester, Derby, Lincoln, Nottingham and Stamford – back under their control.

The project continued with Æthelstan, Edward's eldest son and Alfred's grandson. However, Æthelstan was fostered in Mercia with his Aunt Æthelflæd, making his succession to the throne much more acceptable to the Mercians, for he was, effectively, one of their own and probably spoke their dialect of Old English rather than the Wessex dialect. Æthelstan completed the reconquest of the Norse kingdoms by taking York. In 927, he signed a treaty with the kings of the northern kingdoms in which they recognised Æthelstan as their overlord. The coinage minted in his name has him as *Rex totius Britanniae* ('King of all Britain'), and in charters and dedications he was called the king of the English.

Through his domination of all the other kings in Britain and indeed in Ireland, Æthelstan had brought to reality the idea that had been implicit in Bede's history, written two centuries earlier: of a Britain made up of separate nations but all under the overall leadership of the English and their king. That fixed idea would continue to play out, in wars and revolts, for centuries to come. By the end of his rule, Æthelstan ruled an area that maps well on to what is today England. If you want to know who the first king of England was, Æthelstan has a better claim to that title than anyone else.

That a West Saxon dynasty should produce the first kings of England was a result of Bede's baptising the nation in his *History*. It was also true that three of the four great Anglo-Saxon kingdoms, Mercia, Northumbria and East Anglia, were seen as being realms of the Anglians while only Wessex was Saxon. As Æthelstan took control of the old Anglo-Saxon kingdoms and sought to weld them together under his rule, it made political sense to style himself as the king of the English to lessen the smack of conquest that would have attached to him calling himself the king of the Saxons.

Some 400 years later a Florentine poet named Dante Alighieri set to writing an epic of human and divine love in the vernacular. But being an Italian, the question was which vernacular he was to write in, as Italian was split into many, widely differing dialects. In an essay, Dante set about analysing the different dialects, seeking to discover which of these was most suited to his purpose of writing an epic in a language that matched Latin for grandeur, flexibility and beauty. Having considered the other Italian dialects, Dante concluded that the dialect most suited to his purposes was, in fact, his own dialect, the Tuscan version of Italian. So that was the language in which Dante wrote his *Commedia* and, by doing so, he made his dialect of Italian into an instrument of unsurpassed power and felicity and the foundation for modern Italian. By the power of his poetry, his anointing of the Tuscan dialect as the best form of Italian became validated by the power of his *Commedia*.

Centuries before, when Bede started to tell the history of his people, his decision to identify his own people, the Angles, with all the different tribes speaking his language in the British Isles did the same thing.

Bede invented the country before it was born and christened the English as its inhabitants.

CHAPTER 16

# Long, long ago . . .

It doesn't look like one of the most important sites in English history. Visiting St Peter's Church in Sunderland today is, if I am honest, something of a disappointment. The church itself sits in a neat little park, the grass close cut and speckled with daisies in summertime. The church itself betrays little of its past. From the outside it's a trim building built of grey stone that looks not dissimilar to other Victorian suburban churches. The ceiling is painted in patterned squares. There is an organ and pretty embroidered kneelers stacked at the back of the pews. It has the feel of so many old churches today, sitting in the quiet of its prayered past, little visited but looked upon fondly as part of the landscape.

Outside the church, to its south, paths and blocks mark out the outline of Rosemary Cramp's excavations here, with notices providing brief blocks of information as to what was there a long time ago.

The church is surrounded on three sides by the quiet St Peter's Way and to the north by the bustling A4183, Dame Dorothy Street. Although I knew that the River Wear flows to the sea just south of the church, it's impossible to see the river from the church. The area between the church and the river has been built over, the buildings mainly belonging to the University of Sunderland, although the Northern Gallery for Contemporary Art and the National Glass Centre cut off the view to the river to the east. It's a built-up area not far from the centre of Sunderland. As such, it takes a considerable exercise of archaeological imagination to picture the surroundings as they were when Bede walked here.

It's much easier to picture Bede and the other monks at St Paul's Church in Jarrow. The area around the church there is much less developed. The church is set among trees and paths with some evocative but later ruins to its south (these are the remains of the attempt to refound the monastery in the twelfth century). Past the ruins the ground slopes sharply down to the River Don which, turning north, flows into the River Tyne. What is left of the mudflats of Jarrow Slake – not very much – lies to the east of the church. The building itself is austere and rather imposing from without, its nave bisected by a central tower. The interior continues its austere exterior, with walls of bare stone. The chancel at the east end of the church dates from Bede's time and set into the southern wall are three tiny windows, one of which is glazed with pieces of glass that Rosemary Cramp excavated here, making it the oldest stained-glass window in the country. The windows were set in the south wall of the church to make the most of the sunlight.

The dedication stone from when the church was first built is now set into the wall above the chancel arch. There's a helpful ground-level replica below. Sitting in the church, looking up at the stone and then peering into the chancel is a humbling and strangely moving experience. Bede himself breathed the air of this church; his voice was one of those raised in song to fill the quiet and make it sing.

St Paul's is more visited than St Peter's because just to the north of it is the splendid Jarrow Hall museum and Anglo-Saxon village and farm. Jarrow Hall is a regular stop for local schoolchildren and a popular attraction at weekends with local people stopping by to feed the animals and ramble the paths that line the Don and the Tyne. When the church is open, a fair number of the visitors stop in there, too, pausing to appreciate its quiet and deep sense of the past.

Bede died at this outpost of the twin monastery. But he died here a long time ago. Nearly 1,300 years ago. Most people are forgotten within two or three generations of their deaths. If they are childless, they are forgotten quicker. Bede obviously never had any children, but he is still remembered, even down to having a contemporary museum and visiting centre built in his honour. Not many monks are feted in such a manner.

It is clear that even in his own lifetime, Bede's contemporaries recognised that he stood outside the ordinary for his scholarship and knowledge. Although highly regarded by his brethren, there is no suggestion that he was ever put forward for any ecclesiastical office higher than that of priest. His talents were needed in the school-room and the scriptorium, not at Church councils or negotiating with local farmers over the price of calf skin.

That renown was spread both by Bede's pupils but also by correspondence. He maintained a surprisingly extensive list of corre-spondents, men and women who sought his advice on many matters but chiefly on the interpretation of difficult passages of the Bible. Many of Bede's correspondents went on to important positions within the Church. Nothhelm became archbishop of Canterbury, Acca the bishop of Hexham, while his pupil Cuthbert later became the abbot of the twin monastery. Another of Bede's pupils, Ecgbert, became bishop of York and set about establishing a school in the city that came to rival the twin monastery in its learning and its library.

Among the students who studied at York was a young man named Alcuin who swiftly revealed himself to be as brilliant as his peers. Alcuin was appointed the head of the school and became one of the king's chief advisors. As such, Alcuin was dispatched to Rome. On his way back, Alcuin stopped in Parma in Italy where he met the king of the Franks, Charles, soon to be named Charlemagne, who was not just engaged with conquest; he wanted to spark a renewal of learning and scholarship in his kingdom, too. To that end, he was engaging eminent scholars to come and live in his kingdom, to teach and learn there. It was an offer Alcuin could not refuse. He moved to Aachen and became the head of the palace school. Together with the other scholars Charlemagne had gathered to his court, Alcuin sparked and then fed the Carolingian Renaissance that produced a renewal of interest in literature, jurisprudence, music, architecture and the visual arts.

Indeed, such was Bede's importance to the Carolingian scholars that we owe them thanks for ensuring the survival of his work. It was the Carolingian scriptoria that copied Bede's works in numbers large enough to ensure their survival during the chaos of the Viking incursions that followed the Carolingian Renaissance. These copies also ensured Bede's European fame: in the *Commedia*, Dante places Bede in the heaven of the sun alongside such figures of intellectual brilliance as Thomas Aquinas and Boethius. It's notable that Bede is the only English character to appear in the *Divine Comedy*. By the fourteenth century, Bede's fame had transcended his origin.

Within his own country, Bede came again to unwitting prominence following the Norman Conquest. The Anglo-Norman historians who chronicled the history of the conquest and the subsequent rule of the house of Normandy used Bede as part of their justification for the invasion. In an ironic reversal of the intellectual device by which Bede had justified the usurpation of the land of the Britons by the Anglo-Saxons, the Normans argued that the falling away of the Anglo-Saxons from the moral and intellectual standards of Bede's time made them into the same divine scourge that Bede argued God had sent against the Anglo-Saxons.

Coming into the modern period, the translation of Bede's work into English, particularly the *Ecclesiastical History*, brought it renewed popularity. The 1896 translation by Charles Plummer proved particularly popular, and there have been many new translations since.

I first read Bede when I was working on the history of Northumbria for my book *Northumbria: the Lost Kingdom*. I am, on the face of it, an unlikely enthusiast for an eighth-century Anglo-Saxon monk. I was born in London to an Italian mother and Sri Lankan father (himself half Sinhala and half Tamil) and all my school friends were the children of other immigrants; indeed, until I went to university I had no friends who were English. My wife, however, is English. But that is English with the usual caveats of the wider empire into which her parents had been born and the usual mixing of this island. Harriet's mother is South African but of English descent and her father was English and Welsh. So I found myself marrying into a thoroughly 'English' family and, for the first time, trying to work out how I fit into the identity of this land. I could not have asked for better in-laws. They were accommodating, kind, polite and courteous: everything that my mother said marked the proper English.

But who were these English? Growing up in London, the rest of the country was something of a mystery, particularly anywhere north of about, well, Peterborough. It was strange country there, a country to which I had no direct access via family or friends. I had, however, travelled to many parts of the country while growing up in books. The first book I remember reading was *The Wind in the Willows*; it was a window into that brief Edwardian idyll when it was always summer before the winter of war drew that world to its close. The Lone Pine novels of Malcolm Saville introduced me, in print, to places such as Shropshire, the Yorkshire Moors, Dartmoor and Sussex. I had a sense of England, of its past and the quiet mysticism of its landscape, through these and other books, but little direct contact with that world. England existed, but in my head, as a construct of children's books and Arthurian tales.

But as I grew older I met, and became friends with, and eventually married, more and more of the English, this mysterious people among whom I had been living without actually knowing. I liked them. And with my wife, and our children once we had them, I started visiting some of the places I had seen only on the page: Shropshire, Yorkshire, Cornwall, Norfolk. Each was different, with landscapes and towns and villages that were unique to themselves, but they were united by an underlying sense of shared identity – except, perhaps, for Cornwall, which did have the sense of standing outside that shared identity. England was seeping into my bones.

Then we received an invitation to go up to Bamburgh. Harriet's sister, Rosie Whitbread, was an archaeologist and married to another archaeologist, Paul Gething. Together with two other archaeological friends they had set up the Bamburgh Research Project to excavate in and around Bamburgh Castle in Northumberland and by that point they had been digging there for four seasons. When we received the invitation to visit, I had never even heard of Bamburgh Castle and, frankly, I was dubious about using up our summer holiday to go and visit somewhere cold and windswept and northern. But I could not really think of an excuse, so bundling our one-year-old into the car we drove up. This was in the days when my internet connection was still dial-up, so I didn't search for any pictures of our destination before going.

Turning north on the road out of Seahouses, I still remember the jaw-dropping impact of seeing Bamburgh Castle squatting atop a huge outcrop of granite, dominating land and sea and sky. We arrived at the castle and went, open-mouthed in wonder, up to where they were digging. From its ramparts, I could see low-lying islands out to sea and, further north, what appeared to be another castle sticking out on a headland. Asking what these were, Paul told me that they were the Farne Islands, where St Cuthbert had had his hermitage, while the castle was on Lindisfarne, Holy Island.

Cuthbert was just a name to me, and Lindisfarne the name of the band who sang 'Lady Eleanor'. It took the rest of that holiday, and patient explanations from Rosie, Paul and the rest of the Bamburgh Research Project to learn just how important these places had once been. My own history education had pretty well skipped over the years between the Romans leaving and the Normans arriving, and then I had swerved towards the sciences for a while, thinking with the arrogance of the young that, since history was the story of dead people, it didn't matter. I couldn't think that any longer. Not when standing on the battlements of the castle, looking down at the vast beach stretching out below, which, Paul informed me, had arrived in one fell swoop in the eighteenth century following a truly apocalyptic storm that had lifted and shifted the sand banks from Budle Bay south to Bamburgh Castle.

Over that first week, I learnt of Oswald and Cuthbert, of Aidan and Edwin, and of Bede, the monk who had written about them all. And I decided to write about them in my turn. So, with Paul, I wrote a book about the history of Northumbria, and then another (*Warrior*) and a third (*The Perfect Sword*). Learning the stories of

Kings Edwin, Oswald and Oswiu, I realised that they made a perfect narrative arc and thought that surely someone must have written these as novels before. But no one had. So I decided to.

Without expecting it, I was diving deep into the history of England, so deep that, at the start of these stories, England as an idea did not even exist. But now I was learning what had turned this land into my country. For England was becoming my country.

Growing up, I did not really know what I was. I wasn't English. I was a dark little Asian boy who was called 'Paki' often enough to know that whatever I was, I wasn't what those children who called me 'Paki' thought of as one of their own. But I wasn't Italian and nor was I Sri Lankan. I did not speak Italian, Sinhala or Tamil. My parents' shared language was English, and that was what I spoke. But apparently I wasn't English, either. And I could see why that was the case: I knew my parents had come here as immigrants. Although I couldn't hear them (and still can't), I'm told that they each retain strong accents. English people, I thought, had to be the children of English parents, of people who had lived here for generations. By that criterion, I wasn't English. Not having the languages, I could not fit into the language-defined groups of Italians who lived in north London, although we knew many of them. We fitted even less well among the Sri Lankans, for they divided themselves into Sinhala and Tamil enclaves and, by reason of my father's mixed parentage, we fitted neither. As the civil war in Sri Lanka escalated, both sides in that country retreated further from each other, divorcing us further from that side of our past.

But if I wasn't Italian, or Sri Lankan, or English, then what was I?

It was Bede who gave me the answer, positively and negatively. Reading him, I immediately appreciated that, despite the gulf of years, he was a man after my own heart. For while his greatest faith was given to God, it seemed clear to me that coming not far behind that faith was another belief, well nigh as fervent: Bede believed in books. He believed in them as sources of knowledge, as things of beauty, as objects of truth and tellers of wonders. He believed in books, and I did, too.

Bede took that belief and spun it into a story about his people, the English, and, in telling that story, he made them into a people where before they had not been: he weaved them into his story and they became living threads within it. That was the power of books: it could take people and incorporate them into their stories.

Bede put the English into a story where they were a special people, a chosen people, living in a land of promise and wonder. He made of England, this England, a place where one can believe that those feet really did walk this green and pleasant land. He made England holy.

I was still not English, but I was living in a new holy land.

Bede achieved this by setting the English apart and against the other peoples of this island: the Britons, the Picts and the Irish. Bede was a Northumbrian. He loved his own people and their land. Rather as Dante did for Italian, he made his own people the paradigm for the whole country. But there came with that a bitter edge: the centuries of conflict between England and Wales, and between England and Scotland.

But from the twelfth century onwards, there arose a competing origin story, that told in Geoffrey of Monmouth's *The History of the Kings of Britain*. A Welshman, Geoffrey told stories of Arthur and his knights that popularised the Arthurian legends and led to the whole medieval cycle of Arthurian romances. So, by the strange process of osmosis and intermingling that occurs in the legend ground of a people's imagination, the stories of Arthur, a hero of the Britons, slowly merged into the stories of the English, creating a national legend that united the ancient foes. Now, Arthur and his knights sleep, under hill or on Avalon, waiting to be summoned at England's need.

There is a story there that unites and transcends the different countries, that holds England and Wales and Scotland, and even maybe parts of Ireland, together. And that's the story of Britain, and the British, a people defined only by their presence living here, in these islands. To be British is to partake of the mystery of a holy land, to have roots that dig back to saints and warriors, to Rome and Boudica, and to mix in Spitfires and kings, Shakespeare and

Tolkien, 'Flower of Scotland' and 'Land of My Fathers', reggae and bhangra and the Beatles.

Bede taught me that I am British and that this land, this Great Britain, is more than the sum of its parts. I am grateful to him for that and much besides.

Not bad for a monk who lived 1,300 years ago and never moved far from Jarrow.

# Endnotes

## Chapter 1

1 In a long letter he wrote to Milton Waldman in late 1951, J.R.R. Tolkien said that as a young man, and with a young man's confidence, he had set out to write a whole mythology for England but the years and the scale of the task he had set himself showed his aim to be beyond any one man.

2 As well as the Matter of Britain, there was the Matter of France – the legends of Charlemagne and his knights, in particular Roland – and the Matter of Rome, derived from classical mythology.

## Chapter 2

1 The only work dedicated to Benedict Biscop is Eric Fletcher's Jarrow lecture from 1981. It is not too easy to track down, although the last time I visited they did have copies for sale at St Paul's Church, Jarrow.

2 Apart from Bede, the most important primary source for Wilfrid's life is the biography written of him by his disciple, Stephen of Ripon. There is an excellent translation of his *Life of Wilfrid* in Penguin's *Age of Bede*.

3 For the fascinating history and archaeology of the isle, see Gerald Moody's *The Isle of Thanet, from Prehistory to the Norman Conquest*, published by the History Press.

4 The *Oxford Dictionary of National Biography* entry on Balthild, written by Janet Nelson, is an excellent starting point on this extraordinary woman.

5 For more on the relationship between the Anglo-Saxons and Rome in the early medieval period, see *England and Rome in the Early Middle Ages*, edited by Francesca Tinti and published by Brepols.

6 The fascinating research about Theodore is in *Archbishop Theodore*, edited by Michael Lapidge and published by Cambridge University Press.

7 For the best overview of this crucial but often overlooked figure, see Nicholas Higham's *Ecgfrith: King of the Northumbrians, High King of Britain*, published by Paul Watkins.

8 Rosemary Cramp wrote up her excavations of the two sites in two magnificent volumes, *Wearmouth and Jarrow Monastic Sites, volumes 1 and 2*, published by English Heritage. Unfortunately, the paper books are unfeasibly expensive for anything other than university libraries but thankfully pdfs of both volumes are available from the website of Archaeology Data Service: https://archaeologydataservice.ac.uk/

9 The Battle of Nechtansmere (also known as the Battle of Dún Nechtain) was generally thought to have been fought near Dunnichen in Angus. However, Alex Woolf has advanced an interesting argument for the battle having taken place much further north, near Dunachton in the Scottish Highlands – see: https://works.hcommons.org/records/je0k4-za182. The argument for the traditional site is put well in Peter Marren's *Battles of the Dark Ages*, published by Pen and Sword.

### Chapter 3

1 Translation by Sonny Topsom.

### Chapter 4

1 John Haywood's *Dark Age Naval Power*, published by Anglo-Saxon Books, provides an excellent overview of the historical and archaeological evidence, including the vexed and still-

unanswered question as to whether the Anglo-Saxons used sails in their boats.

2 This was in Bede's *30 Questions on the Book of Kings*.

3 Also from *30 Questions on the Book of Kings*.

4 For more on Bede as a teacher, see Rosalind Love's chapter, 'The world of Latin learning', in *The Cambridge Companion to Bede*, edited by Scott DeGregorio and published by Cambridge University Press.

5 As recounted in his *Lives of the Abbots of Wearmouth and Jarrow*.

## Chapter 5

1 By far the most entertaining general survey of Christian monasticism is Peter Levi's *The Frontiers of Paradise*, published by the Harvill Press. Reading it is like taking tea with a slightly bibulous elderly monk who regales you with all the best gossip while taking sips from what he assures you is really just a cup of weak tea.

2 Larry Hurtado was the scholar who brought this preference most forcefully to our attention. Although Professor Hurtado died in 2019, his entertaining and thought-provoking blog remains online at https://larryhurtado.wordpress.com/. See also his book, *The Earliest Christian Artifacts*, published by William B. Eerdmans.

3 See his book *At Day's Close*, published by Weidenfeld & Nicholson, for a history of night-time.

4 *Source:* https://www.medievalists.net/2016/01/how-did-people-sleep-in-the-middle-ages/.

5 I was seventeen and, taking a new book, I sat down on the floor in my bedroom, opened it and began to read. The book was *Silent Music* by William Johnston, now long out of print. Turning the first pages, I came to an epigraph, the lines by the sixteenth-century mystic St John of the Cross quoted above. I read them and . . . my mind went splat. I have no recollection whatsoever of what happened for the next ten minutes. I woke slowly again to myself, the book still in my hands, bewildered by the impact these words had had on me. No words before or since have affected me in such a way.

## Chapter 6

1 The standard work on early Christian Ireland is T.M. Charles-Edwards' *Early Christian Ireland*, published by Cambridge University Press.

## Chapter 8

1 As you, like me, will probably never get to touch, let alone physically open the *Codex Amiatinus*, read Christopher de Hamel's wonderful account of what it is like to struggle with it in *Meetings with Remarkable Manuscripts*, published by Allen Lane.
2 Drawings of the Church of the Holy Sepulchre, the Abbey of the Dormition on Mount Zion and the Dome of the Ascension on the Mount of Olives, which is now a mosque.
3 Source: https://blogs.bl.uk/digitisedmanuscripts/2014/06/the-burden-of-writing-scribes-in-medieval-manuscripts.html.

## Chapter 9

1 This short extract shows why I have decided not to go into the technical details of *computus* in this book!
2 For how medieval thinkers laid the foundations for modern science, see James Hannam's *God's Philosophers*, published by Icon Books.
3 For the many technological innovations of the medieval period, see Frances and Joseph Gies' *Cathedral, Forge and Waterwheel*, published by HarperCollins.

## Chapter 11

1 The best, and most comprehensible, account of the technical difficulties in calculating the date of Easter is in Faith Wallis's introduction to her translation of *The Reckoning of Time*, published by Liverpool University Press; she even makes epacts and embolisms accessible!

## Chapter 12

1 See Michelle Brown's *Bede and the Theory of Everything*, published

by Reaktion Books. Brown identifies text marks that Bede used to indicate quotations and identifies the passages that she believes Bede wrote. The book is also a marvellous overview of Bede and his work.

## Chapter 14

1 Richard Shaw's *How, When and Why Did Bede Write his Ecclesiastical History?* published by Routledge, was very helpful in writing this chapter.

## Chapter 15

1 Source: https://en.wikipedia.org/wiki/De_Excidio_et_Conquestu_Britanniae#Part_III].

2 Richard Shaw's *The Gregorian Mission to Kent in Bede's Ecclesiastical History*, published by Routledge, has opened up fascinating new lines of inquiry about Bede's sources and methods.

# APPENDIX 1

# Bede's Books

At the end of the *Ecclesiastical History*, Bede does something unusual. He provides a short autobiography (to the frustration of generations of scholars who would have wished him to expand beyond the bare-bones outline he supplies) and a much longer list of the books he had written to that time. He did miss out a few works from the list, but it's pretty comprehensive. What's particularly impressive about Bede's bibliography is its length – he wrote a lot of books! – and its breadth: his books covered a very wide range of knowledge.

It's not just the number of books he wrote that is remarkable but also their length. The Penguin edition of the *Ecclesiastical History* has 290 pages of closely packed text. The Liverpool University translation of *The Reckoning of Time* has 372 pages. Bede's original Latin texts would have been shorter, since Latin is a terser language than English, but they wouldn't have been that much shorter. And that's just two of his works. When you consider the physical labour involved in writing with a quill pen, as well as the work undertaken by the monastery to copy Bede's work, you get some sense of the importance that they all attached to what he was doing. This was work to push back the darkness.

In honour of that, here's a table giving the complete list of Bede's works, including the few that he omitted from his own bibliography, with their original Latin title, the English title, its date of composition if known, and a short note on what each book was about and whether it survived.

| **Commentaries on the Old Testament. The commentaries Bede wrote on the Old and New Testaments comprised the major part of his work and were his most copied books in the centuries after his death.** | | | |
|---|---|---|---|
| **Latin title** | **English title** | **Probable date of completion if known** | **Notes** |
| *Capitula lectionum in Pentateucum Mosi, Iosue, Iudicum* | *Chapters of readings on the Pentateuch of Moses, Joshua and Judges* | | No surviving manuscript |
| *De aedificatione Templi* | *On the building of the Temple* | | |
| *De tabernaculo* | *On the Tabernacle* | Around 721 | |
| *In Cantica Canticorum* | *On the Song of Songs* | | |
| *In Canticum Habacum* | *On the Song of Habakkuk* | | Unusually, Bede dedicated this work to a nun, but he does not name her |
| *In Ezram et Neemiam* | *On Ezra and Nehemiah* | Between 725 and 731 | |
| *In Isaiam, Danhihelem, duodecim Prophetas, et partem Hieremiae* | *On Isaiah, Daniel, the 12 prophets, and part of Jeremiah* | | No surviving manuscript |
| *In Isaiam, Ezram et Neemiam* | *On Isaiah, Ezra and Nehemiah* | | No surviving manuscript |
| *In Job* | *On Job* | | No surviving manuscript |
| *In libros Regum, et Verba dierum* | *On the books of King and Chronicles* | | No surviving manuscript |

| | | | |
|---|---|---|---|
| *In Parabolas, Ecclesiasten, et Cantica Canticorum* | *On Proverbs, Ecclesiastes and the Song of Songs* | | No surviving manuscript |
| *In primam partem Samuhelis libri IIII* | *On the first part of Samuel* | 716 | Bede wrote the first three books before June 716, when Ceolfrith unexpectedly left for Rome, and the fourth book when Hwætberht had been elected abbot |
| *In principium Genesis* | *Commentary on the beginning of Genesis* | | Bede initially wrote two books of commentary, later expanding this to four books |
| *In Proverbia Salmonis* | *On the Proverbs of Solomon* | | |
| *In Tobiam* | *On the book of Tobit* | | |

**Commentaries on the New Testament**

| | | | |
|---|---|---|---|
| *Capitula lectionum in tutum Novum Testamentum, except Evangelio* | *Chapters of readings on all the New Testament, except the Gospels* | | No surviving manuscript |
| *Collectio Bedae presbyteri ex opusculis sancti Augustini in Epistulas Pauli Apostoli* | *Excerpts from the Works of Augustine on the Pauline Epistles* | | |
| *In Actus Apostolorum* | *On the Acts of the Apostles* | Within a year or two of 709 | |
| *In Apocalypsin* | *On Revelation* | Between 707 and 709 | |

| | | | |
|---|---|---|---|
| *In Epistolas vii Catholicas* | *On the seven universal epistles* | The commentary on John I was written in 709; unknown dates for the others | Commentary on the seven letters addressed to the whole Church rather than particular congregations |
| *In Evangelium Marci* | *On the Gospel of Mark* | After 716 | Commentary on Mark |
| *In Evangelium Lucae* | *On the Gospel of Luke* | Between 709 and 716 | Commentary on Luke |
| *Omeliarum Evangelii* | *Of Homilies on the Gospels* | | |
| *Retractiones* | *Retractions* | Between 725 and 731 | Bede became dissatisfied with the previous work and later corrected it |

| **Hagiographies** | | | |
|---|---|---|---|
| *Librum vitae et passionis sancti Anastasii* | *The book of the life and passion of St Anastasius* | | Bede notes that this 'was ill translated from the Greek, and worse amended by some unskilful person, I have corrected to the sense as I was able' |
| *Librum vitae et passionis sancti Felicis* | *The book of the life and passion of St Felix* | | Bede took four poems by St Paulinus of Nola on the life of St Felix and produced a prose life based on them |
| *Martyrologium* | *The Martyrology* | Between 725 and 731 | |
| *Vita Cudbercti metrica* | *The life of St Cuthbert* | Between 705 and 716 | First version in heroic verse |
| *Vita Cudbercti prosaica* | *The life of St Cuthbert* | Around 721 | Prose version |

| Historical works | | | |
|---|---|---|---|
| *Chronica maiora* | *The Greater Chronicle* | 725 | Contained within *The Reckoning of Time* |
| *Chronica minora* | *The Lesser Chronicle* | 703 | A shorter timeline included in *On Times* |
| *Historiam abbatum monasterii huius* | *History of the abbots of Wearmouth and Jarrow* | Between 725 and 731 | |
| *Historia ecclesiastica gentis Anglorum* | *Ecclesiastical History of the English People* | Completed 731, but likely composed over a much longer period | |
| Scientific works | | | |
| *De natura rerurm* | *On the Nature of Things* | 703 | |
| *De temporibus* | *On Times* | 703 | |
| *De temporum ratione* | *On the Reckoning of Time* | 725 | A much-expanded version of his earlier book *On Times* |
| Teaching books | | | |
| *De arte metrica* | *On the art of poetry* | | |
| *De orthographia* | *On Orthography* | | |
| *De schematibus et tropis* | *The Figures of Rhetoric* | | |
| Collected sermons | | | |
| *Homeliarum euangelii* | *Homilies on the Gospels* | | Many later sermons were attributed to Bede and added to this collection |

| Letters. Bede was, for the time, a great correspondent and some of his letters were saved and copied. | | | |
|---|---|---|---|
| *Aliquot questionum liber* | *On Eight Questions* | | Letter written to Nothhelm, later archbishop of Canterbury |
| *De eo quod ait Isaias* | *On What Isaiah Said* | | Letter to Acca, bishop of Hexham |
| *De mansionibus filiorum Israel* | *On the Resting Places of the Children of Israel* | | Letter to Acca, bishop of Hexham |
| *Epistula ad Albinum abbatem* | *Letter to Abbot Albinus* | After 731 | Albinus was the abbot who first commissioned the *Ecclesiastical History*. Bede wrote to thank him for providing information for it |
| *Epistula ad Ecgbertum episcopum* | *Letter to Bishop Ecgberht* | 5 November 734 | Ecgberht was bishop of York. Bede wrote to apologise for being unable to visit him (his declining health probably precluded that) and to complain about bad practice among contemporary churchmen |
| *Epistula ad Helmuualdum* | *Letter to Helmwald* | | |
| *Epistula ad Pleguinam* | *Letter to Plegwin* | | Plegwin was a monk who wrote to Bede advising him that others had accused him of heresy. This is Bede's reply, defending himself |

| | | | |
|---|---|---|---|
| *Epistula ad Uuicthedum* | *Letter to Wicthed* | | A monk friend of Bede |
| *In Regum librum XXX quaestiones* | *Thirty Questions on the Book of Kings* | Possibly about 725 | Written to Nothhelm answering, as it says, 30 queries about the Book of Kings |

| **Geography** | | | |
|---|---|---|---|
| *De locis sanctis* | *On the Holy Places* | Before 709; probably between 702 and 703 | |

| **Poetry** | | | |
|---|---|---|---|
| *Librum hymnorum diverso metro sive rhythmo* | *A book of hymns in different meters and rhythms* | | No surviving manuscript |
| *Librum epigrammatum heroico metro sive elegiaco* | *A book of epigrams in heroic or elegiac meter – poems* | | No surviving manuscript |

We also know that Bede was working on a translation of St John's Gospel into English in the final months of his life which, according to the account of his death written by his pupil Cuthbert, he finished shortly before he died. Unfortunately, this was one of his works which did not survive. If it had survived, it would have been the oldest and longest piece of Old English prose we possess.

APPENDIX 2

# Gazetteer of Bedan Sites

History churns, burying the past in its passage. But there are a few places and things that still provide us with a physical and tangible link back to Bede and his time. These are the most important of them.

## St Paul's Church, Jarrow

Church Bank, Jarrow, Tyne and Wear, NE32 3DY.
Telephone 0191 489 7052. Website: https://www.parishofjarrowand
simonside.info/our-churches-and-congregations/st-pauls/

This was where Bede spent the greater part of his life. The church of St Paul mostly dates from later than Bede's time, but the church's chancel was a free-standing chapel for Bede's community in which he would have sung the Office many times. The original dedication stone is now set into the chancel arch. It's astonishing to think that Bede would have looked at that stone every day as he went into the church to do the work of a monk – he might even have helped put it in place when it was first raised. As the dedication stone is set high on the arch, there is a replica at ground level that visitors can inspect more closely.

During Rosemary Cramp's excavations the archaeologists found small pieces of the original glass that had gone into the windows in the church. After analysis was complete, the fragments were put into a circle of glass and reinstalled in one of the original window frames – it's the middle of the three small windows on the right-hand side of the church looking towards the altar. The glass pieces are a mix of clear, blue, yellow, orange and green.

It's also worth going round the outside to look at the north porch. In it, there's a stone shouldered, drying-out coffin. The hole in the bottom was to allow decomposition liquid to drain away. Outside the church, there are remains of the later Benedictine monastery that was refounded on the site where Bede lived and worked.

If there's one Bedan place worth visiting, this is it. During opening hours there are usually helpful and knowledgeable volunteers on hand to show visitors around while also allowing you to take as much time as you want. And I must mention the excellent bookshop in the church. Not only does it stock all my books, but it's one of the few places where you can find copies of the excellent Jarrow Lectures, annual talks given by experts in Bedan and Anglo-Saxon studies.

The church has escaped urban sprawl and sits in green fields and copses, cut through with footpaths. The Don curves round the church, jagging north to join the Tyne. It's not too hard to imagine yourself back to Bede's day, particularly on days when the sea mist, the haar, rolls in, laying nets of wet on tree and branch and throwing a shroud of quiet over the old church. Then, if you stand and listen, you might hear the faint echo of prayer and psalm, spun down the centuries from a time when faith was young in a country already grown old.

### Jarrow Hall

Anglo-Saxon Farm, Village and Bede Museum, Church Bank, Jarrow, South Tyneside, NE32 3DY. Telephone 07966 330022. Website: https://jarrowhall.com

Just a few minutes' walk north from St Paul's Church is Jarrow Hall. This is the best sort of living history, with a reconstructed Anglo-Saxon farm and village, as well as a museum dedicated to Anglo-Saxon life in general and Bede in particular. They are all excellent and the museum, in addition to fascinating exhibits about Bede and the monastery, also has a life-size replica of the *Codex Amiatinus*. It's only when you see it that you can really appreciate the scale of the enterprise the monks undertook when writing it – and its two, now lost, companion Bibles.

## St Peter's Church, Sunderland

St Peter's Way, Sunderland SR6 0DY. Telephone: 0191 5160135. Website: https://stpeters-wearmouth.org.uk/

The first church that Benedict Biscop built still stands, although only a small part of the current church is original: the porch and the west wall. The wider monastery was largely destroyed. However, following Rosemary Cramp's excavations, low walls and pavements outside the church now show where the monastery's buildings once stood.

The church is surrounded by a pleasant small park but it sits firmly within modern-day Sunderland, so it takes a greater effort of the imagination to see how it might have looked in Bede's day. However, the website has a useful audio guide that you can listen to when visiting the church and surrounding site. Still, if you only have time to visit one Bedan site, then St Paul's is the better choice.

## *Codex Amiatinus*

The *Codex Amiatinus* is now held at the Laurentian Library in Florence, Italy. It's not normally on public display but the codex has been digitised and can be seen online here: https://www.loc.gov/resource/gdcwdl.wdl_20150/?st=gallery. Going through the pages, it's enjoyable to speculate which ones Bede wrote.

## Lindisfarne

Bede famously did not do much travelling during his lifetime, but he did visit Lindisfarne to collect information for his *Life of St Cuthbert*. The monastery that Aidan founded, and Bede stayed at, was subject to the first Viking attack on Britain in 793 and later abandoned; the monastic ruins there now are the remains of a later refoundation that was in turn despoiled by Henry VIII. The tidal island nevertheless retains a unique atmosphere, particularly if you stay on after the tide flows in and the daytrippers depart.

## Hexham Abbey

Beaumont Street, Hexham, Northumberland NE46 3NB.
Telephone: 01434 602031. Website: https://www.hexhamabbey.org.uk/

The monastery in Hexham was founded by Wilfrid in 674 and, when Acca became bishop there, it housed a famous library that Bede consulted when visiting the bishop. Acca was one of Bede's main correspondents and sponsors for many years. The crypt is the original Anglo-Saxon one. After the dissolution of the monasteries, the abbey became the parish church of Hexham but, in a rather delicious twist, in 2014 it regained control of its old monastic buildings and turned them into a museum and visitor centre telling the abbey's history.

## Bamburgh Castle

Bamburgh NE69 7DF. Telephone: 01668 214208.
Website: https://www.bamburghcastle.com/

This is one place that doesn't need a road address. Anyone driving towards Bamburgh will see the castle, squatting on a vast outcrop of the Whin Sill, looming over the village. Rather than being a picturesque ruin like Dunstanburgh Castle further south, the castle is home to a number of lucky people as well as containing museums, a café and gift shop. It owes its state of repair to the Victorian industrialist William Armstrong, a native of Newcastle who kept his money in the area and who paid for the restoration of the castle after it had fallen into disrepair in the nineteenth century. His descendants still own the castle.

As such, most of the castle is fairly modern. However, if you head down to the end of the West Ward you will come to St Oswald's Gate, which was the original entrance to the stronghold during its heyday as the principal defensive bastion of the kings of Northumbria. This entrance led down to a small harbour where boats could land (the beach was much narrower then); the castle was oriented towards the sea, from where most visitors arrived. Much of the stonework leading down to the gate is original.

Within the castle, inside the keep, there is the well. The key weakness of the original stronghold was that it had no water source. So one of the early Anglo-Saxon rulers, reputedly King Æthelfrith, had a hole excavated into the bedrock deep enough to reach water. To dig down through that amount of rock – 210 feet (44 metres) of hard dolerite – they probably banked fires on top of the stone and then, with the stone still hot from the fire, poured cold water onto the rock. The thermal stress made the surface rock shatter, allowing it to be dug out. Then, fire and repeat, for 200 feet.

The view from the castle battlements is both extraordinary and interesting. To the north, you can clearly see Lindisfarne. Journeys between Bamburgh and Lindisfarne by boat, in good weather, would only have taken a couple of hours (the land route is much longer, requiring a long inland detour around Budle Bay). There, laid out across the sea, is the route of influence that ran between the political and spiritual centres of Northumbria.

But looking east, and lying much closer to the castle, are the low shapes of the Farne Islands. Exactly how many islands there are depends on the state of the tide. The islands are further upcrops of the Whin Sill. It was on Inner Farne, the island lying closest to the walls of the castle, that St Cuthbert made his hermitage, living there in isolation but in view of the royal family across a mile of sea. It was a very public place to live in retreat.

The kings who lived at Bamburgh supported Bede's monastery, gifting it land, supporting and encouraging it. There must have been much contact between the two centres, contact facilitated by the relatively easy travel between them by sea. Bede dedicated the *Ecclesiastical History* to King Ceolwulf, to whom he also sent draft copies for comment. It doesn't seem unlikely that he personally took the book to the king, taking passage in a boat up the coast with the precious manuscript wrapped in an oil cloth to keep it safe from the sea.

## Ad Gefrin

Just off the B6351, Yeavering, Wooler NE71 6TH. Website: https://www.
northumberlandnationalpark.org.uk/places-to-visit/the-cheviots/ad-gefrin/

It is, admittedly, a field. But this field is, for me, one of the most evocative sites in Northumberland. It was from looking at aerial photos taken of the area during a particularly dry summer that Brian Hope-Taylor noticed marks that suggested to him there would be something worth looking at under the grass. That dig became his investigation into what he concluded was the great hall of King Edwin, and the report he wrote of it became one of the great classics of archaeology. While it's true that recent re-evaluations have cast some doubt on his conclusions (although I'm not convinced the doubts are justified) I still find walking this field peculiarly haunting. Maybe it's the wind that sets waves running through the grass, as if I am walking through the sea of time. To the south rises Yeavering Bell, its summit necklace clad with the tumbledown remnants of what was once a great hill fort. The rock used to make the ramparts is andesite. When andesite is first quarried, it's a bright, salmon pink. So Yeavering Bell, and the many surrounding hills with their own hill forts, would once all have had pink necklaces thrown around their summits.

Kings lived here, on field and hill. Their works have decayed but their echo, receding, comes to the walker gently down the centuries.

## Ad Gefrin Museum

South Road, Wooler NE71 6NJ. Telephone: 01668 281554.
Website: https://adgefrin.co.uk/

This new museum in Wooler provides an immersive experience of what being inside an Anglo-Saxon hall would have been like, as well as a fascinating collection of artefacts excavated from the original Ad Gefrin, the site of King Edwin's royal residence in the shadow of Yeavering Bell where Paulinus preached to the Northumbrians. It's the best small museum on Northumbria and the Anglo-Saxon world that I have visited. The atrium to the museum is an architectural wonder, a cupola of wood to a central flame core. Standing under it, looking upwards, the music of an all but forgotten song came to mind: 'Set the Controls for the Heart of the Sun', by Pink Floyd. There's also a distillery on site, producing local whisky and gin.

## Maelmin

Off the A697, near Millfield, Wooler NE71 6HL.
Website: https://www.maelmin.org.uk/

When King Penda burnt down the great hall at Ad Gefrin, the kings of Northumbria decided to move their hall a little further north. They chose a site two miles away, near the village of Millfield, in the Till Valley. The valley had been an important route in prehistory, with eight henges lining the valley. The Northumbrians built their new great hall to the east of modern-day Millfield. Although the Anglo-Saxons did not build castles, to provide better defences for the new hall they surrounded it with a double palisade. The enclosed area contained the great hall and a hundred other houses, sheds, warehouses and workshops. This location is near one of the main crossing points of the River Till, which is probably why it was chosen.

In the late 1990s a group of archaeologists got together and, after slightly too much to drink, decided that it would be a great idea to reconstruct one of the henges that had once lined the valley, using only the tools available to the original builders, while wearing authentic clothing and eating and drinking, so far as was possible, appropriate provender. With a team of thirteen volunteers assembled, including my sometimes co-writer, Paul Gething, all led by Clive Waddington, the group settled on the first two weeks in April 2000 to do the work. That avoided the worst winter weather as well as summer heat, when dried-out ground can make digging all but impossible.

What they hadn't bargained upon was the wettest April in recorded history. Paul can now personally vouch for the fact that Neolithic clothing does a reasonable job of keeping you warm even when soaked. Despite the dreadful conditions, the team built their henge. It's 100 feet (33 metres) in diameter with 30 inner posts and 21 outer posts.

It's still there, as part of the free-to-visit Maelmin trail. A couple of hundred yards from the henge there's a reconstructed house, based upon the excavation of local houses dating between 410 and 570 – so possibly belonging to Britons or Anglo-Saxons. Along the trail there are excellent and informative panels, taking the visitor on a journey from the Ice Age right through to the early medieval.

Not many people visit, which makes it all the more fascinating. Take the trail and walk through centuries.

## St Oswald's Church, Heavenfield

Just north of the B6318, Heavenfield, Northumberland NE46 4HB.
Website: https://www.nationalchurchestrust.org/church/st-oswald-heavenfield

Oswald fought his critical battle against Cadwallon near the church that bears his name and commemorates his victory. The church itself was built in 1817, replacing a medieval church that itself stood on Anglo-Saxon foundations. Although not old in itself, the church has never been connected to the electricity network: light is provided by gas burners with mantles and candles. The church might mark the place where Oswald raised up the cross that he and his men venerated on the eve of the battle. It's an evocative place to visit.

## Escomb Saxon Church

Saxon Green, Escomb, Bishop Auckland DL14 7SY.
Website: https://escombchurch.co.uk/

There are only four intact surviving Anglo-Saxon churches. This one, in County Durham, was built between about 670 and 675, so around the time that Bede was born. We don't know if he ever visited the church, but it does represent a direct link back to the types of churches erected during this first phase of the conversion of the Anglo-Saxons. The church was built using stone recycled from the nearby Roman fort at Binchester, rather as Biscop did with his foundation. Having fallen into relative dilapidation, the church was restored in the 1870s, with rather more sympathy for the original than was often the case with Victorian restorations. The keys for the church are kept at 28 Saxon Green; take the keys and let yourself in (but remember to return the keys afterwards).

## St Cadwaladr's Church, Llangadwaladr

Just off the A4080, Llangadwaladr, Anglesey LL62 5LB. Website: https://www.nationalchurchestrust.org/church/st-cadwaladr-llangadwaladr

The nemesis of King Edwin and the foe of King Oswald was Cadwallon, king of Gwynedd. This church is a long way from Northumbria, but it is near Aberffraw, the ancient capital of the kings of Gwynedd. Cadwallon died in Northumberland and his body never came home. But his father, Cadfan ap Iago, died around 634 and his tombstone was engraved with a Latin epitaph. At some point, Cadfan's memorial was brought into the church and set into the wall, where it remains to this day, a direct physical link to a time very long ago. The stone, which is carved somewhat unevenly but still legibly, reads: *CATAMANUS REX SAPIENTIS MUS OPINATISM US OMNIUM REG UM* ('King Cadfan, the Wisest and Most Renowned of All Kings').

## Whitby Abbey

Abbey Lane, Whitby YO22 4JT. Website: https://www.english-heritage.org.uk/visit/places/whitby-abbey/

The famous ruins that brood on the clifftop overlooking Whitby are the remains of a Benedictine monastery that was established here by Reinfrid, one of the soldiers brought over from France by William the Conqueror. Given that Reinfrid founded the monastery around 1078, it's plausible that one reason for Reinfrid laying down his sword and donning the habit of a monk was in atonement for his role in the Harrying of the North, William's devastating campaign against the people in the north of England to punish them for their support of rebellions against his rule. Reinfrid's abbey flourished and became a notable centre of learning until Henry VIII, as great a vandal as William, destroyed it, leaving the ruins that Bram Stoker used to such dramatic effect in *Dracula*.

However, this was not the abbey that Bede knew. That abbey was founded around 657 by Hild, a kinswoman of King Edwin of Northumbria, as Streanaeshalch. It was a double monastery, for men and women, but under the rule of an abbess, with Hild as its foundress. Such was Hild's reputation for wisdom and discretion that the abbey was chosen as the location for what we now call the Synod of Whitby but which was presumably called the Synod of Streanaeshalch at the time. Hild died in 680, when Bede was still a boy, so it's very unlikely that he had any direct contact with her. There is no surviving evidence of any correspondence between Bede and Hild's successors at the abbey, but Bede does include in his history the story of Cædmon, an illiterate cowherd employed by the abbey who was inspired by a dream vision to compose a song of creation in Old English. Impressed by his poetry, Hild took him into the abbey as a monk, where he continued to compose vernacular songs on biblical themes. His eight-line poem, *Cædmon's hymn*, is the oldest surviving example of Old English poetry. Bede put his Latin translation of *Cædmon's hymn* in the *Ecclesiastical History*; we owe the survival of its Old English text to later copyists, who added the original version of the poem to their transcriptions of *Bede's* History.

The Streanaeshalch abbey was abandoned, probably because Viking raids made it untenable, in the ninth century. No traces of the old abbey survive above ground.

# Glossary

*bookland* – land granted to church establishments in perpetuity through a written and witnessed charter. Later expanded to include other recipients of land.

*Compline* – one of the monastic hours. Prayers before retiring to bed.

*folkland*, or folcland – family land held in ownership through long custom and, as such, ownership could not normally be transferred outside the family, not even by sale.

*gesith* – member of the king's warband. From about the time of Alfred to the Conquest, it was replaced by *thegn*.

*insular majuscule* – the form of majuscule letters developed in Ireland and Britain (Ireland first because scriptoria in Ireland were active before any in Britain).

*insular minuscule* – the form of minuscule letters developed in Ireland and Britain.

*Lauds* – a later name for *Matins*, the monastic dawn.

*loanland*, or lænland – land given, usually by the king to one of his servants, where ownership was retained by the giver.

*majuscule* – essentially, writing where all the letters are the same height. Majuscule developed into insular forms in Ireland and Britain. These letters developed into capitals.

*Matins* – the first of the monastic hours at dawn.

*minuscule* – letters with ascenders (b, d, etc.) and descenders (g, y, etc.) that stretch above and below the main letter zone. Lower-case letters developed from minuscule.

*Nocturns* – the night-time monastic Office.

*Nones* – one of the monastic hours. The ninth hour, so about mid-afternoon.

*Prime* – one of the monastic hours; the first hour of daylight.

*Sext* – one of the monastic hours. Six hours after dawn, or about noon.

*Terce* – one of the monastic hours; the third hour of daylight, or roughly 9 a.m.

*Thegn* – member of the Anglo-Saxon nobility.

*uncial* – a script using rounded letters that are not joined up. Capital letters developed from uncial, which was used by Anglo-Saxon scriptoria when copying important books such as the Bible.

*Vespers* – one of the monastic hours. Prayers said at sunset.

*Vigils* – an alternative but later name for the night-time monastic Office.

# Acknowledgements

As publishing chance would have it, I am writing the acknowledgements for two different books on the same day. That's unusual – writing a book is a reasonably lengthy process and I write my acknowledgements at the end of the production process to try to make sure that I don't forget anyone. However, on this occasion, because of the vagaries of production schedules, two different books that I wrote one after the other are coming out at roughly the same time, so I find myself writing the acknowledgements for both of them while sitting in a café waiting for my youngest son. (If you're interested, the other book is called *The Man Who Stopped the Sultan: Gabriele Tadino and the Defence of Europe*.)

I'm writing this one second and, as with the other, I will begin with saying that while writing a book is usually, for me, a one-man job (although it wasn't in this case, which I will go into later), producing a book ready for readers is a task to which many people contribute.

Those who contributed to it most are Robert Dudley, my agent, and Hugh Andrew, my publisher. In Robert's case, I could ask for no better agent, a man who has championed my work for the last ten years and ensured that my books have found an audience. He is also great company.

As for Hugh, I am profoundly grateful for his feedback on the first, and subsequent, drafts of this book. Hugh put his deep knowledge of Bede, and the times in which he lived, to the service of the book and it is much, much better as the result of his criticisms and suggestions. The faults that remain are entirely my own.

On the production side, I also want to thank Andrew Simmons at Birlinn for his encouragement and Craig Hillsley for his detailed and meticulous copy edit – Craig took the text and polished it until it shone!

Deborah Warner has piloted the book calmly through the production process, coping nobly with authorly anxieties. Allison McKechnie proofread the book, catching many mistakes, Nina Mcpherson designed the splendid cover, and Alistair Hodge created the fabulous maps (books are always better with maps!). My grateful thanks to them all.

Sonny Topsom helped me greatly with the research on the book, personifying the worth of having a living, breathing researcher rather than relying on the ersatz aid of artificial intelligence. Should you, dear reader, ever need a researcher, I recommend Sonny wholeheartedly (contact me through my website and I will put you in touch with him).

The volunteers at the church of St Paul, Jarrow, are unfailingly kind, knowledgeable and enthusiastic. To step where Bede himself sang and prayed is an incalculable privilege and I urge any of you who can to pay the church a visit.

Finally, and always, I would like to thank my wife, Harriet, and my boys, Theo, Matthew and Isaac. What's more, Harriet allowed me to get a dog, on the proviso that he not be big and definitely not a German shepherd. Barnaby is only three-quarters German shepherd (the other quarter is Border collie, making him a shollie) and perhaps a little bigger than she anticipated, but being the wonderful woman that she is, Harriet has taken him to her heart – and Barnaby is a little puppy in her hands.

All six of us (Barnaby too) visited St Paul's in the summer of 2025. It was a memorable visit although, looking back, I was too busy taking photographs to pray. Now, to make up for that, I ask Bede for his intercession: may this book bring his life, times and work to a new audience and those who need it.

# Bibliography

This book includes a number of direct quotations, particularly from books that Bede wrote himself. These are the works quoted from:

Bede (1990). *Ecclesiastical History of the English People*. London: Penguin Books.

Colgrave, Bertram and Mynors, R. A. B. (1969). *Bede's Ecclesiastical History of the English People*. Oxford: Clarendon Press. https://archive.org/details/x-bede-s-ecclesiastical-history/

Martin, Lawrence T. and Hurst, Dom David (2010). *Homilies on the Gospels by the Venerable Bede*. Piscataway: Gorgias Press.

Trent Foley, W. and Holder, Arthur G. (1999). *Bede: A Biblical Miscellany*. Liverpool: Liverpool University Press.

Wallis, Faith (2004). *Bede: The Reckoning of Time*. Liverpool: Liverpool University Press.

Webb, J. F. and Farmer, D. H. (1998). *The Age of Bede*. London: Penguin Books.

Whitelock, Dorothy (1979). *English Historical Documents; volume 1, 500–1041*. London: Eyre & Spottiswoode.

\*

Abels, Richard P. (1988). *Lordship and Military Obligation in Anglo-Saxon England*. London: British Museum Publications.

Adams, Max (2013). *The King in the North*. London: Head of Zeus.

Adams, Max (2015). *In the Land of Giants: Journeys through the Dark Ages*. London: Head of Zeus.

Adomnán of Iona (1977). *Life of St Columba*. Harmondsworth, Middlesex: Penguin.

Alexander, Michael (translator) (1977). *The Earliest English Poems*. Harmondsworth, Middlesex: Penguin.

Anonymous (1998). *The Anonymous History of Abbot Ceolfrith*. In Webb, J. F. and Farmer, D. H. (1998). *The Age of Bede*. London: Penguin Books.

Anonymous (1998). *The Voyage of St Brendan*. In Webb, J. F. and Farmer, D. H. (1998). *The Age of Bede*. London: Penguin Books.

Arwidsson, Greta and Berg, Gosta (1983). *The Mästermyr Find: A Viking Age Tool Chest from Gotland*. Lompoc, California: Larson.

Backhouse, Janet (2010). *The Lindisfarne Gospels*. Oxford: Phaidon.

Bede (1990). *Ecclesiastical History of the English People*. London: Penguin Books.

Bede (1998). *Life of Cuthbert*. In Webb, J. F. and Farmer, D. H. (1998). *The Age of Bede*. London: Penguin Books.

Bede (1998). *Lives of the Abbots of Wearmouth and Jarrow*. In Webb, J. F. and Farmer, D. H. (1998). *The Age of Bede*. London: Penguin Books.

Blair, John (2000). *The Anglo-Saxon Age: A Very Short Introduction*. Oxford: Oxford University Press.

Blair, Peter Hunter (1976). *Northumbria in the Days of Bede*. London: Victor Gollancz.

Blair, Peter Hunter (1977). *An Introduction to Anglo-Saxon England*. Cambridge: Cambridge University Press.

Blair, Peter Hunter (1990). *The World of Bede*. Cambridge: Cambridge University Press.

Brøndsted, Johannes (1965). *The Vikings*. Harmondsworth, Middlesex: Penguin Books.

Bromwich, Rachel (2017). *Trioedd Ynys Prydein: The Triads of the Island of Britain*. Cardiff: University of Wales Press.

Brooks, Nicholas (1984). *The Early History of the Church of Canterbury*. Leicester: Leicester University Press.

Brown, Michelle P. (2023). *Bede and the Theory of Everything*. London: Reaktion Books.

Brown, Peter (1989). *The World of Late Antiquity: AD 150–750*. London: Thames & Hudson.

Brown, Peter (2013). *The Rise of Western Christendom: Triumph and Diversity A.D. 200–1000*. London: John Wiley & Sons.

Brown, Terry (2006). *English Martial Arts*. Ely: Anglo-Saxon Books.

Campbell, James (1982). *The Anglo-Saxons*. Oxford: Phaidon.

Campbell, James (2000). *The Anglo-Saxon State*. London: Hambledon and London.

Carman, John and Harding, Anthony (1999). *Ancient Warfare*. Stroud: Sutton Publishing.

Carver, Martin (1998). *Sutton Hoo. Burial Ground of Kings?* London: British Museum Press.

Charles-Edwards, T. M. (2013). *Wales and the Britons 350–1064*. Oxford: Oxford University Press.

Clarkson, Tim (2017). *The Picts: A History*. Edinburgh: Birlinn.

Connolly, S. (1995). *Bede: On the Temple*. Liverpool: Liverpool University Press.

Corfe, T. (1997). 'The Battle of Heavenfield', *Hexham Historian*, 7.

Crawford, Sally (2009). *Daily Life in Anglo-Saxon England*. Oxford: Greenwood World Publishing.

Crocker, Richard and Hiley, David (eds) (1990). *The New Oxford History of Music: The Early Middle Ages to 1300*. Oxford: Oxford University Press.

Crumplin, Sally (2004). *Rewriting History in the Cult of St Cuthbert from the ninth to the twelfth centuries*. St Andrew's University Thesis.

Davidson, H. E. (1998). *The Sword in Anglo-Saxon England*. Woodbridge: Boydell.

DeGregorio (2006). *Bede: On Ezra and Nehemiah*. Liverpool: Liverpool University Press.

DeGregorio, Scott (ed) (2010). *The Cambridge Companion to Bede*. Cambridge: Cambridge University Press.

Dickinson, T. and Harke, H. (1992). *Early Anglo-Saxon Shields*. The Society of Antiquities of London.

Dunn, Marilyn (2009). *The Christianization of the Anglo-Saxons c.597–c.700*. London: Continuum.

Eddius Stephanus (1998). *Life of Wilfrid*. In Webb, J. F. and Farmer, D. H. (1998). *The Age of Bede*. London: Penguin Books.

Evans, A. C. (2008). *Sutton Hoo Ship Burial*. London: British Museum Press.

Fletcher, Eric (1981). *Benedict Biscop*. Jarrow: Jarrow Lecture.

Fletcher, Richard (1998). *The Barbarian Conversion from Paganism to Christianity*. New York: Henry Holt.

Foster, Sally M. (2014). *Picts, Gaels and Scots*. Edinburgh: Birlinn.

Fraser, James E. (2009). *From Caledonia to Pictland: Scotland to 795*. Edinburgh: Edinburgh University Press.

Frodsham, Paul and O'Brien, Colm (eds) (2015). *Yeavering: People, Power & Place*. Stroud: The History Press.

Geoffrey of Monmouth (1966). *The History of the Kings of Britain*. London: Penguin.

Gething, Paul and Albert, Edoardo (2012). *Northumbria: The Lost Kingdom*. Stroud: The History Press.

Gildas (2009). *On the Ruin of Britain*. Rockville: Serenity Publishers.

Groves S.E., Roberts C.A., Lucy S., Pearson G., Nowell G., Macpherson C. G., Gröcke D., Young G. (2013). Mobility histories of 7th–9th century AD people buried at Early Medieval Bamburgh, Northumberland, England. *American J Physical Anthropology* 151(3): 462–476.

Groves, S.E. (2010). The Bowl Hole Burial Ground; A Late Anglian cemetery in Northumberland. In J. Buckberry and A. Cherryson (eds): *Burial in Later Anglo-Saxon England, c.650 to 1100AD*. 114–125. Oxford: Oxbow Books.

Groves, S.E. (2011). Social and Biological Status in the Bowl Hole Early Medieval burial ground, Bamburgh, Northumberland. In D. Petts, S. Turner (eds): *Early Medieval Northumbria*. Belgium: Brepols

Hawthorne, J. G. and Smith, C. S. (1979). *Theophilus On Divers Arts*. New York: Dover Publications.

Haywood, John (2006). *Dark Age Naval Power: Frankish and*

*Anglo-Saxon Seafaring Activity*. Hockwold-cum-Wilton: Anglo-Saxon Books.

Higham, N. J. (1993). *The Kingdom of Northumbria AD 350–1100*. Stroud: Sutton Publishing.

Higham, N. J. (1994). *The English Conquest: Gildas and Britain in the Fifth Century*. Manchester: Manchester University Press.

Higham, N. J. (1995). *An English Empire: Bede, the Britons and the Anglo-Saxon Kings*. Manchester: Manchester University Press.

Higham, N. J. (1997). *The Convert Kings: Power and Religious Affiliation in Early Anglo-Saxon England*. Manchester: Manchester University Press.

Higham, N. J. (2006). *(Re-)Reading Bede*. Abingdon: Routledge.

Higham, Nicholas J. and Ryan, Martin (2013). *The Anglo-Saxon World*. New Haven: Yale University Press.

Higham, N. J. (2015). *Ecgfrith: King of the Northumbrians, High-King of Britain*. Donnington: Shaun Tyas.

Hill, David (1981). *An Atlas of Anglo-Saxon England*. Oxford: Blackwell.

Hill, Paul (2012). *The Anglo-Saxons at War 800–1066*. Barnsley: Pen & Sword Books.

Hindley, Geoffrey (2006). *A Brief History of the Anglo-Saxons*. London: Robinson.

Holder, A. (1994). *Bede: On the Tabernacle*. Liverpool: Liverpool University Press.

Hope-Taylor, B. (1977). *Yeavering: an Anglo-British Centre of early Northumbria*. London: English Heritage.

Ingram, Rev. James (translator) (1912). The Anglo-Saxon Chronicle. London: Everyman Press.

Jackson, K. H. (1969). *The Gododdin: The Oldest Scottish Poem*. Edinburgh: Edinburgh University Press.

Johnston, Bob (2004). *Dalriada: The Land that Scotland Forgot*. Isle of Gigha: Ardminish Press.

Kendall, C. B. (2008). *Bede: On Genesis*. Liverpool: Liverpool University Pres.

Kendall, C. B. and Wallis, Faith (2010). *Bede: On the Nature of Things and On Times*. Liverpool: Liverpool University Press.

Kirby, D. P. (2000). *The Earliest English Kings*. London: Routledge.

Lang, Janet (2007). *The Rise and Fall of Pattern Welding: an investigation into the construction of pre-medieval sword blades*. University of Reading Thesis.

Lapidge, Michael, Blair, John, Keynes, Simon and Scragg, Donald (eds) (2001). *The Blackwell Encyclopaedia of Anglo-Saxon England*. Oxford: Blackwell Publishing.

Lapidge, Michael (1995). *Archbishop Theodore*. Cambridge: Cambridge University Press.

Leahy, Kevin. (2010). *Anglo-Saxon Crafts*. Stroud: The History Press.

Leahy, Kevin and Bland, Roger (2009). *The Staffordshire Hoard*. London: British Museum Press.

Lucy, Sam (2000). *The Anglo-Saxon Way of Death*. Stroud: Sutton Publishing.

Magennis, Hugh (1999). *Anglo-Saxon Appetites*. Dublin: Four Courts Press.

Marren, Peter (2009). *Battles of the Dark Ages*. Barnsley: Pen & Sword Books.

Marsden, John (1992). *Northanhymbre Saga: The History of the Anglo-Saxon kings of Northumbria*. London: BCA.

Mayr-Harting, Henry (1991). *The Coming of Christianity to Anglo-Saxon England*. London: B. T. Batsford Ltd.

McKinney, Windy (2011). *Creating a gens Anglorum*. York: University of York.

Moffat, Alistair (2001). *The Sea Kingdoms*. London: Harper Collins.

Moffat, Alistair (2013). *The British: A Genetic Journey*. Edinburgh: Birlinn.

MoLAS (2004). *The Prittlewell Prince*. London: Museum of London.

Nennius (2008). *History of the Britons*. Book Jungle.

O'Brien, Colm (2015). 'The Great Enclosure' in *Yeavering: People, Power & Place*, edited by Frodsham, Paul and O'Brien, Colm. Stroud: The History Press.

Oswald, Al, Ainsworth, Stewart and Pearson, Trevor (2006). *Hillforts: Prehistoric Strongholds of Northumberland National Park*. Swindon: English Heritage.

Ottaway, Patrick (1992). *Anglo-Scandinavian Iron Work from 16–22 Coppergate, York: c.850–1100 A.D.* York: University of York Press.

Pirie, Elizabeth, J. E. (2000). *Thrymsas, Sceattas and Stycas of Northumbria.* Llanfyllin: Galata Print.

Pollington, Stephen (1996). *The English Warrior from Earliest Times to 1066.* Ely: Anglo-Saxon Books.

Renfrew, Colin and Bahn, Paul (1996). *Archaeology: Theories, Methods and Practice.* London: Thames and Hudson.

Reynolds, Andrew (2009). *Anglo-Saxon Deviant Burial Customs.* Oxford: Oxford University Press.

Robertson, A.J. (1956). *Anglo-Saxon Charters.* Cambridge: Cambridge University Press.

Rollason, David (2003). *Northumbria, 500–1100: Creation and Destruction of a Kingdom.* Cambridge: Cambridge University Press.

Rowland, T. H. (1987). *Medieval Castles, Towers, Peles and Bastles of Northumberland.* Warkworth: Sandhill Press.

Rushton, Sara et al. (eds) (n.d.) *Bamburgh: Archaeology in Northumberland: Discovery Series 1.* Northumberland: Northumberland County Council.

Sawyer, Peter (2013). *The Wealth of Anglo-Saxon England.* Oxford: Oxford University Press.

Shaw, Richard (2018). *The Gregorian Mission to Kent in Bede's Ecclesiastical History.* Abingdon: Routledge.

Shaw, Richard (2022). *How, When and Why Did Bede Write his Ecclesiastical History?* Abingdon: Routledge.

Siddorn, Kim J. (2000). *Viking Weapons and Warfare.* Stroud: Tempus Publishing.

Smith, Scott Thompson. (2007). *Writing Land in Anglo-Saxon England.* University of Notre Dame, Indiana, Thesis.

Stancliffe, Clare and Cambridge, Eric (eds) (1995). *Oswald: Northumbrian King to European Saint.* Stamford: Paul Watkins.

Stenton, Frank (2001). *Anglo-Saxon England.* Oxford: Oxford University Press.

Stephenson, I. P. (2002). *The Anglo-Saxon Shield*. Stroud: Tempus Publishing.

Theophilus (1980). *On Divers Arts*. New York: Dover Publications.

Trent Foley, W. and Holder, Arthur G. (1999). *Bede: A Biblical Miscellany*. Liverpool: Liverpool University Press.

Tweddle, Dominic (1992). *The Anglian Helmet from Coppergate*. York Archaeological Trust.

Underwood, Richard (1999). *Anglo-Saxon Weapons and Warfare*. Stroud: Tempus Publishing.

Waddington, Clive (1999). *Land of Legend: Discovering ancient Northumberland*. Milfield, Wooler: Country Store Publishing.

Waddington, Clive (2001). *Maelmin: An Archaeological Guide*. Milfield, Wooler: Country Store Publishing.

Wallis, Faith (2004). *Bede: The Reckoning of Time*. Liverpool: Liverpool University Press.

Wallis, Faith (2013). *Bede: Commentary on Revelation*. Liverpool: Liverpool University Press.

Ward-Perkins, Bryan (2005). *The Fall of Rome and the End of Civilization*. Oxford: Oxford University Press.

Watkins, Ann E. (translator) (n.d.) *Aelfric's Colloquy*. https://www.vikingage.org/wiki/wiki/Aelfric%E2%80%99s_Colloquy

Webb, J. F. and Farmer, D. H. (1998). *The Age of Bede*. London: Penguin Books.

Welch, Martin (1992). *English Heritage Book of Anglo-Saxon England*. London: BCA.

Whitelock, Dorothy (1979). *English Historical Documents; volume 1, 500–1041*. London: Eyre & Spottiswoode.

Wickham, Chris (2009). *The Inheritance of Rome*. London: Penguin.

Williams, Allan. (2011). *Estudio Metalurgic De Algunas Espadas Vikingas*. Gladius PDF.

Wood, Michael (2003). *In Search of the Dark Ages*. London: BBC Worldwide Ltd.

Young, Graeme (2003). *Bamburgh Castle: The Archaeology of the Fortress of Bamburgh AD 500 to AD 1500*. Bamburgh: Bamburgh Research Project.

# Index